the Birthday Oracle

Discover what your birth date says about you

the Birthday Oracle

Discover what your birth date
says about you

Pam Carruthers

ARCTURUS

ARCTURUS

This edition published in 2010 by Arcturus Publishing Limited
26/27 Bickels Yard, 151–153 Bermondsey Street,
London SE1 3HA

Created for Arcturus Publishing by Omnipress Limited,
Eastbourne, Sussex.

ISBN: 978-1-84837-577-2
AD001282EN

Printed in Singapore

Contents

Introduction

Have you ever wondered why we all have different characteristics and why the planets and celestial bodies have an effect on us? An astrologer uses the position of the planets to create a horoscope – an interpretation of the way ahead for a certain person. They use this information as a tool to try and understand who we are, where we are going, and why we do certain things at certain times of the year.

The Birthday Oracle is broken down into the 365 days of the year, and as you read through these you will notice that a pattern of qualities starts to appear. You will not only learn a lot about yourself, but also the characteristics of many of your colleagues, friends and family. Hopefully, it will all start to make sense and explain why you may get on with one star sign better than another as you learn how the signs interact with one another. Your star sign will fall into one of twelve Zodiac signs – Aries, Taurus, Gemini, Cancer, Leo, Virgo, Libra, Scorpio, Sagittarius, Capricorn, Aquarius and Pisces. Each of these signs is governed by a planet or planets, whose position in the birth charts provides clues as to how we should best channel their energy to our advantage.

THE PLANETS

SUN
The Sun tells us about the fundamental essence of a person and their inner self.

MOON
This planet represents our feelings and emotions and also has an effect on our general body rhythms and our ability to cope with change.

MERCURY
Mercury is the planet that controls our common sense, our ability to learn and our sense of reason.

VENUS
Venus governs our enjoyment of pleasure, our libido and general aesthetic awareness of beauty.

MARS
Mars represents our energy and drive; it also signifies courage and our readiness for action.

JUPITER
Jupiter gives us our sense of justice and also our optimism.

SATURN
Saturn rules our conscience and governs the way we choose to live. It can also tell us about our powers of endurance and ability to concentrate.

URANUS
Uranus gives us our intuition and our insights into anything new or unusual.

NEPTUNE
Neptune governs our supersensory perception and opens doors to mystical experiences.

PLUTO
Pluto governs our regenerative powers and also controls the cycles of birth and death.

TAROT CARDS

Tarot and astrology have always been closely linked. So what exactly is tarot? The Tarot is a deck of cards that is believed to have originated over 500 years ago in northern Italy. The art of tarot has always been shrouded in mystery and controversy, but there will always be something irresistible in the notion of shuffling a pack of cards and having your destiny laid out in front of you.

Many people regard tarot-reading as a so-called 'dark art' and are not comfortable with its use, while to some it is a magical way of unlocking the future.

THE MAJOR ARCANA

A typical tarot deck is comprised of 78 cards, which are split into two different tiers. The Minor Arcana are split into four suits – swords, staves, cups and coins (also known as disks or pentacles), corresponding loosely to the hearts, diamonds, spades and clubs in a modern deck of playing cards. The Major Arcana were apparently added later and number 22 cards in total including the Fool – the tarot equivalent of the joker card. The Major Arcana are the most powerful cards in the tarot deck. They tell the story of a journey through space and time with the Fool as the central character, representing the new-born infant or the basic human element in all of us. It is the cards of the Major Arcana that can be successfully used in conjunction with numerology and astrology to unlock the secrets of our inner selves. Here is a description of each card in the Major Arcana as it relates to your astrological profile:

0 – The Fool represents the wide-eyed innocent beginning a new journey. He is brimming over with youthful exuberance but prone to impetuousness. He doesn't always look before he leaps. The knapsack he carries is too small to sustain him for very long. The dog at his heels represents loyalty and faith.

Keywords: beginnings, innocence, simplicity, fresh starts, blind faith

1 – The Magician can be seen either as the fool who has been reborn, having ditched the tiny knapsack in favour of real life-experience, or as a separate character altogether. He is the master of the elements – regal, powerful, graceful, confident and above all able to make things happen. He is in control of his own thoughts and therefore his potential for achievement is limitless.

Keywords: power, action, awareness, application, resourcefulness

2 – The High Priestess is the keeper of secrets and inner knowledge. She is knowing like the magician, but her unquestionable power comes from a female energy rooted in the unseen forces of nature. The contents of the scroll she holds are known only to her and she controls how much she imparts to others.

Keywords: influential, psychic, secretive, knowing

3 – The Empress represents the mother figure of the tarot deck. She offers love and abundance and nurtures growth in everything and everyone around her. She reminds us that there is always enough for everyone to enjoy, we just need to learn to look in the right places.

Keywords: promise, femininity, abundance, creativity, assurance

4 – The Emperor is the father figure of the tarot deck and the meanings of this card are tied up with qualities traditionally expected from a father figure – wisdom, authority and grounding. The emperor has achieved his wisdom through life experience; he wears the battle armour – and probably scars – to prove it. He can be sceptical at times and he is not easily fooled. He is a great source of strength and advice for others.

Keywords: strategy, rulership, authority, practicality

5 – The Hierophant means 'holy man' and this card is the card of dogmatic knowledge. Just as a priest represents his chosen religion, the hierophant is the bearer of great responsibility because it is his job to impart his knowledge to his flock. The hierophant is the well-versed and educated teacher of accepted, conventional knowledge. He has it within him to guide the masses.

Keywords: respect, law, holiness, ceremony, tradition, conformity

6 – The Lovers is the card of the heart and of partnership, and was originally just called love. It represents a kind of crossroads in the tarot journey at which the fool, our central character, meets his soulmate and chooses to travel on a rockier road with her, rather than amble along an easier path alone. Love doesn't always listen to reason, and it often influences our decisions in ways we, not to mention others in our lives, cannot fully understand.

Keywords: sex, love, health, union, trust, passion, temptation, vulnerability, communication

7 – The Chariot is all about determination, skill and action. It depicts a warrior riding a chariot with his two horses champing at the bit.

Keywords: tact, skill, action, control, focussed, driven, balance, physicality

8 – Strength This card depicts a young woman subduing a fierce lion, but her clothing is unruffled and her countenance is calm and serene. She doesn't appear to be exerting any physical strength, so we can conclude that the power she's drawing on comes from inside.

Keywords: balance, strength, courage, patience, compassion, understanding

9 – The Hermit has a deep sense of perspective and takes the time needed to really observe situations before he acts. When he does act, he does so with great integrity and wisdom. The hermit has tapped into an important truth in life, that all our actions are like bricks in a wall, each one helping to build our own reality. It is this realization that gives him power.

Keywords: stillness, solitude, wisdom, humility, deliberate detachment

10 – The Wheel of Fortune is about consequence as well as luck, indicating that we need to learn how to turn the wheel to our advantage. It is all about the way life unfolds – through luck, change and fortune.

Keywords: luck, chance, destiny, change, revolution, consequence

11 – Justice represents our conscience, and when this card shows up in a conventional tarot reading the seeker should see it as a sign that there is an issue in their life that requires urgent attention. As part of an astrological profile however, justice is the card of those with a passion for truth.

Keywords: truth, balance, justice, equality, congruence, admission, examination, accountability

12 – The Hanged Man's strength is in the Fool's state of purposeful surrender. If this is your card you possess the ability to remain still and, as Rudyard Kipling put it, 'keep your head, when all around are losing theirs'. People look up to you because you always seem to be calm and collected, even when your world has been turned upside down.

Keywords: yield, suspend, surrender, sacrifice, submission, non-action, stillness, calm

13 – Death This card, ironically, does not actually represent death, and it is very significant that this card appears around the middle of the sequence and not at the end. The death card is all about the inevitability of change, and people whose card this is know instinctively that nothing is forever.

Keywords: eternal change, exposure, transition, termination, inevitability

14 – Temperance is the card of balance in all things. It is all about harmony and those born under it are natural healers who are able to revive and invigorate everyone around them. They are naturally tapped into the flow of all things, and therefore posses a certain magnetism that draws people close and keeps them there, mesmerized.

Keywords: balance, healing, connection, chemistry, fluidity, moderation

15 – The Devil can be slightly alarming, but this card is not all about evil. While it does have some negative connotations, it is the card of the ego and we need our ego to function as human beings; this is what differentiates us from all other living things. The devil card is very powerful – it taps into our base nature – and is also the key to transcendence and freedom.

Keywords: ego, addiction, illusion, disruption

16 – The Tower tells us straight away that something is afoot and is an unsettling card. In a conventional tarot reading, the tower foretells an event, a sudden shift in the seeker's life; change that is not always for the better. The change is usually gradual, giving us time to adapt, but on occasion it can be quick and explosive if the individual needs to be made more responsive.

Keywords: change, eruption, upheaval, exposure, sudden shifts

17 – The Star card is all about assurance, and those born under it are able to offer comfort and hope to people around them. They are also at ease in their own skin, and this too helps people to feel happy in their company. The stars on the card glitter against a clear blue sky. Blue is the colour of inspiration, creativity and aspiration.

Keywords: hope, promise, healing, guidance, cleansing, assurance, ascension, rejuvenation

18 – The Moon holds great influence over the earth, as she holds sway over the ocean tides and human emotions and no one is immune to her power. The moon possesses the power to influence others and this card in a spread represents fear. Sometimes this fear is quite literally a fear of

the dark, or a fear of the unknown, but it is usually a fear that is based on a previous negative emotional experience. The moon encourages us to walk away from difficult relationships and start afresh.

Keywords: cycles, emotion, intensity, reflection, confusion, influence, emergence, perplexity

19 – The Sun, in direct contrast with the moon, is constant. He doesn't wax or wane and his power is obvious, not mysterious or shrouded like that of his sister. The sun card celebrates life and happiness and if this turns up in a reading, the individual can be prepared to celebrate success.

Keywords: life, energy, growth, clarity, vibrancy, understanding, illumination, new beginnings, breakthrough

20 – Judgement This card can be seen as complex and confusing, but if you look carefully its message becomes clear. The characters on the card are holding their hands up in a gesture of surrender towards a higher power. In a conventional tarot reading this card signifies that the seeker needs to stop and listen to their higher calling, to leave the past behind and give themselves up to it. The judgement card can be difficult to read, but it usually signifies that a big change is about to take place. It asks us to face our past wounds, move on and put them to rest irrevocably.

Keywords: faith, honesty, judgement, resurrection, transformation

21 – The World is the last card in the Major Arcana and it represents the end of the Fool's difficult journey. It is therefore the card of completion, achievement and fulfilment. Absolute contentment is not about how much we earn, what car we drive or even how liked we are – it's about something much deeper. This is a wonderful card portraying happiness, wholeness, perfection and satisfaction, especially when we about to finish a long project.

Keywords: value, success, achievement, fulfilment, enrichment, satisfaction

1 ♈

Aries
March 21 – April 20

TAROT CARD: The Emperor

ELEMENT: Fire

QUALITY: Cardinal

NUMBER: 1

RULING PLANET: Mars

GEMSTONES: Bloodstone, coral, malachite, jasper

COLOURS: Scarlet, magenta, claret, carmine

DAY OF THE WEEK: Tuesday

COMPATIBLE SIGNS: Sagittarius, Leo

KEY WORDS: Fighting spirit, the desire to succeed, dynamic creation and destruction

ANATOMY: Head, adrenals, the blood, muscles

HERBS, PLANTS AND TREES: Hot peppers, ginger, radish, onion, garlic, horseradish, mustard, aloe, basil, broom, capers, nettles, briars, cactus and all trees with thorns

KEY PHRASE:
I am

Aries as a sign is all about 'me', pure and simple. It corresponds to the head of the body and consequently you tend to go through life headfirst. You need to forge ahead, to assert yourself. However, as you act on impulse, you have a tendency to make mistakes and, in your rush to get things done, can be accident-prone.

Yours is the first sign of the zodiac. It marks the Spring Equinox where equal day and night meet. This is the turning point in the year, as we rise from the darkness of winter ready for the birth of a new cycle and the adventure of life.

The Sun is exalted in your sign and you possess all the solar qualities of creativity, enthusiasm and courage. You are the pioneer of the zodiac.

PLANETARY RULER AND QUALITIES
Aries is a cardinal fire sign. As the first fire sign it ignites the flame, so Aries excels at initiation. It's governed by Mars, the red planet and God of War. Planets represent energy and Mars is action. The Greek Ares was a 300-foot giant and rather clumsy. The Roman version was Mars, a skilled and honourable warrior. Mars in our astrological birth charts shows us how we get our needs met, our inner and outer drive and our sexuality. Mars can be a two-year-old having a tantrum or a paladin, a spiritual warrior.

RELATIONSHIPS
You are a romantic with chivalrous ideals. Quick to begin a relationship, you may not always stop to consider if a partner is really suitable. The male is the knight in shining armour, the female the huntress who chooses her mate. You are attracted by the other fire signs, Leo and Sagittarius, and are powerfully magnetized by Libra, your opposite. Your best friends are Gemini and Aquarians and you can have challenging, but ultimately rewarding, relationships with Capricorn and Cancer.

MYTH
Aries lies in the constellation of The Ram. The Greek myth of Jason and the Golden Fleece is one of the oldest stories of a hero's quest. Jason with his Argonauts overcomes impossible challenges and fights a guarding dragon to recover the magical fleece and reclaim his kingdom.

STRENGTHS AND WEAKNESSES

Aries represents new life and birth, so you possess enthusiasm, courage, willpower and the urge to do something, to take action and get things done. This is the fighting spirit of the hero archetype. Aries would dash into a burning building to save a child's life with no thought of the risk to self. You act on pure instinct. Arians are to be found at the gym or on the sports field. You love to initiate new projects, are in constant motion and always busy. You can be a workaholic and get burnt out if you don't slow down and take time out to care for yourself. You are direct, can be quick tempered, but you don't bear grudges and appreciate honesty and truth. Passionate and warm-hearted, impulsive and at times naive, you act first and think later.

As an Aries you aren't interested in completion or maintenance, and tend to ignore the instruction manuals, preferring to push all the buttons to see how it works. You can have almost no concept of time, preferring to live in the here and now.

TYPICAL ARIES:
MARLON BRANDO

'Acting is the expression of a neurotic impulse. It's a bum's life. Quitting acting, that's the sign of maturity'

ARIAN POWERS: A natural leader, energetic, accepts challenges readily.

ARIAN NEGATIVES: Must be the boss, dislikes being dictated to, can be impulsive, insensitive and selfish.

March 21

BORN ON THIS DAY:
Johann Sebastian Bach
(composer and musician)
Matthew Broderick
(actor)
Rosie O'Donnell
(actor and chat show host)
Russ Meyer
(filmmaker and photographer)
Gary Oldman
(actor and filmmaker)
Florenz Ziegfeld
(Broadway impresario)

MEDITATION:

Perfect stillness can sometimes deliver more than directionless energy.

You are a lively person who communicates passionately. Your sharp mind can be used to solve practical problems and you are very quick to learn but consequently can easily get bored. You are always ready for action, adaptable and highly versatile, and will take up any challenge offered. A natural debater, you think on your feet and have a ready wit. However, you do have a tendency – on many an occasion – to speak first and think later, which can lead to a reputation for being outspoken and slightly insensitive. Your mind works so fast you tend to interrupt others – which they can find annoying. Never fire off an email or text if upset or angry – wait to cool down. Divert yourself with a sport or martial art that needs mental agility or you could try gentle, stress-reducing t'ai chi.

TAROT CARD: The World
PLANETS: Mercury and Mars
QUOTE: *'The aim and final end of all music should be none other than the glory of God and the refreshment of the soul.'* J.S. Bach

STRENGTHS: Dynamic, perceptive.
WEAKNESSES: Blunt and sometimes thoughtless.

March 22

BORN ON THIS DAY:
George Benson
(singer and guitarist)
Marcel Marceau
(mime artist)
Chico Marx
(actor and comedian)
William Shatner
(actor and writer)
Stephen Sondheim
(composer and lyricist)
Reese Witherspoon
(actor and film producer)

MEDITATION:

When we are helping others, we are nourishing the soul.

You are a highly emotional and sensitive person who can become moody and cantankerous when upset. You are fiercely protective of the things in your life that you care about, especially your family and home, and will defend them at all costs. You are brilliant at sensing the public mood and can absorb others' feelings like a sponge. You can be overly concerned with what people feel about you – remember not to take things personally. Always on the go, you can easily burn out. You love fast food – it was invented for you! However, you need to ensure you never eat while upset. You love to keep everyone happy so can take on too many things. Ask for time to reflect before committing to projects, to make sure you really want to do them. Channel your energies into home improvements.

TAROT CARD: The Chariot
PLANETS: The Moon and Mars
QUOTE: *'Do not the most moving moments of our lives find us without words?'* Marcel Marceau

STRENGTHS: Caring and intuitive.
WEAKNESSES: Moody, prone to emotional outbursts.

March 23

You are a theatrical, big personality, with a strong desire to compete and win. You love being in the limelight, and radiate confidence and self-assurance. You appreciate honesty and directness and can't stand deceit. You are not known for your subtlety or finesse. You are always coming up with creative projects where you can take the leadership role. You take risks, will speculate and gamble. You have the willpower to succeed when others give up. You have courage and strength and boundless enthusiasm. As a natural leader with masses of physical energy, you need to acknowledge the contribution of others. You can be a workaholic and find it hard to delegate. Amateur dramatics, or solo sports, such as tennis, where you excel, will bring you satisfaction. The car you drive has to look as glamorous as you.

TAROT CARD: The Hierophant
PLANETS: Sun and Mars
QUOTE: *'I am just too much.'*
Joan Crawford

STRENGTHS: Inspired, passionate.
WEAKNESSES: Egotistical, slightly stubborn.

BORN ON THIS DAY:
Damon Albarn
(singer/songwriter and record producer – Blur and Gorillaz)
Roger Bannister
(athlete – the four minute mile)
Donald Campbell
(record breaking car racer)
Joan Crawford
(actor)
Chaka Khan
(singer)
Steve Redgrave
(Olympic rower)

MEDITATION:
To conquer oneself is more of a challenge than conquering others.

March 24

You are a productive and busy person who thrives on handling a variety of projects at once. You use up a lot of nervous energy which can cause inner tension and headaches. Your need to get things right is strong, which is great when dealing with written communication and editing. Excellent at detailed work with your hands, you are a natural craftsman or artisan. You love to design systems and enjoy complex and demanding mental tasks. You want others to do things your way – the right way! You worry that what you produce isn't up to your high standards and this can produce negative energies, so working to a deadline helps you finish. When feeling mentally overwhelmed, time is well spent in decluttering and reorganizing your work and living space.

TAROT CARD: The Hermit
PLANETS: Mercury and Mars
QUOTE: *'Have nothing in your house that you do not know to be useful, or believe to be beautiful.'* William Morris

STRENGTHS: Flair for detail, excellent multi-tasker.
WEAKNESSES: Perfectionist and overly critical.

BORN ON THIS DAY:
Fatty Arbuckle
(silent film actor)
John Harrison
(clockmaker)
Harry Houdini
(magician)
David Irving
(historian)
Steve McQueen
(actor)
William Morris
(artist, designer and writer)

MEDITATION:
Strive for excellence not perfection.

March 25

MEDITATION:
*Compare yourself only
to yourself.*

You are a charming, gregarious person who needs a life partner to find out who you are. They can bring out the best in you. A born romantic – and a bit of a flirt – you are highly creative and love the idea of love. Your heart can rule your head and you constantly need to be appreciated. You act confidently but can be rocked by the mildest negative comment. Your critics say you are self-centred, but those who know you appreciate how kind-hearted you really are. You have a childlike creativity that touches people's hearts. Your heroism can be an inspiration. However, your tendency to emotionally see-saw can have you reaching for wine or chocolate as comfort – that's when you need to call friends over to talk things through instead of battling through it alone.

TAROT CARD: The Chariot
PLANETS: Venus and Mars
QUOTE: *'The great thing about rock and roll is that someone like me can be a star.'* Elton John

STRENGTHS: Endearing and sociable.
WEAKNESSES: Indecisive, too eager to please.

March 26

MEDITATION:
*A truth with a
nasty intent
is worse than a lie.*

You are a hypnotic and powerful person with magnetic appeal. You are unstoppable and once you set your mind on something you make sure you get it, by whatever means. You have a sharp mind and a sardonic sense of humour which serves to balance the underlying determination of your actions. You are unstoppable and push yourself to the limits. People admire your courage as you are gracious in defeat, but you always come back to fight another day. There is a refreshing honesty in what you say; you tell it how it is. Some call this brutal, others love your frankness. In relationships and work, once you commit, you are in it for the duration. You are a passionate lover. To relax you need to let off steam; strengthening exercises – such as weightlifting or digging up the garden – are excellent.

TAROT CARD: Strength
PLANETS: Pluto and Mars
QUOTE: *'If I have someone who believes in me, I can move mountains.'* Diana Ross

STRENGTHS: Magnetic, enterprising.
WEAKNESSES: Ruthless and brutally honest.

March 27

You are larger than life, an adventurer who travels far in many ways. You are highly intuitive, very friendly and warm-hearted but can occasionally be highly strung and impatient with others who do not share your ideals. You have an intense moral certainty. A born philosopher and talker, you can speak for hours when campaigning about your pet cause. You have strong entrepreneurial skills. A big personality with fire in your belly, you can motivate others. When you're in love you give yourself wholeheartedly. You suffer badly if let down, because rarely do you anticipate this possibility. Heal your wounds by escaping to the great outdoors; you'd enjoy going on safari or a camping trip to somewhere exotic and hot. Adventure re-inspires you and restores your high spirits.

TAROT CARD: The Hermit
PLANETS: Jupiter and Mars
QUOTE: *'My mother is Irish, my father is black and Venezuelan, and me - I'm tan, I guess.'* Mariah Carey

STRENGTHS: Highly intuitive and adventurous.
WEAKNESSES: Prone to exaggeration, overly optimistic at times.

BORN ON THIS DAY:
Mariah Carey
(singer/songwriter and record producer)
David Janssen
(actor)
Romulus
(Italian founder of Rome)
Henry Royce
(engineer and car manufacturer)
Gloria Swanson
(actor)
Quentin Tarantino
(filmmaker and actor)

MEDITATION:
To exaggerate is to weaken.

March 28

You are a tough-minded individual with a droll sense of humour. You are the boss, a realist who approaches life as a series of challenges to be conquered. You are a creative entrepreneur with ideas that are grounded and have longevity. You have talents that work well in the political arena. You respect those who have the audacity to teach you something new. In love you need to let your hair down and relax more; taking work home with you is guaranteed to get under the skin of your partner. You are thick-skinned so partners learn quickly that you respond best to straight talking. Take short breaks in the course of your working day, enjoy simple pleasures: eat an ice cream, walk barefoot in the grass. Remembering your inner child will rejuvenate you.

TAROT CARD: The Wheel of Fortune
PLANETS: Saturn and Mars
QUOTE: *'My sense of humour has served me well.'* Vince Vaughn

STRENGTHS: Droll sense of humour, creative entrepreneur.
WEAKNESSES: Workaholic, uptight.

BORN ON THIS DAY:
Dirk Bogarde
(actor and writer)
Maxim Gorky
(writer)
Ken Howard
(actor, writer, musician, producer)
Charles Edward Isaacs
(jazz musician)
Richard Kelly
(film director)
Vince Vaughn
(actor)

MEDITATION:
How beautiful it is to do nothing, and then to rest afterward.

March 29

MEDITATION:
*Blessed are the flexible,
for they shall not be
bent out of shape.*

You are an extremely friendly and sociable person with a passion for justice and human rights. Your leadership abilities combined with your progressive ways of thinking make you a natural campaigner for social causes. You are a rebel who does things their way. You have the capacity for being very successful because you possess a sharp intellect as well as charisma and a gift for persuasion. You should never be underestimated. Yours is a different vision for the world and others sit up and take note when you speak of it. You love to be with a group so relationships come naturally to you. You need intellectual stimulation with your partner and a lot of personal space. You run on nervous energy, so need to de-stress with some form of yoga – experiment until you find what suits you.

TAROT CARD: Justice
PLANETS: Uranus and Mars
QUOTE: *'You cannot belong to anyone else, until you belong to yourself.'* Pearl Bailey

STRENGTHS: Gift of the gab, friendly.
WEAKNESSES: Over rational, easily bored.

March 30

MEDITATION:
*Patience is the companion
of wisdom.*

You are a born optimist and your *joie de vivre* lights up a room when you enter. You have a strong inner core, you know what you want, but can be easily distracted with too many irons in the fire. Your gifts are many and your versatility is your asset – and this is the reason people like you – you can relate. You have musical talent and can easily imitate others – you have an ear for the latest slang. Your energetic approach can wear others out and because you speak so fast some can find you too abrupt. Learning the art of pausing will serve you well. Your soulmate has to be someone who adores you and gives you the stability you need. You enjoy the cut and thrust of city life and your idea of relaxing is hanging out at a buzzing cafe or bar. Take time to watch and listen, so your ideas can focus.

TAROT CARD: The Empress
PLANETS: Mercury and Mars
QUOTE: *'I often think that the night is more alive and more richly coloured than the day.'* Vincent Van Gogh

STRENGTHS: Zest for life, adaptable.
WEAKNESSES: Brash and impatient, a fast-talker.

March 31

You are a natural carer and protector, with huge ambitions to do something positive for the planet. You can be daring and original with your ideas, taking them out into the world and never fretting about how others will perceive them. You have the ability to tune into what people need and will give it to them by saying exactly what they want to hear. You also have the drive to get things done. A secure family base is a necessity, providing a much-needed refuge after your travels. You can rush into things and fling yourself headfirst into projects without thought, then get upset when things don't turn out as you expected. If you swallow your feelings, your frustration can take its toll. Participating in team games for all the family – which have the element of fun rather than competition – is the answer.

TAROT CARD: The Emperor
PLANETS: Moon and Mars
QUOTE: *'In order to improve the mind, we ought less to learn, than to contemplate.'* Rene Descartes

STRENGTHS: Responsible, intuitive, devoted to family.
WEAKNESSES: Clannish, clingy.

BORN ON THIS DAY:
Rene Descartes
(mathematician and philosopher)
Al Gore
(American politician)
Gordie Howe
(ice hockey player)
Maximilian I
(Holy Roman Emperor)
Ewan McGregor
(actor)
Pope Benedict XIV

MEDITATION:
Teamwork divides the task and multiplies the success.

April 1

You are a one off, a truly courageous person who leads the way with a pioneering spirit. You are prepared to risk everything, moving fast and without undue thought into uncharted territory. You are a true hero, never stopping to think of your own safety when your instincts tell you that someone or something needs your help. You have a forceful personality that people either love or loathe – you are not subtle! You can be very independent so a partnership can create difficulties. You can't bear to be number two. It works best if your partner has a life of their own, so when you do get together it's a honeymoon rather than a fight. You can burn out and neglect your body so your diet is of vital importance to keep your energy levels high. Remember that even the best-made engine needs an oil change!

TAROT CARD: The Magician
PLANETS: Mars and Mars
QUOTE: *'Laws are like sausages, it is better not to see them being made.'* Otto von Bismark

STRENGTHS: Bold and heroic, a pioneer and individual.
WEAKNESSES: Rash and impulsive with a blunt approach.

BORN ON THIS DAY:
Otto von Bismarck
(Prussian statesman)
Ferruccio Busoni
(composer and pianist)
Lon Chaney
(actor)
Samuel Ray Delany
(writer)
Dan Flavin
(artist)
Method Man
(rapper with Wu Tang Clan)

MEDITATION:
The trees that are slow to grow bear the best fruit.

April 2

MEDITATION:

Nature does not hurry, yet everything is accomplished.

You are both gentle yet tough, diplomatic yet tactless. You are an enigma and very attractive to be with. You adore the opposite sex and they feel your admiration. You ooze a self-confidence which others envy. You love the material world and love to spend the considerable amount of money you can earn. You are determined to get what you want and you can rush in with undue haste which you regret later. Your sense of humour borders on the risqué, but you can get away with it if the occasion is right. You make an adorable companion and always have a partner on your arm. A special relationship is essential for you, and two weeks alone has you climbing up the walls. You know how to take care of yourself. A good massage is essential for your peace of mind.

TAROT CARD: The High Priestess
PLANETS: Venus and Mars
QUOTE: *'Life itself is the most wonderful fairy tale.'* Hans Christian Andersen

STRENGTHS: Self-assured, sexy.
WEAKNESSES: Hasty, tactless.

April 3

MEDITATION:

Silence is the true friend that never betrays.

You are direct and very persuasive, you can sell anything to anybody. A natural comic, you come across as light and eternally youthful. You are constantly on the move and creative ideas flow from you. A notepad or dictaphone is an essential tool. You talk fast and people struggle to keep up with you. Your *joie de vivre* helps everybody feel more alive in your presence. You are a natural companion but get easily bored in relationships. You blow hot and cold and this is disconcerting for those of a steadier constitution. You have the gift of the gab, so be careful not to mislead others with false expectations. Keep your options open and don't make promises you can't keep. You can burn out with too much talking, so take time out to restore your energy by walking barefoot and grounding yourself.

TAROT CARD: The Empress
PLANETS: Mercury and Mars
QUOTE: *'I've always had confidence. It came because I have lots of initiative. I wanted to make something of myself.'* Eddie Murphy

STRENGTHS: Quick witted, persuasive, young at heart.
WEAKNESSES: Short concentration span, unpredictable.

April 4

Your charisma appeals to all ages. An artist with a rich imagination, you have innate charm, with a natural flair in all you accomplish. You can stun people with your unique talents. Your creativity comes in fits and starts and you can be unpredictable depending on how you feel about a project. Your sensitivity is both a blessing and a curse. When upset you sulk and nurse your wounds, but, like a child, you are ready to play the next day. In love, you are seeking to be mothered, and will test your partner to see if they care for you even when you throw a tantrum. You can get homesick and gain great comfort from childhood comforts – an old teddy bear or a home-made apple pie will make you feel rested once more. Once you learn to mother yourself, you'll be an excellent partner.

TAROT CARD: The Emperor
PLANETS: Moon and Mars
QUOTE: *'I know very little about acting. I'm just an incredibly gifted faker.'* Robert Downey Jr.

STRENGTHS: Charismatic, artistic flair, action-orientated.
WEAKNESSES: Over-emotional, moody and prone to self-pity.

BORN ON THIS DAY:
Maya Angelou
(writer and artist)
Paul Bertrand
(artist)
David Blaine
(magician and endurance artist)
Robert Downey Jr.
(actor, writer and producer)
Pierre Lacotte
(ballet dancer)
Heath Ledger
(actor)

MEDITATION:
Self-pity is self-destruction – think positive.

April 5

You are a showman, a natural leader with an appetite for life. You know that you're the centre of the universe and it comes as no surprise that you have many admiring followers who want to know your secret. You are an inspiration to others by just being you. Innately warm and enthusiastic, you are a natural star who just has to shine. You can act like a prima donna and you do have a strong ego, so you need to take the leadership position or you will act like a child having a temper tantrum. You need passion and adoration from your partner and if they can help promote your career, all the better. Whatever you do, you need applause, so make sure you use your creativity and natural acting ability to entertain others. Your playfulness will always win them over in the end.

TAROT CARD: The Hierophant
PLANETS: Sun and Mars
QUOTE: *'I will not retire while I've still got my legs and my make-up box.'* Bette Davis

STRENGTHS: Generosity of spirit, contagious enthusiasm.
WEAKNESSES: Emotionally immature, vain.

BORN ON THIS DAY:
Albert R. Broccoli
(film/TV producer)
Bette Davis
(actor)
Arthur Hailey
(writer)
Joseph Lister
(founder of antiseptic surgery)
Gregory Peck
(actor)
Spencer Tracy
(actor)

MEDITATION:
The only cure for vanity is laughter.

19

April 6

You are straightforward and direct in your approach to life yet there's an undercurrent of timidity and shyness. You have an ability to focus on the smallest thing and can be obsessive if everything isn't up to your exacting standards. At times you let loose and live life on a grand scale, but there is always a nagging inner critic highlighting your imperfections and holding you back. You can be too hard on yourself at times and need to learn to overlook mistakes in yourself and others. In romance you can veer between an almost Neanderthal approach and appearing to be so shy and retiring you lose out completely. When you get trapped in being too obsessive, try doing something that requires precision and shows off your talent for eye and hand coordination, such as needlework or playing snooker.

TAROT CARD: The Lovers
PLANETS: Mecury and Mars
QUOTE: *'At the age of 80, everything reminds you of something else.'* Lowell Thomas

STRENGTHS: Modest, orderly.
WEAKNESSES: Obsessive and timid.

MEDITATION:
Whether you think you can or you think you can't, you are right.

April 7

You are eager for life, a passionate person with an enthusiasm that is endearing yet tinged with emotional naivity. You are a lover, who needs a leading man/lady to play opposite you. As an idealist, you seek the truth, but can often argue for an opposing view just to create lively debate and get people stirred up! You are prone to jealousy and this leads to fights with your lover. However, for you, anger is a form of foreplay which leads to the pleasure of making up, but be aware that this way of behaving can be difficult for a lover to cope with. Nevertheless a committed relationship would be the making of you. Once you master your emotions you are a born leader, skilled in the art of diplomacy. Vigorous physical activity – such as a good workout at the gym – is the best release when your temper gets too hot.

TAROT CARD: The Chariot
PLANETS: Venus and Mars
QUOTE: *'I don't think there's any artist of any value who doesn't doubt what they're doing.'* Francis Ford Coppola

STRENGTHS: Tactful, passionate about life.
WEAKNESSES: Emotionally reserved, insecure.

BORN ON THIS DAY:
Jackie Chan
(actor and martial arts master)
Francis Ford Coppola
(filmmaker)
Russell Crowe
(actor)
David Frost
(TV presenter)
James Garner
(actor)
William Wordsworth
(poet and writer)

MEDITATION:
In jealousy there is more of self-love than love.

April 8

You are a charismatic, intense person and are on this Earth to make a statement with your life. You believe in your own abilities and your inner core is strong and resourceful. Whatever life throws up, you can survive; crises are the making of you. You have a penchant for investigating the dark side of life. While mainly quietly purposeful, you can be overly dramatic and come on too strong. You care what people think of you and need their approval, so cooling down your approach is necessary if you want to win them over. You need a strong partner to match you. Once you have found them you make a formidable team. You have enormous powers of endurance. Hard physical exercise – such as rowing or hitting the dancefloor with a strenuous routine – helps you release excess energy.

TAROT CARD: Strength
PLANETS: Pluto and Mars
QUOTE: *'It is not possible for a man to be elegant without a touch of femininity.'* Vivienne Westwood

STRENGTHS: Resolute, captivating.
WEAKNESSES: Overbearing with a tendency to overreact.

BORN ON THIS DAY:
Albert I
(Belgian monarch)
Kofi Annan
(UN secretary-general)
Betty Ford
(feminist and activist)
Julian Lennon
(musician, son of John Lennon)
Giuseppe Tartini
(violinist)
Vivienne Westwood
(fashion designer)

MEDITATION:
No one can whistle a symphony – it takes a whole orchestra to play it.

April 9

You are a visionary with a large appetite for life. You see the big picture and your schemes are on the grand scale but the details bore you. Your enjoyment of life comes before anything else, and you are quite likely to drop everything and hop on a plane just for the fun of it. You are resilient and can easily handle setbacks – they are just challenges for you to overcome with innovative solutions. You are competitive and can wield a powerful influence over others. Love is a grand affair and you relish the experience of falling in love, which you do often – essentially you are in love with life and everything and everybody it has to offer. When someone puts a dampener on one of your ideas, you need to get to higher ground. This you can do literally – hot-air ballooning or sky-diving was made for you.

TAROT CARD: The Hermit
PLANETS: Jupiter and Mars
QUOTE: *'Always be a poet, even in prose.'* Charles Baudelaire

STRENGTHS: Fun loving and resilient.
WEAKNESSES: Lack of attention to detail, restless.

BORN ON THIS DAY:
Severiano Ballesteros
(professional golfer)
Charles Baudelaire
(poet)
Alexandre Bisson
(dramatist and composer)
Hugh Hefner
(owner of Playboy business empire)
Leopold II
(Belgian monarch)
Mary Pickford
(actor)

MEDITATION:
The greatest glory is not in never falling, but in rising every time we fall.

21

April 10

BORN ON THIS DAY:

BORN ON THIS DAY:
Eugene d'Albert
(composer and pianist)
Chuck Connors
(actor and sportsman)
Joseph Pulitzer
(publisher)
Steven Seagal
(actor, film producer and martial artist)
Omar Sharif
(actor)
Paul Theroux
(writer)

MEDITATION:

Cultivate your sense of humour – as laughter is the best medicine.

You are a determined person with a forceful manner. You possess considerable flair and a talent for organizing. You are ambitious from a young age and set your sights high. You are a winner, and although you respect tradition you can shock people out of their stagnant ways. You have a wicked sense of humour, a scathing wit and can use sarcasm to get your point across. You do what you say you're going to do, which is refreshing in the modern world. You choose your life partner with the same common sense approach you have to your work. Love is a business partnership and you value the marriage contract highly. When your head is fit for bursting, you need to let go of the responsible you and do something silly. Watch a movie just for the fun of it – a Disney classic is perfect.

TAROT CARD: The Wheel of Fortune
PLANETS: Saturn and Mars
QUOTE: *'Tourists don't know where they've been, travellers don't know where they're going.'* Paul Theroux

STRENGTHS: Determined, with great management skills.
WEAKNESSES: Emotionally restrained, solemn.

April 11

BORN ON THIS DAY:
Oleg Cassini
(fashion designer)
Jeremy Clarkson
(TV presenter)
Joel Grey
(entertainer and dancer)
Bill Irwin
(actor and dancer)
James Parkinson
(doctor and palaeontologist)
Joss Stone
(singer/songwriter)

MEDITATION:

Impatience is the ruin of strength.

You are full of bright ideas and a real people-person. You have an offbeat way of looking at the world. You can express your controversial views with such passion that people pull back, then they hear what you have to say and become fervent supporters. Routine bores you and you're not great at finishing what you've started. You thrive on change. You are best being self-employed and will work long into the night if the inspiration takes you. You are an anarchist and can find your niche in the media, fashion or film industries where you can express your originality. In romantic relationships you are looking for a friend first, a lover second. Your ideal partner keeps you guessing as well as being your best companion. You would do well to combine physical exercise with having fun, so frisbee was invented for you.

TAROT CARD: Justice
PLANETS: Uranus and Mars
QUOTE: *'Sure it's quiet, for a diesel. But that's like being well-behaved … for a murderer.'* Jeremy Clarkson

STRENGTHS: Quirky and canny.
WEAKNESSES: Easily distracted, tendentious.

April 12

You are a paradox: brave and single-minded, but quaking with doubt inside. You can run the show or give in to the feelings of others and shrink from the excessive exposure that the spotlight brings, drifting off into your own dream world. But you have a fertile imagination and this needs to be channelled into artistic creations. Your feelings have to be expressed and putting them down on paper is essential for your growth. You can be too easily influenced by others and give up your personal ambitions or go into sacrifice mode. In relationships you need a partner who nurtures and supports you and gives you space to follow your dreams. When you are feeling out of balance and in need of inspiration, take to the water, either sailing or swimming – even a long shower will nourish your soul.

TAROT CARD: The Empress
PLANETS: Neptune and Mars
QUOTE: *'I think there's a great beauty to having problems. That's one of the ways we learn.'* Herbie Hancock

STRENGTHS: Ingenious, courageous.
WEAKNESSES: Self-contradicting, emotionally impressionable.

BORN ON THIS DAY:
David Cassidy
(singer and actor)
Robert Delaunay
(artist)
Andy Garcia
(actor)
Herbie Hancock
(pianist and composer)
Edward O'Neill
(actor)
Tiny Tim
(performer and entertainer)

MEDITATION:
A strong person and a waterfall always channel their own path.

April 13

You are a man or woman who can act as a spokesperson for people who can't stand up for themselves. You understand how others feel, and can express empathy by taking a stance on behalf of the underdog. Your compassionate nature appeals to both the heads and hearts of others and this quality brings you the friendship of people from all walks of life. Nevertheless, you are a complex, volatile person and you create many dramas in your personal life. If you find people steering clear of you, you can bet you've gone too far. When you're feeling strong you assert yourself and command the stage of your life with supreme confidence. Your relationship is your rock and truly assists you in advancing your career. When you're depressed, a steam bath or sauna can do wonders to revitalize you.

TAROT CARD: The Emperor
PLANETS: Moon and Mars
QUOTE: *'There's man all over for you, blaming on his boots the fault of his feet.'* Samuel Beckett

STRENGTHS: Empathetic and warm-hearted.
WEAKNESSES: Temperamental, with a tendency to over-dramatize.

BORN ON THIS DAY:
Robert O. Anderson
(entrepreneur and oil magnate)
Samuel Beckett
(playwright)
Al Green
(singer)
Seamus Heaney
(poet)
Thomas Jefferson
(US President)
Howard Keel
(actor and singer)

MEDITATION:
Never write a letter while you are angry.

April 14

Your noble manner and integrity have been part of who you are since childhood. You have a social magnetism that exudes vitality. People respect you and want to be in your inner circle. Your intensity, deep convictions, warmth and intelligence are the ingredients to your success in life. Your streak of 'devil may care' can lead you to risk all for love and romance. For your relationships to work, you need to have respect for your partner. You have very high standards – only the best will do. If your pride is hurt or you are ignored, you suffer loudly and march off. This can lead you to extravagance, and indulgence in retail therapy on a grand scale. If you really need some pampering and to be made to feel special, having a facial or a great haircut might be easier on the wallet.

BORN ON THIS DAY:
Robert Carlyle
(actor)
Julie Christie
(actor)
Sarah Michelle Gellar
(actor)
Loretta Lynn
(singer/songwriter)
Peter Rose
(baseball player)
Rod Steiger
(actor)

MEDITATION:

A bargain is only a bargain if it is something you need.

TAROT CARD: Temperance
PLANETS: Sun and Mars
QUOTE: *'I was born under the sign of the Ram, which means I'm headstrong. I don't like people telling me what to do.'* Loretta Lynn

STRENGTHS: Honourable with great reverence for others.
WEAKNESSES: Self-important and wasteful.

April 15

You are outspoken and have clear ideas of how things should be done. You get impatient if you aren't at the centre of any action, with you taking the leading role. You are dutiful and highly disciplined, especially when it comes to performing daily tasks. You love routine yet long to break free and throw caution to the wind. You can be reckless one minute and then overly careful and cautious the next. Learning to trust yourself and others can enable you to be carefree – and that is your ultimate goal. You are creative and you get great satisfaction from a job well done. In affairs of the heart, you desire excitement and adventure and are torn between settling down and playing the field. Your tendency to self-doubt can give you sleepless nights, so a warm bath and lavender can help you to relax.

BORN ON THIS DAY:
Jeffrey Archer
(British politician and writer)
Evelyn Ashford
(champion Olympic sprinter)
Claudia Cardinale
(actor)
Théodore Rousseau
(artist)
Emma Thompson
(actor and screenwriter)
Leonardo da Vinci
(artist)

MEDITATION:

Search for the person you aspire to be.

TAROT CARD: The Devil
PLANETS: Mercury and Mars
QUOTE: *'A well-spent day brings happy sleep.'* Leonardo da Vinci

STRENGTHS: Controlled, conscientious.
WEAKNESSES: Domineering, attention-seeker.

April 16

You are a forthright, impulsive person who wears their heart on their sleeve. In every relationship you come up against the question, who's in charge, them or me? This is due to the delicate balancing act you perform in your life. The courage you have to bounce back after a heartbreak is admirable; in this respect you are a hero and your life is spent seeking the fairy tale ending. You need a partner who loves adventure and excitement, someone who enjoys the highs and lows of the drama that is your life. Teamwork gives you the support you need and helps to put you in the spotlight where you belong. You need to learn to express your feelings when hurt – a close friend can help heal your tender heart. Never eat when upset, you are more sensitive than you let on.

TAROT CARD: The Chariot
PLANETS: Venus and Mars
QUOTE: 'A day without laughter is a day wasted.' Charlie Chaplin

STRENGTHS: Courageous, determined.
WEAKNESSES: Emotionally naive and confrontational.

BORN ON THIS DAY:
Kingsley Amis
(writer)
Charlie Chaplin
(entertainer and producer)
Henry Mancini
(conductor and composer)
Spike Milligan
(writer and comedian)
Jimmy Osmond
(singer)
Dusty Springfield
(singer)

MEDITATION:
The walls we build keep out the joy as well as the sadness.

April 17

You embody a range of admirable qualities being highly motivated, ambitious and tenacious. Your powers of persuasion are endearing. You show sincerity and integrity once you are on your chosen path. You excel in the world of theatre or sport where your powerfully dramatic style comes into its own. You can be underhanded and play a political game which can embroil you in conflicts and leave you wondering why friends have turned on you. This can result in self-doubt. Recognize that you have the ability to transform your life and begin anew. A strong relationship is your biggest asset. You are faithful unless betrayed. When angry it's best to relieve your tension by boxing a punchbag or pillow rather than getting into a shouting match with your sweetheart.

TAROT CARD: Strength
PLANETS: Pluto and Mars
QUOTE: 'Bombs do not choose; they will hit everything.' Nikita Khrushchev

STRENGTHS: Determined, influential.
WEAKNESSES: Narcissistic, scheming.

BORN ON THIS DAY:
Victoria Beckham
(fashion desiger, singer – Spice Girls and entrepreneur)
William Holden
(actor)
Nick Hornby
(writer)
Nikita Khrushchev
(Soviet politician)
James Last
(musician and bandleader)
Tamerlane
(military leader and conqueror)

MEDITATION:
Keep cool, anger is not an argument.

April 18

You are spontaneous and here to enjoy life. You are ardent and passionate and love to gamble – you will risk all for what you believe in. Foreign cultures excite you and you are keen to explore different religions. You always see the good in people and are unaware of the flaws in some of your enterprises. Your optimism is contagious and people love your openness and childlike trust in life. You are gregarious and in all your relationships you are uncomplicated, and direct. A partner needs to understand that you require freedom and space to do your own thing. At times you can verge on being bawdy which surprises your more delicate colleagues. In an argument you feel you are right which results in a showdown. Back off and ask the question, do you want to be right or happy?

TAROT CARD: The Hermit
PLANETS: Jupiter and Mars
QUOTE: *'Insincerity is always weakness; sincerity even in error is strength.'*
George Henry Lewes

STRENGTHS: Free and easy, optimistic.
WEAKNESSES: Bombastic and coarse.

BORN ON THIS DAY:
Suri Cruise
(daughter of Tom Cruise)
America Ferrera
(actor)
Bob Kaufman
(poet)
George Henry Lewes
(philosopher)
Hayley Mills
(actor)
James Woods
(actor)

MEDITATION:
Remember that cleverness is not wisdom.

April 19

You are a real go-getter, a person with a certain cheekiness that comes out of the blue as you can adopt a serious manner on first meeting. You are prodigious in your output, and your work is your life. You are devoted to truth and can get quite arrogant if someone dares to challenge your belief. Although you make fun of the establishment, you respect the law. You are unwavering in your rise to the top, and you get there – however long it takes you. You have an essentially practical way of looking at life with an earthiness that people respect. When you fall in love it is with a passion that takes your beloved by surprise. Commitment is second nature for you so you can marry young but to an older person. Unwind by exploring the child's world of play: build sandcastles and swim with dolphins.

TAROT CARD: The Sun
PLANETS: Saturn and Mars
QUOTE: *'If you're going to do something wrong, do it big, because the punishment is the same either way.'* Jayne Mansfield

STRENGTHS: Cheeky, fun-loving and unpretentious.
WEAKNESSES: Strident, arrogant.

BORN ON THIS DAY:
Tim Curry
(actor, composer and singer)
Kate Hudson
(actor)
Etheridge Knight
(poet)
Jayne Mansfield
(actor, singer and glamour model)
Dudley Moore
(actor, musician and composer)
Paloma Picasso
(jewellery designer)

MEDITATION:
Smile when it hurts most.

April 20

You have a flair for living, with a strong sensuality and magnetic appeal to both men and women. In public life you are dominant, yet in private you are yielding and soft. You possess formidable drive and energy that can be overwhelming for some. If you don't want to do something no one can persuade you, you just dig your heels in. You enjoy your successes, you know you deserve them. You never like to be taken for granted by your lover and are possessive and prone to jealousy, maybe due to your own roving eye. You can brood if you're ignored and sometimes you find it hard to throw off your moods. Once you get going again – a splendid meal and a glass of wine helps – you are irresistible once more. If that fails, a good night's sleep always works to restore your bonhomie.

BORN ON THIS DAY:
Michael Brandon
(actor)
Carmen Electra
(actor and glamour model)
Adolf Hitler
(Austrian-German dictator)
Ryan O'Neal
(actor)
Joan Miró
(artist)
Edie Sedgwick
(actor, model and Andy Warhol muse)

TAROT CARD: Judgement
PLANETS: Venus and Mars
QUOTE: *'I try to apply colours like words that shape poems, like notes that shape music.'* Joan Miró

STRENGTHS: Sensual, with an electrifying magnetism.
WEAKNESSES: Insecure and stubborn.

MEDITATION:
Concentrate the mind on the present moment.

TYPICAL ARIES:
MAYA ANGELOU

'I believe the most important single thing, beyond discipline and creativity, is daring to dare.'

ARIES TRAITS:
Aries love to start new things and are not scared of the unknown – the A for Aries is also for adventure. This means that they are very instinctive; however, it can also result in them not finishing what they start.

27

Taurus

April 21 – May 21

TAROT CARD: The Empress

ELEMENT: Earth

QUALITY: Fixed

NUMBER: 2

RULING PLANET: Venus

GEMSTONES: Diamond, quartz, crystal

COLOURS: White and multi-colours

DAY OF THE WEEK: Friday

COMPATIBLE SIGNS:
Virgo, Capricorn

KEY WORDS: Steadfast and loyal,
affectionate and tactile, practical
and firm, over-indulgent, lazy
and materialistic

ANATOMY: Throat and neck

HERBS, PLANTS AND TREES: Moss, spinach,
lilies, daisies, dandelions, beets,
larkspur, flax and myrtle

KEY PHRASE:
I have

Taurus is the lover of the zodiac. This sign corresponds to the neck and throat and as a result you tend to suffer from sore throats and thyroid problems, although you may also have a lovely voice and sing extremely well. Above all, you value stability and security. Known to be stubborn, your powers of endurance are legendary. Starting over again feels like a backward step – so you keep going when others would give up.

This is the second sign of the zodiac, when the darling buds of May blossom and nature shows off her best outfit. The moon is exalted in this sign and Taureans love to touch, to hold and to be physically present. This, in conjunction with your innate stability, helps provide children and adults with the emotional growth they relish. Taurus represents the early years of life when a young child begins to explore its body and its physical environment.

PLANETARY RULER AND QUALITIES

Taurus is a fixed earth sign. As the first earth sign it secures the seed planted by Aries, so Taurus excels at grounding and loves gardening. Taurus is governed by Venus, the most brilliant and beautiful planet, also known as the Morning or Evening Star. She is Aphrodite, the Goddess of Love. Planets represent energy and Venus is all about relationships, harmony and money. In the Greek myths Aphrodite was renowned for her beauty and vanity. She was not faithful and enjoyed taking lovers, much to the annoyance of her husband. Venus in your astrological birth chart shows us what you love and how you like to be loved. It reflects your taste in fashion and your style. For a man it's the type of woman he is attracted to. Venus can be a spoilt princess in need of constant attention or the Goddess herself.

RELATIONSHIPS

Taurus is a sensualist, so physical love, touch and pleasure is right at the top of your agenda. You are patient and take your time in a relationship. You definitely need to be sure that your partner is faithful to you. Both sexes are skilled in the art of love. The male is the steady and reliable type, the woman can teach others how to attract and keep a mate. Taureans are attracted to the other earth signs, Virgos and Capricorns, and also powerfully magnetized by Scorpios, your opposite. Best friends are Librans and Pisceans. There can be challenging, but rewarding, relationships for you with both Leos and Aquarians.

Pl. 17.

TYPICAL TAURUS:
AUDREY HEPBURN

'I was born with an enormous need for affection, and a terrible need to give it.'

TAUREAN POWERS: Extremely loyal, affectionate, sensual.

TAUREAN NEGATIVES: Materialistic, resistant to change, lack sense of urgency.

MYTH

Taurus lies in the constellation of The Pleiades, the Seven Sisters. Taurus is the Latin name for 'bull' and therefore this sign is associated with the myth of Theseus and the Minotaur, and with Zeus, who assumed the form of a magnificent white bull to abduct Europa, a legendary Phoenician princess. Both involve beautiful women, bulls and desire.

STRENGTHS AND WEAKNESSES

Taureans appreciate the sensual delights of food and drink so you can often be found at restaurants and wine bars. You love all worldly pleasures and can easily relax to the extent that you turn into a couch potato, watching cookery programmes or gardening shows.

You prefer things to stay the same, so can be very resistant to change of any sort. You have a comfortable home and take pride in what you own. However, you can be possessive, holding onto people and things that are long past their sell-by date.

As a Taurean you are able to bring stability and keep a project going, but you can appear too slow for some. You love the rhythms of the day and are happy with routine.

29

April 21

MEDITATION:
*Learn to focus –
for concentration is the
secret of strength.*

You are a person who has a way with words. You combine a lightness of touch with a delightful turn of phrase that is sheer poetry. You can use your gifts as a writer commercially and make a superb copywriter in advertising. You are immensely witty and persuasive, so selling comes naturally to you. An eloquent speaker, people love listening to you. You adore being with people of all ages and backgrounds. You have a chameleon quality that allows you to blend in and mix in a variety of groups. Your youthful, enquiring spirit demands that your love partner is forever learning something new to keep the relationship alive. At times you can be absent-minded, restless and easily distracted, so soft music rather than watching TV restores your soul at the end of the day.

TAROT CARD: The Empress
PLANETS: Mercury and Venus
QUOTE: *'I'm just going to write because I cannot help it.'* Charlotte Brontë

STRENGTHS: Persuasive, an articulate wordsmith.
WEAKNESSES: Daydreamer, restless, has trouble focussing.

April 22

MEDITATION:
*Make one new decision
a day as a way out of
the habitual routine.*

You are a strongly kinesthetic person, highly sensual and totally at ease with your body. You are creative, resourceful and in tune with what the public need. You are gifted at understanding how people feel and offer true sympathy. You are an excellent listener and make an ideal counsellor and therapist. You are also a wonderful friend and are always there when the people close to you need a shoulder to cry on. You have a strong sense of the intrinsic value of things and what they are worth, and this makes you good at business. Relationships are a bedrock for you and you settle down early. You can get too cosy at times and become complacent with your partner, staying in too often. Recognize this tendency, go out and do something different – it will greatly enhance your love life.

TAROT CARD: The Emperor
PLANETS: Moon and Venus
QUOTE: *'Beer, it's the best damn drink in the world.'* Jack Nicholson

STRENGTHS: Trustworthy, strong, sympathetic.
WEAKNESSES: Driven by habit, fixed.

April 23

You are a vibrant person who shines in the world with your gift of beauty. You radiate warmth and are immensely attractive. You have a gift of concentration and follow through what you start in a consistent manner. At times you are quiet and introverted so enjoy working alone on your creative project. People look to you as their leader because of your enthusiasm and social ability. You love to entertain at home and play host to eminent people. A character with strong but fixed opinions, your blind spot can be failing to see others' points of view. You are a born lover and relationships matter to you. You are passionate and playful, highly sensual and need to be appreciated and adored. When feeling down, you need colour and beauty – surround yourself with yellow flowers when this happens.

TAROT CARD: The Hierophant
PLANETS: Sun and Venus
QUOTE: *'A fool thinks himself to be wise, but a wise man knows himself to be a fool.'* William Shakespeare

STRENGTHS: Warm-hearted, focussed.
WEAKNESSES: Need to be adored, single-minded.

BORN ON THIS DAY:
Catherine de Medici
(French monarch)
Roy Orbison
(singer/songwriter)
Sergei Prokofiev
(composer)
William Shakespeare
(poet and playwright)
Shirley Temple
(child actor)
Joseph M. Turner
(artist)

MEDITATION:
The best quality a human can possess is tolerance.

April 24

You are a highly skilled person who loves to create beautiful things. You have a natural talent for intricate work using your hands. You pay great attention to detail and can become obsessed with the tiniest of blemishes or imperfections. Whatever you do is to a high standard of excellence that people will pay for. You are a true professional and work hard, long hours. You are patient and will save up to afford the best-quality items for your home. You are a good organizer and planner and an invaluable member of a team because you consider everyone's needs. In romance you are affectionate and thoughtful. At home, with your family, you need to let go of your need to keep everyone on a strict timetable. Use your sense of humour, laugh at yourself and you'll endear yourself to your loved ones even more.

TAROT CARD: The Lovers
PLANETS: Mercury and Venus
QUOTE: *'There is nothing more important in life than love.'* Barbra Streisand

STRENGTHS: Thoughtful, a natural craftsperson.
WEAKNESSES: Rigid planner, tendency to over-organize.

BORN ON THIS DAY:
Jean Paul Gaultier
(fashion designer)
Willem De Kooning
(artist)
Shirley MacLaine
(dancer and actor)
Henri Petain
(French prime minister)
Barbra Streisand
(actor and singer)
Robert Penn Warren
(first US poet laureate)

MEDITATION:
Learn to mix routine with spontaneity for a well-rounded life.

April 25

MEDITATION:

Each person's opinion is as important as the next, including your own.

You are a refined person with brilliant skills of diplomacy and making people feel at ease. You are well suited to working in any aspect of fashion or beauty. Your impeccable taste and good manners would help you thrive in the upmarket retail business. You could well study ballet or classical dance, because you adore rhythmic movement and are extremely graceful. You inspire others with your beauty and could be a muse for an artist or poet. Relationships are vital to you so you are never alone for long. You revel in the trappings of romance – the candlelit dinner and the box of chocolates. You can suffer from the constant need to be liked, tending to hide your true feelings so as not to upset people. This can appear fake, so being direct and honest with people would win their respect.

TAROT CARD: The Chariot
PLANETS: Venus and Venus
QUOTE: *'It's easy to fool the eye but it's hard to fool the heart.'* Al Pacino

STRENGTHS: Elegant and light-footed, romantic.
WEAKNESSES: Inhibited, submissive.

April 26

MEDITATION:

When anger rises, think of the consequences.

You are a shrewd person, perceptive and clear thinking. You are fascinated by the darker side of life. You are very sensual and have a magnetism that appeals to both sexes. You impress people with the courage and power of your convictions. A force to be reckoned with, you always make a memorable impression. Even if people only meet you once, they never forget you. You have an ability to find the treasure that is buried under the pile of rubbish. You would make an excellent antiques dealer with your love of restoring damaged and discarded goods to their former beauty. You are a passionate partner and need an equal who can handle your intensity and occasional temper. Vigorous exercise such as boxing would help you vent your feelings when life isn't going to plan.

TAROT CARD: Strength
PLANETS: Pluto and Venus
QUOTE: *'A weapon isn't good or bad, depends on the person who uses it.'* Jet Li

STRENGTHS: Passionate and intuitive.
WEAKNESSES: Short-tempered, overbearing.

April 27

You are a practical and grounded person who is also a high-flyer and a born voyager. You love to gamble and take risks but never go that step too far – you always have your safety belt on! Higher education is vital for you and if you didn't go to college you will take up study later on. You adore adventure stories. Your rich imagination enables you to spin a yarn and be totally believed. You love to travel and since you have an eye for good value and beauty you would be adept at importing foreign artefacts. Relationships are synonymous with adventure for you, so you may well marry a foreigner and end up living abroad. You can be restless and always craving new experiences. Planning your next journey or watching educational films is your way of relaxing.

TAROT CARD: The Hermit
PLANETS: Jupiter and Venus
QUOTE: *'What I did in my youth is hundreds of times easier today. Technology breeds crime.'* Frank Abagnale

STRENGTHS: Explorer, innovative with a rich imagination.
WEAKNESSES: Story-teller, gambler.

BORN ON THIS DAY:
Frank Abagnale
(forger turned US security consultant)
Sheena Easton
(singer)
Ulysses S. Grant
(US president)
Coretta Scott King
(civil rights leader)
Jack Klugman
(actor)
Samuel F.B. Morse
(inventor of the Morse Code)

MEDITATION:
Channel restlessness into creating something that is new to you.

April 28

You are an extremely ambitious person who nevertheless appreciates traditional ways. You are keen to preserve the status quo and would do well working in a long-established heritage institution, running a large estate or museum or working with valuable antiques. You set a goal and work hard to reach the top. You are suited to management or owning your own company. You are a father figure to your employees – whatever your gender – and they respect your dedication and dependability. People know where they stand with you. You make a loyal and faithful partner but you can be highly possessive and demand equally high standards from your spouse. You need to learn to take a few risks to avoid being boring – comedy is a hidden talent and people need to see that side of you more often.

TAROT CARD: The Wheel of Fortune
PLANETS: Saturn and Venus
QUOTE: *'Many receive advice, only the wise profit from it.'* Harper Lee

STRENGTHS: Reliable, enterprising.
WEAKNESSES: Unimaginative at times, overly cautious.

BORN ON THIS DAY:
Ferruccio Lamborghini
(car designer)
Harper Lee
(writer)
Jay Leno
(TV presenter)
James Monroe
(US president)
Terry Pratchett
(writer)
Franco Rossi
(film director)

MEDITATION:
Believe that you have it, and you have it.

33

April 29

MEDITATION:

You must be happy in yourself before you enrich the lives of others.

You are an innovative person with high ideals and the resourcefulness to put them into practice. You have an excellent mind and a strong sense of identity. You are clear and frank in your communications. You are creative and what you produce has a refreshing originality about it. You are best suited to being self-employed. You love working with the public and interacting with lots of people. You are utterly honest and highly principled in your dealings. You are attracted to unusual people as potential love partners. A strong mental rapport is essential if a relationship is to last. Your ideal partner is one you see as your best friend. You can be grumpy if things don't go your way. You are prone to inertia and mood swings and need to relax in the evenings to rest your nervous system.

TAROT CARD: Justice
PLANETS: Uranus and Venus
QUOTE: *'I love to just hang out with my daughter, I love to work in my garden. I'm not a gaping hole of need.'* Uma Thurman

STRENGTHS: Ingenious and artistic.
WEAKNESSES: Cantankerous, prone to mood swings.

April 30

MEDITATION:

If passion drives you, let reason hold the reins.

You are a witty conversationalist and a charming person to be around. You rarely have to bulldoze your way into conversations and can easily convince people to agree with you. You so love chatting that you need to channel your communication skills into what you do, or you will be accused of time wasting. You can blow hot and cold – you can be seen as solid and conservative one minute and spontaneous and flippant the next. In love you are like a butterfly, darting from flower to flower as you play the field – the problem being that you can tease and play with people's affections. You might well marry more than once as you are very changeable and easily tempted. You can eat without thinking, so sitting down and focussing at mealtimes is a good habit to adopt.

TAROT CARD: The Empress
PLANETS: Mercury and Venus
QUOTE: *'My greatest gift that I have in life is basketball.'* Isiah Thomas

STRENGTHS: Playful, quick-witted.
WEAKNESSES: Inconsistent and easily seduced.

May 1

You are a determined person who knows what they want and gets it. You have artistic talents and a musical flair. Your inner drive and forcefulness make a dynamic combination. As well as charisma you have qualities that mark you out as a leader. You have an infectious – verging on outrageous – sense of humour that others find entertaining. At times your temper gets the better of you; you're prone to become impatient when things aren't moving fast enough. You want a secure and comfortable home life. Partnership comes easily to you – as long as you are the one in charge! Your love life will be passionate with lots of ups and downs, until you learn to calm your need to create dramas. Physical exercise, especially with a buddy, is vital to help you let off steam.

TAROT CARD: The Magician
PLANETS: Mars and Venus
QUOTE: *'Next to a battle lost, the greatest misery is a battle gained.'*
Duke of Wellington

STRENGTHS: Tenacious and artistic, with a contagious wit.
WEAKNESSES: Quarrelsome and prone to mood swings.

BORN ON THIS DAY:
Antonio Banderas
(actor)
Scott Carpenter
(astronaut and aquanaut)
Rita Coolidge
(singer)
Glenn Ford
(actor)
Joseph Heller
(writer)
Duke of Wellington
(British general and statesman)

MEDITATION:
Listen to the voice within more than the voice that comes out.

May 2

You are a smooth operator with an overwhelming attraction to beauty in all forms. You naturally gravitate to the worlds of fashion, art and the cosmetics industry. You are a very tactile and physical person, extremely down to earth and with excellent powers of endurance. You care about your appearance, but exercising is a bit hit or miss – you either take pride in training your body so you are fit and toned or you are the couch potato! You work at a slow and steady pace and have a deep desire for calm in your life. This control means you can swallow your anger and push down feelings, yet at times you unexpectedly blow your top. You are attracted to fiery types who are imaginative and intuitive. Dancing to rock music is a great way for you to release some of your control and let your hair down.

TAROT CARD: The High Priestess
PLANETS: Venus and Venus
QUOTE: *'Fashion is all about happiness. It's fun. It's important. But it's not medicine.'*
Donatella Versace

STRENGTHS: Persistent and pragmatic.
WEAKNESSES: Repressive with the tendency to explode with anger.

BORN ON THIS DAY:
David Beckham
(soccer player)
Catherine the Great
(Prussian-Russian empress)
Edward II
(English monarch)
Engelbert Humperdinck
(singer/songwriter)
Dwane 'the Rock' Johnson
(actor and wrestler)
Donatella Versace
(fashion designer and entrepreneur)

MEDITATION:
The only thing that gets destroyed with anger is self-respect.

35

May 3

BORN ON THIS DAY:
Mary Astor
(actor)
Henry Cooper
(champion professional boxer)
Bing Crosby
(singer and actor)
Marcel Dupré
(musician)
Horatio Hale
(anthropologist)
Sugar Ray Robinson
(champion boxer)

MEDITATION:

Do not worry about the future – as you will forget to enjoy today.

You are an agile and flexible person with considerable ability to sway people to see things your way. You do this in such a subtle manner that they think the idea is theirs, which is fine with you – as long as they come round to your way of thinking, you are happy. This talent makes you a superb negotiator and mediator. You have fine reasoning powers and would make a good teacher because people like you. You are quick to grasp concepts and apply what you learn in a practical manner. You work well with young people and students, who see you as one of them, even if you are considerably older. When you're in love you can stay up all night talking to your beloved. High intakes of caffeine or sugar can make you edgy and difficult, so be kind to your body – your friends will thank you for it.

TAROT CARD: The Empress
PLANETS: Mercury and Venus
QUOTE: *'To be a champ, you have to believe in yourself when nobody else will.'*
Sugar Ray Robinson

STRENGTHS: Good intermediary, a flexible learner.
WEAKNESSES: Tense and anxiety prone.

May 4

BORN ON THIS DAY:
Ron Carter
(jazz and classical musician)
Andre Collins
(NFL player)
Moshe Dayan
(Israeli general)
Audrey Hepburn
(actor and humanitarian)
Thomas Huxley
(scientist and zoologist)
Randy Travis
(singer)

MEDITATION:

Set your love free – the wild bird sings the prettiest tune.

You are a private and quiet person with tremendous nurturing qualities. People feel at ease in your company as you are as much of a listener as you are a talker. You care deeply about your friends and family and there is always a welcoming meal and a hug when they arrive. You are a natural earth-mother type, whatever your gender, and could make a success out of the hotel or catering business. You are canny and able to spot a bargain, so are a great person to have at an auction or garage sale. You are protective and can be overly possessive and protective of your family. On the other hand, you can be hyper-sensitive and far too easily upset by criticism. You need a partner who shares your concerns, yet has a more objective viewpoint to balance you. Watch your diet; you are prone to eat when upset.

TAROT CARD: The Emperor
PLANETS: Moon and Venus
QUOTE: *'Some find success. Some don't.'*
Andre Collins

STRENGTHS: Loving and astute.
WEAKNESSES: Possessive and easily hurt.

May 5

You are a regal person with a deep inner belief that you were born to lead. You put your whole heart in anything you do and will take risks. You are a shining example to others, who admire your confidence and self assurance. When you walk into a room it is lit up by your presence. You are great fun and are always ready to entertain friends with a song and dance. You have conventional values and a respect for authority. In a love-relationship you are very affectionate and tactile. As long as your partner gives you attention, you are perfectly content and happy. Problems arise when you feel neglected and your pride is hurt. Pouring your energy into hosting a fancy-dress party or some other celebratory social event would release your creativity and help to restore your natural lust for life.

TAROT CARD: The Hierophant
PLANETS: Sun and Venus
QUOTE: *'From each according to his abilities, to each according to his needs.'* Karl Marx

STRENGTHS: Wholehearted, calm in a crisis.
WEAKNESSES: Attention-seeker, needy.

BORN ON THIS DAY:
James Beard
(first TV chef)
Anne Boleyn
(wife of Henry VIII)
Kurt Loder
(actor and journalist)
Karl Marx
(Communist and philosopher)
Christopher Morley
(writer)
Michael Palin
(comedian, actor and writer)

MEDITATION:
Give others their time in the spotlight – back stage is just as important.

May 6

You care for the well-being of others and give wise guidance and practical help. You aspire to a life of simplicity close to nature, yet find yourself caught in trivia – bogged down with paperwork, for example. You feel that your work is never done and can spend long hours at the office or running the household. You set impossibly high standards and so are best working for yourself. Ethical and very good with money, you have a large dose of common sense, although at times you can lose your vision and what you are really working to achieve. You are a loyal and faithful partner and attracted to physical beauty. You really enjoy yourself when you get to indulge in a good meal and a fine bottle of wine with that special someone. For your own sake, make sure you relax and learn to put work aside in the evenings.

TAROT CARD: The Lovers
PLANETS: Mercury and Venus
QUOTE: *'Being entirely honest with oneself is a good exercise.'* Sigmund Freud

STRENGTHS: Virtuous and insightful into the needs of others.
WEAKNESSES: Workaholic, uptight.

BORN ON THIS DAY:
Andreas Baader
(militant anarchist)
Tony Blair
(British prime minister)
George Clooney
(actor and filmmaker)
Sigmund Freud
(psychiatrist and philosopher)
Berndt Maximilien Robespierre
(French politician and revolutionary)
Orson Welles
(actor and filmmaker)

MEDITATION:
Place as much importance on leisure time as work time.

May 7

You are immensely charming and a delight to be around because you create a soothing, relaxed atmosphere. Innately sophisticated and blessed with the ability to fit in with any social class, you make a perfect escort to any function. You could be a top model or run your own interior decoration business. You will be noticed in whatever you do and well rewarded for it, so will most likely be elevated into a wealthy lifestyle. You have a rational mind and love intellectual discussion. You can over-emphasize logical solutions to problems and can be out of your depth when an understanding of deep emotions is required. You crave the ideal relationship and place high value on physical beauty. When stressed, essential oils are wonderful for you; ylang ylang is perfect to alter your mood.

BORN ON THIS DAY:
Johannes Brahms
(composer)
Robert Browning
(poet)
Angela Carter
(writer)
Gary Cooper
(actor)
Edward IV
(English monarch)
Eva Perón
(Argentinian first lady)

MEDITATION:
By all means love yourself, but love others equally as much.

TAROT CARD: The Chariot
PLANETS: Venus and Venus
QUOTE: *'I am my own woman.'* Eva Perón

STRENGTHS: Endearing, logical and intelligent.
WEAKNESSES: Vain and superficial.

May 8

You are a charismatic person with a magnetic effect on those you meet. Your quiet and affable demeanor hides an intensely creative and forceful personality who prefers to let their actions speak for them. You are a night owl and are happy working late into the small hours. People know they need to keep on your right side because there is a hint of danger about you. You take risks and live on the edge. You are strategic in business and your instinct for survival ensures that you rarely get caught out. Your strong fighting spirit will see you through the worst situations. You are devoted to your partner and remain true to them through good times and bad. Your secrecy can be tough on them, so open up – they will love you more for it. Martial arts are a wonderful antidote to the stress that comes with your way of life.

BORN ON THIS DAY:
Henry Dunant
(founder of the Red Cross)
Enrique Iglesias
(singer/songwriter)
Ricky Nelson
(singer/songwriter)
Roberto Rossellini
(film director)
Gary Snyder
(poet)
Harry S. Truman
(US president)

MEDITATION:
Trust your own instincts and do so with all your heart.

TAROT CARD: Strength
PLANETS: Pluto and Venus
QUOTE: *'All my life, whenever it comes time to make a decision, I make it and forget about it.'* Harry S. Truman

STRENGTHS: Judicious and full of magnetism.
WEAKNESSES: Reticent, risk-taker and domineering.

May 9

You are an inspired person who is searching for truth. In youth you are rather wild and attracted by physical beauty, but as you grow older, it's wisdom that turns you on. You always see possibilities and grasp opportunities as they come your way. This impulsiveness is based on a gut feeling that is invariably right. You have the soul of a gypsy. Living on a desert island just for the experience would be the thrill of a lifetime. Your life has an epic quality about it and you are born to roam. In your relationships you need someone who is both physically beautiful and willing to explore with you what life has to offer. Despite your bohemian nature, you are not suited to casual flings. If you get itchy feet, still them by studying philosophy, or take short breaks to the world's sacred sites.

TAROT CARD: The Hermit
PLANETS: Jupiter and Venus
QUOTE: *'The good ole days weren't always good, and tomorrow ain't as bad as it seems.'* Billy Joel

STRENGTHS: Inspired, a natural explorer.
WEAKNESSES: Unsettled, a roamer.

BORN ON THIS DAY:
Candice Bergen
(actor)
John Brown
(radical abolitionist)
Fernandel
(actor and mime artist)
Albert Finney
(actor)
Glenda Jackson
(actor)
Billy Joel
(singer/songwriter)

MEDITATION:
Explore to learn the value of other people.

May 10

You are a resourceful and conscientious person with a great deal of integrity. As you climb the career ladder you see your work as a labour of love. You appreciate formality and good manners and have a dignified and graceful presence. You value old-fashioned virtues such as honour, politeness and courtesy. You are a serious professional but you also love your home life. You want the highest standards. Nothing but the best will do and you save up until you can afford the things you want. You'll spend on improving your home and take pride in a well-tended garden. Romance brings out the sensualist in you. You are very affectionate with a bawdy sense of humour that only those close to you see. Gardening or pottery will help relax both mind and body, and allow you to express your artistic side.

TAROT CARD: The Wheel of Fortune
PLANETS: Saturn and Venus
QUOTE: *'Truly there would be reason to go mad were it not for music.'* Tchaikovsky

STRENGTHS: Passionate and tender.
WEAKNESSES: Sombre, materialistic.

BORN ON THIS DAY:
Fred Astaire
(dancer and actor)
Paul Hewson – 'Bono'
(singer/songwriter – U2 and activist)
John Wilkes Booth
(actor who shot Abraham Lincoln)
Miuccia Prada
(fashion designer)
Peter Ilich Tchaikovsky
(composer)
Sid Vicious
(bassist – Sex Pistols)

MEDITATION:
Passion flows from the possession of wisdom.

May 11

You are an eccentric and unique person with a love of change and experimentation. You are civilized and avoid conflict at all costs, preferring to slowly win people over to your way of thinking. You make an excellent instructor because you explain things well and are helpful and friendly. You are supremely confident and at times come across as conceited. You work hard and can wear yourself out as your mind is constantly active. You have lots of friends and like being in groups. You are aware of the body and mind connection and could make a profession out of t'ai chi and yoga. Independent and broad-minded, your relationships can be unconventional. You are, however, a real romantic at heart. Stretching and controlled exercises offer the best ways for you to unwind; pilates would be superb for you.

BORN ON THIS DAY:
Irving Berlin
(composer)
Eric Burdon
(singer/songwriter – The Animals)
Salvador Dalí
(artist)
Marco Ferreri
(film director)
Martha Graham
(choreographer and ballet dancer)
Valentino
(fashion designer)

MEDITATION:
Happiness is a choice that requires effort at times.

TAROT CARD: Justice
PLANETS: Uranus and Venus
QUOTE: *'Those who do not want to imitate anything, produce nothing.'* Salvador Dalí

STRENGTHS: Liberal and amiable.
WEAKNESSES: Egocentric, prone to anxiety.

May 12

You are a highly spiritual person, supremely creative, with a compelling vision for life and spellbinding ideas. You could become a visionary musician or artist who inspires others, such is the depth of the field of creativity surrounding you. You aim high and follow your dreams. You travel far – often ending up living overseas – in your search for a place you feel is paradise on Earth. You are an impossible romantic – the corniest of songs appeal to your soft heart. You fall in love with love, and can be deeply disappointed when it all goes wrong, sinking into self-pity. A partner who is faithful is high on your list of priorities. Prone to moodiness and highly sensitive, you need to watch your alcohol intake. Calling up a friend who can console you is the best way to lift your spirits.

BORN ON THIS DAY:
Burt Bacharach
(composer, pianist and singer)
Yogi Berra
(baseball player)
Tony Hancock
(actor and comedian)
Katharine Hepburn
(actor)
Jeddu Krishnamurti
(religious leader and philosopher)
Florence Nightingale
(pioneer of modern nursing)

MEDITATION:
Wasting time on self-pity means that the problem is no closer to being solved.

TAROT CARD: The Hanged Man
PLANETS: Neptune and Venus
QUOTE: *'I can stand out the war with any man.'* Florence Nightingale

STRENGTHS: Imaginative, spiritual and electrifying.
WEAKNESSES: Temperamental and prone to self-pity.

May 13

You are a lyrical, poetic soul whose concern for people extends way beyond your own family. You can touch the hearts of many folk by your natural ability to make them feel cherished. But you can be a soft touch and will put your hand in your pocket any time you are asked, especially if the cause concerns the welfare of animals or children. This is a very special quality but take care not to let others take advantage of it. Your childhood was, and still is, very important to you. Family life suits you. You take time before you commit, because you need to be sure. You are a stable and nurturing partner who mothers people, including your beloved. But make sure you don't smother them – they need to breathe! You need to take time out to give to yourself space; a day being pampered at a spa would be ideal.

TAROT CARD: The Emperor
PLANETS: Moon and Venus
QUOTE: *'Writers should be read, but neither seen nor heard.'* Daphne Du Maurier

STRENGTHS: Profound and nurturing.
WEAKNESSES: Over-protective and easily persuaded.

MEDITATION:
It's not who you are that holds you back, it's who you think you're not.

May 14

You are a generous person with a warm heart, a natural entertainer with immense charm and creativity. You have a vivid imagination and a childlike innocence that people find adorable. You make them feel young again and they love joining in your play. You work well with children and are drawn to the theatrical world, where you can show off to your heart's content! In business you are reliable, and once you start a project you persevere to finish it. You are dedicated to enjoying life and your sunny personality radiates out to all you meet. In your relationships you are 100 per cent involved, but if you are feeling ignored you can over-indulge by spending too much. When this happens, you would do better having a heart-to-heart with your partner and planning a romantic break.

TAROT CARD: The Hierophant
PLANETS: Sun and Venus
QUOTE: *'Cruel leaders are replaced only to have new leaders turn cruel.'* Che Guevara

STRENGTHS: Loving, magnanimous and young at heart.
WEAKNESSES: Exhibitionist, childlike.

MEDITATION:
The inner child can also be the wise old man – it is just a case of balance.

May 15

MEDITATION:

*The future comes
one day at a time.*

You are an earthy, grounded person with a desire to be of service to others. You enjoy methodical work where you create something of long lasting value. You are sensible, caring about nutrition and watching what you eat. Organic food is a priority, as is growing your own vegetables. You like your home comforts and take enormous pleasure in tidying and reorganizing your home on a regular basis. You need to feel useful and willingly take training courses to improve your skills. You excel at home improvements and are a natural craftsperson. Your relationships are for the long term. It is vital that you don't take your partner for granted – choose someone who spurs you on and will help you to fulfill your potential. Dramatic colours will enliven your world and bring some sparkle into it.

TAROT CARD: The Lovers
PLANETS: Mercury and Venus
QUOTE: *'An honest man is always a child.'*
Socrates

STRENGTHS: An artisan, down-to-earth.
WEAKNESSES: Complacent in love, neurotic.

May 16

MEDITATION:

*There will always be
sunshine after rain.*

You ooze sex appeal and elegance. Strangers are immediately won over by your charm and welcoming smile. Flattery gets you everywhere and you make everyone feel special. You would excel in the media, on TV or as a receptionist – yours is the face people want to see. You aim to keep the peace and cannot abide anger or disagreements or anything that disturbs your equilibrium. You work best with a partner because you need someone to complement you. In love you need a lot of physical affection and reassurance because you worry about your looks. When young, you can fall for someone whose outer beauty isn't matched by their character. Your judgement improves with age and you learn to value companionship. Walking in nature is deeply satisfying and restorative for you.

TAROT CARD: The Chariot
PLANETS: Venus and Venus
QUOTE: *'Running is 80 per cent mental.'*
Joan Benoit

STRENGTHS: Hospitable, a charmer and peaceable.
WEAKNESSES: Superficial and insecure.

May 17

You are an enigmatic and glamorous person with a hypnotic gaze. You like to hide behind dark glasses or tinted windows because you prefer to see the world rather than be seen. You move in interesting circles and are not fazed by those who inhabit the sleazier parts of town. People can be fooled into thinking of you as a light-hearted charmer, but you can be a formidable opponent. You love debating and will play devil's advocate just to stir things up and increase the excitement. You are able to make dramatic changes in your life. You either love or hate – for you there are no shades of grey. An ardent and deeply committed lover, you tend to have one mate for life. Sometimes you take life too seriously, and so it is important that you allow yourself to laugh and have fun.

TAROT CARD: Strength
PLANETS: Pluto and Venus
QUOTE: *'Before I fight, I always pray that no one gets hurt.'* Sugar Ray Leonard

STRENGTHS: Loyal and extremely elegant physically and mentally.
WEAKNESSES: Intimidating and uncompromising.

BORN ON THIS DAY:
Dennis Hopper
(actor)
Ayatollah Khomeini
(supreme leader of Iran)
Sugar Ray Leonard
(champion professional boxer)
Tony Parker
(basketball player)
Bill Paxton
(actor)
Ronald Wayne
(co-founder of Apple Inc)

MEDITATION:
Laughter is man's real opposable thumb.

May 18

You are a 'big picture' kind of person, a visionary who is on a mission to bring beauty and inspiration into the lives of others. You can be deeply philosophical and spiritual from an early age – you are always seeking the meaning of life. Because of this you have a strong need to explore and see the world, though you also need a comfortable home base. You travel to expand your mind and broaden your experience; you are attracted to places way off the beaten track and are not fazed by things that are 'different'. Your practicality ensures your success when it comes to manifesting your vision. In love you are warm and generous. You crave excitement and are easily bored, so it is important you find ways of keeping the flame of passion alive. Guard against taking on too much and not giving yourself enough rest.

TAROT CARD: The Hermit
PLANETS: Jupiter and Venus
QUOTE: *'Take your work seriously, but never yourself.'* Margot Fonteyn

STRENGTHS: Contemplative and open-minded, ardent.
WEAKNESSES: Thrill-seeker, prone to exhaustion.

BORN ON THIS DAY:
Frank Capra
(filmmaker)
Perry Como
(singer and entertainer)
Margot Fonteyn
(ballet dancer)
Walter Gropius
(architect – founder of Bauhaus)
Pope John Paul II
Bertrand Russell
(writer, mathematician and philosopher)

MEDITATION:
Happiness never decreases by being shared.

43

May 19

MEDITATION:

Every moment is an experience.

You are a loyal and responsible person commanding of respect; even in childhood you have an air of authority about you. You are a natural leader, a good judge of character and someone people rely on – sometimes too much. You tell it how it is and are direct in your manner, but in such a way that doesn't upset people. You are unflappable and a solid rock when times are bad. You prefer to do things that have been tried and tested. You need to produce something tangible in your life that will stand the test of time. Your relationships are made for life and you work hard to make your marriage work. You have a strong need for security and your home is your castle. You can comfort eat when tired, so take care of your body – a massage does wonders for you.

TAROT CARD: The Wheel of Fortune
PLANETS: Saturn and Venus
QUOTE: *'Love other human beings as you would love yourself.'* Ho Chi Minh

STRENGTHS: Reliable with great leadership skills.
WEAKNESSES: Overly cautious and uptight.

May 20

MEDITATION:

With our thoughts we make the world.

You are a down-to-earth person and yet have enormous style and great taste in clothes and furniture. You are stable and unflappable with a dry sense of humour that people either love or hate. You adore food and wine and the rituals that surround them; this means that you are prone to over-indulging at times. You adore the scents and sounds of life and are well suited to living in the countryside. You are a kind person who offers practical help to people. You are inclined to carry the weight of the world on your shoulders and neglect your own needs. You are prone to illness because what you really want is attention. Sharing with your partner, and letting others help you, is crucial for your well-being. You can get too comfortable and stuck in a rut so you are wise to choose a partner who encourages you to be active.

TAROT CARD: The High Priestess
PLANETS: Venus and Venus
QUOTE: *'Husbands are like fires – they go out when they're left unattended.'* Cher

STRENGTHS: Extremely stylish, kind and faithful.
WEAKNESSES: Easily perturbed, gluttonous.

May 21

You are a Peter Pan, with a butterfly-esque mind, darting from one thing to another. You are a cerebral and self-analysing person who loves facts and collecting information. Surprisingly, you also love playing games, the sillier the better. You are on the move all day long, and were born with a phone in your hand. Sometimes you are so busy multi-tasking and communicating with the world that you forget the person you are with. Loved ones can find this distracting and after a while very irritating. Turning your mobile and the internet off in the evening and focussing your attention on your partner and friends will reap huge rewards. Be aware that your sharp mind can come across as brisk or even cutting, especially when you're tired. Slow down, relax with a cup of tea and allow your partner to truly comfort you.

TAROT CARD: The Lovers
PLANETS: Mercury and Venus
QUOTE: '...can't change the world unless we change ourselves.' The Notorious BIG

STRENGTHS: Good-humoured and engaging.
WEAKNESSES: Easily distracted and manic.

BORN ON THIS DAY:
Malcolm Fraser
(Australian prime minister) Robert Montgomery
(actor and director)
The Notorious BIG
(rapper)
Henri Rousseau
(artist)
Laurence Tureaud – 'Mr T'
(actor)
Fats Waller
(pianist)

MEDITATION:
It is better to conquer yourself than to win a thousand battles.

TYPICAL TAURUS:

MALCOLM X

'I believe in human beings, and that all human beings should be respected as such, regardless of their color.'

TAUREAN TRAITS:

Taurus is the warmest of the three air signs, the lover of nature, of the arts and of fellow humans. Taureans like to feel secure and surrounded by the things they love – including beautiful clothes, cars and jewellery. For a sign that is so in tune with nature, Taurus is also extremely materialistic.

3 ♊

Gemini

May 22 – June 21

TAROT CARD: The Lovers

ELEMENT: Air

QUALITY: Mutable

NUMBER: 3

RULING PLANET: Mercury

GEMSTONES: Emerald, beryl, crystal, garnet, topaz, chrystolite

COLOUR: Green

DAY OF THE WEEK: Wednesday

COMPATIBLE SIGNS: Aries, Capricorn, Virgo

KEY WORDS: Light-hearted, cheerful, intelligent, versatile, clear thinking, talkative, nervous and excitable

ANATOMY: Hands and arms, lungs

HERBS, PLANTS AND TREES: Yarrow, woodbine, vervain, tansy, dog grass, madder

KEY PHRASE:
I think

Gemini is the messenger of the zodiac, and corresponds to the transition between spring and summer. The lungs and arm are ruled by this sign and so Geminis tend to use their hands a lot when in conversation. Immensely curious, they are always seeking new information, but can suffer from nervous exhaustion if they become over-stimulated, so this has to be guarded against.

As the third sign of the zodiac, Gemini explores the neighbourhood that Taurus has cultivated. Mercury governs the roads and rivers, trade and commerce, consequently Geminis love to live in cities and thrive on the buzz and business. Geminis are often found in coffee bars and on the internet in chat forums – anywhere people meet and exchange ideas. Gemini represents the time when a young child starts to talk and relate to their siblings and neighbours.

PLANETARY RULER AND QUALITIES
Gemini is a mutable air sign. As the first air sign it circulates messages and the news, consequently Geminis ask excellent questions and make brilliant journalists. You are ruled by Mercury, which, because it is the closest planet to the sun, often remains invisible. Gemini is like quicksilver, ever changing, fast moving and a chameleon. Mercury (also known as Hermes) was always playing tricks on the other gods. He was a precocious baby, inventing the lyre one day after his birth and stealing Apollo's cattle during the night after. Luckily, the god was enchanted by the lyre and forgave him. Geminis make excellent mimics and linguists and adore playing charades.

RELATIONSHIPS
Geminis are great fun to be with. You are always talking, so a good mental connection with your partner is vital for you. Friendships come easily, and you have a light approach to relationships. You are ever youthful and attractive and need a lot of variety in your life. Due to this, and your need for freedom to play the field and try all that love has to offer, marriage does not top your list of priorities.

However, this does change as you reach your thirties – but not until you find that special someone that you can respect as an equal.

Geminis are attracted to the other air signs, Libra and Aquarius, and are fascinated by Sagittarius, their opposite, with whom they share a love of knowledge. Best friends and marriage partners are Arians; Capricorns make the best business partners. You share a common bond with Virgos, whose sign is also ruled by Mercury.

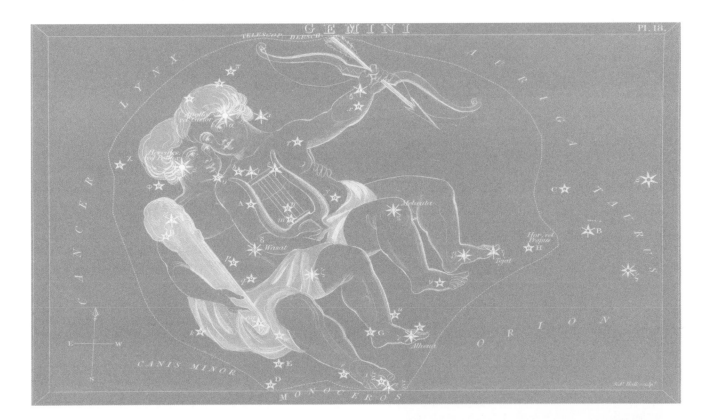

MYTH

Gemini is in the constellation of Castor and Pollux, who were twin brothers. The twins shared the same mother but had different fathers which meant that Pollux was immortal and Castor was mortal. Castor was a skilled horse trainer and Pollux an expert boxer. Inseparable, the brothers were never apart and when Castor died, Pollux asked Zeus to let him share his own immortality with his twin, so they could be together. They were both transformed into the Gemini constellation.

STRENGTHS AND WEAKNESSES

Geminis love variety and often have two of everything – two cars, two homes, two careers and, occasionally, two lovers. The proverbial butterfly, you can be fickle and easily distracted, and find it difficult to stay still and focus. Geminis are the broadcasters of the zodiac, and will tell the world other people's business. You make ideal networkers but can be gossips. This isn't ill-meant – you just love to know what's going on. If you want something 'leaked', tell a Gemini!

You were born with a phone in your hand and enjoy the fast-moving world of the marketplace and commerce. Geminis invented multi-tasking, internet-enabled phones and the art of having more than one project on the go.

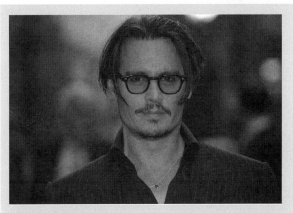

TYPICAL GEMINI:
JOHNNY DEPP

'If there's any message to my work, it is ultimately that it's OK to be different, that it's good to be different, that we should question ourselves before we pass judgement on someone who looks different, behaves different, talks different, is a different colour.'

GEMINIAN POWERS: Lover of diversity, a social butterfly who has a way with words.

GEMINIAN NEGATIVES: A scandalmonger, prone to anxiety.

May 22

MEDITATION:
*Remember what
true love is.*

You have a way with words that can win the hearts of children and adults alike. You are a great thinker yet make decisions that are led by your emotions. You have a light-hearted attitude to life and people adore being in your convivial company. You work well with children because you share their eagerness to learn and absorb new ideas. At times you can appear unsure of yourself as you are impressionable and changeable depending on the latest advice you've been given. You marry young as you adore kids and family life. You fall in love at the drop of a hat and you need constant affection and cuddles. However, your moodiness can drive a partner away. Watch what you eat and take the advice of a nutritionist as your digestive system is sensitive to your swings in emotions.

TAROT CARD: The Emperor
PLANETS: Moon and Mercury
QUOTE: *'We can't command our love, but we can our actions.'* Arthur Conan Doyle

STRENGTHS: Friendly with a carefree approach to life.
WEAKNESSES: Capricious and ambivalent.

May 23

MEDITATION:
*Simplicity is the
ultimate sophistication.*

You are a glamorous star in the show that is your life. Even as a child you had an air of royalty about you, and your friendly nature combined with the warmth you emit toward others makes you immediately popular. You learnt early in life how to exaggerate for effect and no one cares whether what you say is true, as you are extremely entertaining with your stories – keeping people captivated for hours. You are a natural performer and although you are great fun you are also an ambitious person with a strong determination that belies your sometimes fluffy persona. You need a partner who treats you with masses of affection and strokes. This, sometimes desperate, need for flattery can severely upset a partner but so long as you return the favour now and again they'll continue to adore you.

TAROT: The Hierophant
PLANETS: Sun and Mercury
QUOTE: *'I mean, even my dressing room at the studio has candles and cushions and cashmere rugs and things.'* Joan Collins

STRENGTHS: Humorous, compelling.
WEAKNESSES: Emotionally insecure, overly flamboyant.

May 24

You are a down-to-earth person who applies what you learn in a practical way. You desire to be truly in service to others. You are quite critical and have a strong perfectionist streak. This trait can create the frustration of having a lot of projects that never get finished because you can't bear to let them go until they are 'just so'. In spite of this, you have ability to make good decisions and to think on your feet. Working in the fast-moving radio, TV or stock market worlds would be good for you because they would teach you to meet deadlines. You are always on the go and this hectic lifestyle can put a strain on your relationships. Your desire for perfectionism extends to your partner, who has to be good-looking, intellectual and witty! Relax and acknowledge the fact that no one is perfect.

TAROT CARD: The Lovers
PLANETS: Mercury and Mercury
QUOTE: *'A man is a success if he gets up in the morning and gets to bed at night, and in between he does what he wants to do.'* Bob Dylan

STRENGTHS: Unpretentious, a quick thinker.
WEAKNESSES: Perfectionist, fussy.

BORN ON THIS DAY:
Jim Broadbent
(actor)
Eric Cantona
(soccer player and actor)
George Washington Carver
(botanist, naturalist and chemist)
Bob Dylan
(singer/songwriter, musician, artist and poet)
Priscilla Presley
(actor and wife of Elvis Presley)
Queen Victoria
(British monarch)

MEDITATION:
Gold cannot be pure, and people cannot be perfect.

May 25

You are a gifted communicator who can charm the birds from the trees. Extremely sociable, you adore being with people and fill your diary with social events and outings. You love the buzz of city life, even when you're not working; exploring the world's great cities – especially in Europe – is the ideal vacation. You are a good friend and are always available for a chat. You are impartial, so people turn to you when there is a dispute. Your aim in life is to make people happy, and largely you succeed. You have a large circle of friends. Your partner needs to be seen as desirable, because appearance matters to you. They also have to have a good mind or you'll get bored. You cannot bear to be anywhere that's unpleasant. When stressed you need to get away to a peaceful, beautiful sanctuary to restore your inner peace.

TAROT CARD: The Chariot
PLANETS: Venus and Mercury
QUOTE: *'A friend may well be reckoned the masterpiece of nature.'*
Ralph Waldo Emerson

STRENGTHS: Captivating and extremely sociable.
WEAKNESSES: Constantly craving excitement, too impartial at times.

BORN ON THIS DAY:
Ralph Waldo Emerson
(writer and poet)
Ian McKellen
(actor)
Claudio Monteverdi
(composer)
Mike Myers
(actor, comedian, screenwriter and producer)
Padre Pio
(Capuchin monk and healer)
Zim Zimmerman
(cartoonist)

MEDITATION:
Remember that boredom is an insult to oneself.

May 26

You are a complex person with both a light and dark side. You make a powerful first impression as you are a magnetic, effervescent personality. You have a way of moving your body that is hypnotic, graceful and intense. You have immense courage and will never give up once you have committed to a course of action. You go the distance and can bounce back from emotional pain with a joke and cheerfulness that surprises others. You are immensely curious and research everything. Naturally suspicious, you take nothing at face value. Your sexual magnetism is strong and in romance you play the field. Once you settle down you can suffer from jealousy and need to learn to trust your partner. You need a confidant or therapist with whom you can discuss your deepest feelings.

TAROT CARD: Strength
PLANETS: Pluto and Mercury
QUOTE: *'I know what I've done for music, but don't call me a legend. Just call me Miles Davis.'* Miles Davis

STRENGTHS: Vivacious and spirited.
WEAKNESSES: Sceptical and prone to jealousy.

BORN ON THIS DAY:
Zola Budd
(champion long distance runner)
Miles Davis
(musician)
Isadora Duncan
(dancer and child star)
Prince Edward, Duke of York
(British royal)
Peggy Lee
(singer)
John Wayne
(actor, film director and producer)

MEDITATION:
No man becomes a fool until he stops asking questions.

May 27

You are a traveller in both mind and body. Constantly learning something new, you are the eternal student. Depending on your education and how disciplined you are, you will become the philosopher as you get older. You are both the student and the teacher and work well with young people, whatever your age. Your insatiable curiosity can get you into trouble when you overstep the mark by asking too many questions. You are a fascinating companion and would make a great tour guide because you are so well informed. In relationships your thirst for information means you can talk without listening for the answer – this habit can drive partners crazy. Writing down whatever comes into your head every morning for half an hour would help give you focus.

TAROT CARD: The Hermit
PLANETS: Jupiter and Mercury
QUOTE: *'No one will ever win the battle of the sexes; there's too much fraternizing with the enemy.'* Henry Kissinger

STRENGTHS: A deep thinker, adaptable.
WEAKNESSES: Preoccupied and interrogatory.

BORN ON THIS DAY:
Rachel Carson
(marine biologist and green pioneer)
Joseph Fiennes
(actor)
Neil Finn
(lead singer – Crowded House)
Henry Kissinger
(political scientist and diplomat)
Christopher Lee
(actor)
Vincent Price
(actor)

MEDITATION:
Worry often gives a small thing a big shadow.

May 28

You are a serious yet fun person. A disciplined writer and wordsmith, you are prepared to work diligently over a long period of time to craft the finest letter, poem or piece of prose you possibly can. You have an 'old head on young shoulders' and can be promoted early in your career to a high position. Bosses like the respect you give them. You can say 'yes' on impulse then change your mind and take forever to come to a final decision. You are shrewd and have a quick mind, so are well suited to business, especially with your aptitude for maths, finance and admin. In relationships you are serious; you could be content with an older partner. You love solitude and so would get on best with someone who has their own career or is happy to do their own thing without you. Your meditation would be writing your novel.

TAROT CARD: The Wheel of Fortune
PLANETS: Saturn and Mercury
QUOTE: *'Part of me is a sexual exhibitionist.'*
Kylie Minogue

STRENGTHS: Perceptive, well-mannered.
WEAKNESSES: Hesitant, a loner.

BORN ON THIS DAY:
Carol Baker
(actor)
Ian Fleming
(writer – creator of James Bond)
Rudolph Giuliani
(mayor of New York)
Gladys Knight
(singer)
Kylie Minogue
(singer)
William Pitt the Younger
(British politician)

MEDITATION:
Remember the difference beween loneliness and solitude.

May 29

You are a natural reformer, an extraordinary person with an unusual way of expressing yourself that is highly engaging. A free thinker, you are one of a kind, with revolutionary ideas that can be ahead of their time. You come across as being light-hearted, but this impression belies the deep connection you have in your soul with the rest of humanity and your belief that you are here to serve them. Your intention is to make the world a better place by what you say. In love you need an intellectual equal and best friend, but you shy away from deep emotions. Your need for a lot of personal space can prevent true intimacy with your partner. Lack of exercise can be a problem, especially if you tend to spend hours each day working at a desk; try to make time in your schedule for pilates or gentle yoga to stretch your limbs.

TAROT CARD: Justice
PLANETS: Uranus and Mercury
QUOTE: *'I don't feel old. I don't feel anything till noon. That's when it's time for my nap.'*
Bob Hope

STRENGTHS: Progressive, a philanthropist.
WEAKNESSES: Scared of personal emotions, too independent at times.

BORN ON THIS DAY:
Melanie Brown
(singer – Spice Girls and TV personality)
G. K. Chesterton
(writer and poet)
Rupert Everett
(actor)
Patrick Henry
(American revolutionary war leader)
Bob Hope
(actor and comedian)
John F. Kennedy
(US president)

MEDITATION:
By neglecting your own emotions someone you love will get hurt.

51

May 30

You are incredibly versatile and skilful, especially with your hands. You express yourself as much with your hands as your mouth when you speak. You have an agile mind and are sensitive to the nuances of sound and language. Your friendly nature is irresistible. You are very funny and love telling childish jokes. You are inventive and love new things, so much so that you tire quickly of anything that's 'old'. You have masses of contacts in your address book and make the ideal social networker, always connecting people with each other. In romantic relationships you need to know what's going on in the mind of your partner and can be accused of texting far too often. 'Twitter' to the world or watch the 24-hour news programmes to satisfy your thirst for the sound bite.

BORN ON THIS DAY:
Albrecht Durer
(artist and engraver)
Peter Carl Fabergé
(goldsmith and jewellery designer)
Benny Goodman
(clarinetist and bandleader)
Peter the Great
(Russian emperor)
Wynonna Judd
(singer)
Larry G. Spangler
(film director)

MEDITATION:
A single conversation with a wise man is better than ten years of study.

TAROT CARD: The Lovers
PLANETS: Mercury and Mercury
QUOTE: *'I have conquered an empire but I have not been able to conquer myself.'*
Peter the Great

STRENGTHS: Practical, entertaining.
WEAKNESSES: Easily bored, information-hungry.

May 31

You are a lively person with a soft heart. Sensitive to the mood of the public, and with the ability to express the feelings of those who cannot speak for themselves, you are suited to being a spokesperson for a group. You delight in being with people and have a host of friends and family eager to see you. You keep everyone in touch with each other and have the tendency to worry if someone disappears from your radar; remember, they may just want time to themselves. Your chatty and charming persona is well suited to working with the elderly because you can cheer them up just by being you. You often feel your partner is so familiar you've known them all your life, and you can end up marrying the boy/girl next door. At times you can take what people say too personally. Brush off their comments with a winning smile.

BORN ON THIS DAY:
Clint Eastwood
(actor)
Colin Farrell
(actor)
Rainier III
(sovereign of Monaco)
Brooke Shields
(actor and model)
Terry Waite
(humanitarian and released hostage)
Walt Whitman
(poet)

MEDITATION:
You cannot shake hands with a clenched fist.

TAROT CARD: The Emperor
PLANETS: Moon and Mercury
QUOTE: *'The less secure a man is, the more likely he is to have extreme prejudice.'*
Clint Eastwood

STRENGTHS: Compassionate and protective towards others.
WEAKNESSES: Over-sensitive and ruled by emotion.

June 1

You are an effervescent person bubbling over with energy. You can multi-task and are always up to date with the latest news and gossip. You have such a quick mind that people who are slow to catch on are often a source of irritation. Your innate curiosity about life and the entrancing childlike side to your personality keep you forever young – although with this comes an air of naivety. You are highly persuasive. Your biggest assets are your wit and humour. When in love you bore easily, so you need a partner who is as intellectually lively as you are to keep you mentally stimulated. Expressing your innermost feelings can be a difficulty. You can exhaust yourself by talking too much, so getting in touch with your body, and your breathing, by jogging or running is an excellent corrective.

TAROT CARD: The Magician
PLANETS: Mars and Mercury
QUOTE: *'I've been on a calendar, but I've never been on time.'* Marilyn Monroe

STRENGTHS: Inquisitive and vibrant.
WEAKNESSES: Immature and impatient.

BORN ON THIS DAY:
Pat Boone
(singer and actor)
Morgan Freeman
(actor)
Bob Monkhouse
(comedian)
Marilyn Monroe
(actor, singer and model)
Nelson Riddle
(composer and conductor)
Ronnie Wood
(guitarist – The Rolling Stones)

MEDITATION:

Respect yourself and others will respect you.

June 2

You are a sensual person with a strong intellect. There are two sides to you – you can think both with the heart and the head. You are often rushing around the city one minute, then relaxing in a garden with a bottle of wine the next. Luckily, you do realize the need to balance your active social life with some downtime. You are a stylish person who loves to keep up to date with fashion. You tend to take everything at face value, to the detriment of your spiritual side. Relationships are vital for you and you are never alone for long. You flirt outrageously because you love the opposite sex and they love you, too. Yet in your heart you are both incredibly loyal and faithful. You relax best when you are using all your senses, so preparing and cooking an exotic meal is your idea of fun.

TAROT CARD: The High Priestess
PLANETS: Venus and Mercury
QUOTE: *'It is difficult for a woman to define her feelings in a language which is chiefly made by men to express theirs.'* Thomas Hardy

STRENGTHS: Level-headed and easy-going.
WEAKNESSES: Flirtatious and sometimes lacking depth.

BORN ON THIS DAY:
Keith Allen
(actor)
Sir Edward Elgar
(composer)
Thomas Hardy
(poet and writer)
Stacy Keach
(actor)
Marquis de Sade
(writer)
Charlie Watts
(drummer – The Rolling Stones)

MEDITATION:

Beauty is power; a smile is its sword.

53

June 3

BORN ON THIS DAY:
Raúl Castro
(president of Cuba)
Tony Curtis
(actor)
King George V
(British monarch)
Allen Ginsberg
(writer and poet)
Curtis Mayfield
(singer)
Suzi Quatro
(musician, singer/songwriter)

MEDITATION:

Follow your inner moonlight; don't hide the madness.

You are the eternal youth, and retain a childlike air about you, whatever your age. You bubble over with enthusiasm, and are always thinking and talking very fast. It's hard for slower types to keep up with you. You have a gift for languages and can easily mimic voices. This makes you an excellent actor or translator. Your immense curiosity about people means you are always asking questions. This can be misread as flirtatiousness. People can assume you are interested in them, which you are, but not necessarily romantically. You find expressing emotions uncomfortable and are wary of over-intense types. You need nurturing and appreciate a partner who is at home when you return from your busy work life. Learning about emotional intelligence would hugely benefit you, and you'd enjoy the results in your love life.

TAROT CARD: The Empress
PLANETS: Mercury and Mercury
QUOTE: *'How is the Empire?'*
King George V

STRENGTHS: Articulate, youthful outlook on life.
WEAKNESSES: Uncomfortable with feelings of the heart, fast-talker.

June 4

BORN ON THIS DAY:
Gene Barry
(actor)
Matt Gonzalez
(activist and poet)
Angelina Jolie
(actor and humanitarian)
Dennis Weaver
(actor)
Heinrich Otto Wieland
(chemist and Nobel Prize winner)
Noah Wyle
(actor)

MEDITATION:

Don't talk too fast – you may say something you haven't thought of yet.

You are a kind and charming person with a deep connection to the past and to your family and ancestry. Your ability to remember and record is ideally suited to the occupation of diarist or writer, especially of children's fiction. You need to create a home with lots of activity for all the family, and there is always a group activity in full-flow. You love going on outings to places you knew as a child and they bring back memories of the great times you had. The way to your heart is an easy path; you are turned on by the sound of a person's voice and if they can cook like your mother did, all the better. Your partner is undoubtedly your best friend and more like a brother/sister at times. When you're tired of talking, it's best to eat your childhood favourites; you'll feel comforted by the taste and the memories.

TAROT CARD: The Emperor
PLANETS: Moon and Mercury
QUOTE: *'We come to love not by finding the perfect person, but by learning to see an imperfect person perfectly.'* Angelina Jolie

STRENGTHS: Wordsmith, sentimental.
WEAKNESSES: Not focussed, over talkative at times.

June 5

Although you have a regal bearing, you are a relaxed and approachable person at heart. You are a born storyteller and can't resist embellishing your life with brilliantly observed anecdotes which can somewhat stretch the truth. However, you are a person with integrity and the stories are for entertainment purposes only. As a self-dramatist you are ideally suited to the movie or media world. The other field you could do well in is sales because you can convince people to buy anything. Your innate mischieviousness certainly livens up a dull world. In romance you are very fussy and want the best – mere mortals need not apply! Playing charades is a wonderful way for you to let off steam because you are so good at it and you are certain to get the applause you love.

TAROT CARD: The Hierophant
PLANETS: Sun and Mercury
QUOTE: *'The purpose of anthropology is to make the world safe for human differences.'* Ruth Benedict

STRENGTHS: Congenial and playful.
WEAKNESSES: A show-off, a raconteur.

BORN ON THIS DAY:
John Couch Adams
(mathematician and astronomer)
Ruth Benedict
(anthropologist)
William Boyd
(actor)
Igor Stravinsky
(composer)
Pancho Villa
(Mexican revolutionary)
Mark Wahlberg
(actor and film producer)

MEDITATION:
Don't speak unless you can improve on the silence.

June 6

You are a conscientious person who would never let anyone down. You are here to be of service and give your practical expertise to benefit others. You have a dry wit which you sometimes use to flirt discreetly. Your fine analytical mind is suited to work in which detail matters. You have good hand-eye coordination which is brilliant for sport or technical design. You are someone with a lot of hobbies because you get bored if your mind isn't constantly stimulated. In romance you love the chase and need someone who is devoted to you. Marry someone who keeps you young. Your helpfulness is your biggest asset, but be aware of being over-used in this role. Any self-pity is most unattractive so put your energies into creativity – carving or painting will totally absorb you.

TAROT CARD: The Lovers
PLANETS: Mercury and Mercury
QUOTE: *'Everything is politics.'* Thomas Mann

STRENGTHS: Supportive and diligent.
WEAKNESSES: Prone to self-pity, manic.

BORN ON THIS DAY:
David Abercrombie
(businessman)
Sandra Bernhard
(comedian and actor)
Björn Borg
(champion tennis player)
Thomas Mann
(writer and Nobel Prize winner)
Alexander Pushkin
(writer)
Captain Robert Falcon Scott
(explorer – Scott of the Antarctic)

MEDITATION:
Self-pity is self-destruction.

June 7

MEDITATION:

Focus:
Wherever you are,
be there.

You are a charmer and make a delightful host with your ability to bring people together. They love being in your company as you have an uncanny knack of knowing what to say and when to say it – to soothe and make everyone feel at ease. You are artistic by trade or by soul, with a great sense of style. You have a bright and breezy manner which is refreshing and cheers people up. You love travelling to new places. In your love life you thrive when your partner shares your busy life. You are loyal but because you can see both points of view you can seem unsupportive; there are times when your partner needs to know that you are unequivocally on their side. When you're at home relaxing, turn off the TV and give your full attention to your partner. Talking will calm your mind and benefit your relationship.

TAROT CARD: The Chariot
PLANETS: Venus and Mercury
QUOTE: *'I shut my eyes in order to see.'*
Paul Gauguin

STRENGTHS: Charming and hospitable.
WEAKNESSES: Vague, lacking concentration at times.

June 8

MEDITATION:

A proverb is the
wisdom of many
and the wit of one.

You are a natural joker with a scathing wit, which can be used to great effect in politics or when crusading for a cause you believe in. You have a rapier-like skill with words that can make fools out of your enemies, especially those who mistakenly mark you down as a lightweight. You are a wonderful counsellor because you understand human emotions and offer sound advice. Your ability to laugh in the face of adversity gives you a resilience that others admire. At times you scatter your energies and can change allegiance on a whim, completely wrong-footing those who believe in you. You need a passionate partner who understands that your jokes hide a sensitive soul and is not put off when your temper gets the better of you. A long hot bath soothes you when life gets too hectic.

TAROT CARD: Strength
PLANETS: Pluto and Mercury
QUOTE: *'I have flabby thighs, but fortunately my stomach covers them.'* Joan Rivers

STRENGTHS: Sympathetic and hot-blooded.
WEAKNESSES: Indecisive, scathing wit.

June 9

You are warm and enthusiastic with a delightful gift of the gab. You can make intuitive leaps of understanding that take the breath away. You are likeable and popular and have many friends from different backgrounds. You are forever bursting with excitement about a latest project, which tends to involve a host of people from all over the world. You see life as an adventure. You are attracted to study the great thinkers and philosophers in history, and love immersing yourself in ancient knowledge. You fall in love with people from other cultures and it's more than likely that you end up marrying a foreigner. You can be juvenile when it comes to affairs of the heart. Your need for freedom to roam makes it difficult for you to settle in one place. Running is the perfect exercise for you to use up all your excess energy.

TAROT CARD: The Hermit
PLANETS: Jupiter and Mercury
QUOTE: *'I'm perceived as being really young and yet I have the clinical condition of an old man.'* Michael J. Fox

STRENGTHS: An adventurer, charming.
WEAKNESSES: Emotionally immature, restless.

BORN ON THIS DAY:
Matthew Bellamy
(musician, singer/songwriter – Muse)
Patricia Cornwell
(writer)
Johnny Depp
(actor, screenwriter, producer and director)
Michael J. Fox
(actor and writer)
Cole Porter
(composer)
Eugen Verboeckhoven
(artist)

MEDITATION:
Nothing is a waste of time if you use the experience wisely.

June 10

You are a person who appears older in youth and younger in old age! You have a social conscience and can work well with the underprivileged, in particular young people. You are known for your pungent wit and can at times be quite cynical. You are clever and study hard to succeed in life. You can still be studying well into old age. You hide your pessimism and inner doubt under a veneer of brightness and laughter. In relationships you are shy and reserved, but partners are drawn to your grace and elegant manner. You have a common-sense approach to life's problems, but can't be as sanguine when it comes to your personal life because of the difficulty you have sharing your emotions with those you love. You need to be active, and mastering complex dance steps is fun for you.

TAROT CARD: The Wheel of Fortune
PLANETS: Saturn and Mercury
QUOTE: *'If I am a legend, then why am I so lonely?'* Judy Garland

STRENGTHS: Chic, levelheaded.
WEAKNESSES: Cynical and self-doubting.

BORN ON THIS DAY:
Gustave Courbet
(artist)
Faith Evans
(singer)
Judy Garland
(singer and actor)
Patachou
(actor and singer)
Prince Philip
(consort to Queen Elizabeth II)
Henry Morton Stanley
(explorer)

MEDITATION:
Anyone who has never made a mistake has never tried anything new.

3

June 11

MEDITATION:

You can only learn to love by loving.

You are a person who aspires to know the truth and seeks out clever methods to solve the world's problems. Fascinated by people, you love discussing intellectual topics way into the night. You can be expert at organizing networking groups and are up to the minute with new technology. You are an excellent negotiator because you are objective and clear headed. You have the ability to spot business opportunities. You love to hang out with friends, especially oddball types, who you find particularly fascinating. You are seeking mutual understanding at an intellectual level with your love partner and often are an advocate of 'open' relationships. This is really because you feel out of your depth with emotions. Acupuncture that gets your *chi* moving is very helpful for you.

TAROT CARD: Justice
PLANETS: Uranus and Mercury
QUOTE: *'No sooner does man discover intelligence than he tries to involve it in his own stupidity.'* Jacques Yves Cousteau

STRENGTHS: Problem-solver, a good mediator.
WEAKNESSES: Scared of commitment, emotionally naive.

June 12

MEDITATION:

There is no remedy for love but to love more.

You are a highly sensitive soul who uses a lot of words to cover up and disguise your vulnerability. You are prone to sentimentality and can be capricious as your feelings get the better of you. You have an in-built radar for any criticism coming your way. As well as being highly adaptable, you have a rich imagination which is very creative. You possess innate musical talent, and have a talent for writing lyrics. Romance thrills you but you can often be attracted to people who don't return your feelings. You are worth more and need someone who adores the fact that you wear your heart on your sleeve and appreciates your expressions of love. Boundaries are an issue; you can identify too deeply with the world's victims. Your proneness to colds stems from an inability to allow yourself to cry when you feel sad.

TAROT CARD: The Hanged Man
PLANETS: Neptune and Mercury
QUOTE: *'I don't think of all the misery but of the beauty that still remains.'* Anne Frank

STRENGTHS: Loving and inspired.
WEAKNESSES: Moody and over-sensitive.

June 13

You are a chatty and welcoming person who can entertain and charm people with witticisms. You are a quick learner and are mainly auditory, so prefer to listen rather than read. You are torn between deciding what rules you, your head or heart? Some people perceive you as being muddled and you would do well to assess your opinions in private rather than talk too openly with those in authority. You can become defensive when criticized; mostly criticism will relate to your tendency to spread yourself too thin. Your busy social life and caring for those less fortunate can distract you from finding your true love. A partner will need to understand that your natural flirtatiousness is innocent. You need to calm down; lavender in your bath or on your pillow would help when getting to sleep is a problem.

TAROT CARD: Death
PLANETS: Moon and Mercury
QUOTE: *'The worst thing about some men is that when they are not drunk they are sober.'* William Butler Yeats

STRENGTHS: Funny, versatile.
WEAKNESSES: Easily distracted and chaotic.

BORN ON THIS DAY:
Malcolm McDowell
(actor)
Ban Ki-moon
(UN secetary general)
James Clerk Maxwell
(physicist)
Ashley and Mary Kate Olsen
(actor twins)
Basil Rathbone
(actor)
William Butler Yeats
(writer and poet)

MEDITATION:
Turn chaos into art.

June 14

You are a natural game player and view life through the eyes of a child, using your imaginative streak and competitive side in everything you do. By combining humour with a cheerful manner and exuding confidence, you excel at public speaking. You have strong principles which others admire, or hate, depending on their view. You are a born leader and adore the hectic world of business, as long as you are leading the way. You work your way to the top with your affability, making your mark as an individual who has something of importance to communicate. You radiate charisma and it is difficult for you to find someone who you can respect as your equal but who treats you in the manner to which you have become accustomed. When you give yourself, you give wholeheartedly.

TAROT CARD: The Hierophant
PLANETS: Sun and Mercury
QUOTE: *'When you lose a couple of times, it makes you realize how difficult it is to win.'* Steffi Graf

STRENGTHS: Charismatic with high aspirations.
WEAKNESSES: Sore loser and unable to take orders.

BORN ON THIS DAY:
Alois Alzheimer
(pathologist)
Steffi Graf
(champion tennis player)
Burl Ives
(singer and actor)
Nikolaus Otto
(inventor of the combustion engine)
Donald Trump
(entrepreneur)
Sam Wanamaker
(actor)

MEDITATION:
Being gracious is just as important as being a winner.

June 15

MEDITATION:

You, yourself, as much as anybody... deserve your love and affection.

You are a natural comedian, skilled in the art of the one-liner, who delights in having fun. But there is another, very different side to your character, because you also have a sharp, clever mind and love being in an intellectual environment at work and at home. You love to learn, especially if you can apply your studies in a practical way immediately. You can't help but share what you know with others, and so would make a wonderful teacher. In romance you enjoy the dance of courtship and can communicate well with your partner. Your weakness is when you neglect to share your feelings and get caught in the everyday world of trivia. Learning massage with your partner would be of mutual benefit and help you get more in touch with your senses.

TAROT CARD: The Devil
PLANETS: Mercury and Mercury
QUOTE: *'I may be crazy, but it keeps me from going insane.'* Waylon Jennings

STRENGTHS: Cheerful and erudite.
WEAKNESSES: Prone to self-neglect, overwhelmed by minor details.

June 16

MEDITATION:

Life is not a problem to be solved but a reality to be experienced.

You are very persuasive and eloquent with a way of disarming people. You believe strongly that justice and truth matter. You have strong diplomatic skills, and are adept at arbitration and keeping the peace. You are highly civilized and have a graceful air about you. Your ideals can inspire others due to your skills as an orator. You appreciate beauty and love arty parties and being a part of the glitterati. In your personal relationships you need variety, and in your daily life you love being around a lot of people. Just being with one person for long periods of time can be difficult for you. You find it hard to accept that there is a dark side to life. An accusation that can be flung at you by disappointed partners is that you are superficial. Avoid caffeine and staying up late as your sleep patterns are highly sensitive.

TAROT CARD: The Chariot
PLANETS: Venus and Mercury
QUOTE: *'If anyone at my funeral has a long face, I'll never speak to him again.'* Stan Laurel

STRENGTHS: Refined and articulate.
WEAKNESSES: Superficial and blinkered to reality.

June 17

You are a bright and bubbly person with a wickedly competitive side. You love playing games, especially those involving mystery and intrigue and which test your strategic skills. You can appear unsympathetic but underneath you are provocative and intense. Interestingly your rivals are also your friends as you spur each other on to excel. Whatever you do in your life there is an inherent power to the message you deliver. Your heart can rule your head and you can put your career on the line for your beliefs. After a wild youth of experimenting, once married you are a devoted and dedicated partner. When you finally give your heart, it will be forever. You love nightlife and seek excitement which can make you frazzled. Spending time near water will provide the balance your soul needs.

TAROT CARD: Strength
PLANETS: Pluto and Mercury
QUOTE: *'In my mind, I'm always the best. If I walk out on the court and think that person is better, I've already lost.'* Venus Williams

STRENGTHS: Enthusiastic and committed.
WEAKNESSES: Flippant, prone to over-exertion.

BORN ON THIS DAY:
André Derain
(artist)
Greg Kinnear
(actor)
Ken Loach
(film director)
Barry Manilow
(singer/songwriter, arranger and producer)
Igor Stravinsky
(composer)
Venus Williams
(champion tennis player)

MEDITATION:
Talk little and listen much.

June 18

You are inquisitive, eternally young and a flamboyant communicator. You have a storyteller's gift. Your stories are worth listening to because they usually have a deeper meaning and a moral to them. You are an optimist, always seeing the bright side even after you've received one of life's hard knocks. You can be impatient and win most debates because of your agile mind. You learn how to survive by using your wits to get you out of trouble. With close partners you can come across as high and mighty because you truly believe you know best and are right. This will cause fights which you see as a chance to show off your superior way with words and win. Ask yourself, do you want to be right or happy? You need to stretch your body and mind. Hiking in the great outdoors is ideal relaxation for you.

TAROT CARD: The Moon
PLANETS: Jupiter and Mercury
QUOTE: *'South Africa belongs to all who live in it, black and white.'* Thabo Mbeki

STRENGTHS: A raconteur, sanguine.
WEAKNESSES: Argumentative, restless.

BORN ON THIS DAY:
Red Adair
(infamous troubleshooter)
Richard Boone
(actor)
Paul McCartney
(singer/songwriter and musician – The Beatles)
George Mallory
(explorer)
Thabo Mbeki
(South African president)
Isabella Rossellini
(actor)

MEDITATION:
Remember time brings roses.

61

3 ♊

June 19

You are a reliable and methodical person who is both serious and carefree. You are okay with routine and can be guaranteed to find the most efficient way to run things – you delight in finding shortcuts. You make an excellent teacher as you can explain complex subjects in a meaningful and interesting way. You have a gift for understatement and appear dry but when you let your hair down you are very funny and border on being saucy. In love you can appear very controlled so you need a partner who is prepared to reassure you that no one ever died of feeling their feelings! At times you can over organize your partner which isn't always what they want. They married a lover not their father/authority figure. Ballroom dancing is an excellent solution where your control is to be admired.

MEDITATION:
You can't direct the wind but you can adjust the sails.

TAROT CARD: The Sun
PLANETS: Saturn and Mercury
QUOTE: *'A book is a version of the world. If you do not like it, ignore it; or offer your own version in return.'* Salman Rushdie

STRENGTHS: Systematic, cheeky.
WEAKNESSES: Emotionally restrained, controlling.

June 20

You are a natural poet, someone who can translate ideas into form whether it is music, art or letters of verse. As a natural wordsmith you can be seduced by someone with a silver tongue, but you need time to discover if they are genuine. You give the impression of being unpredictable, but deep down you are a stable person who appreciates security. You have an innate common sense and can be depended upon once you commit. You are attracted to wild types who are your exact opposite. You can be a muse for an artist, as you inspire them to greatness. When stressed you crave sugar but over-indulgence only makes you feel worse. Reach for a book of Rumi's poetry instead of a chocolate bar. Alternatively reach out to friends on Facebook – it was invented for you.

MEDITATION:
Every object, every being is a jar full of delight.

TAROT CARD: Judgement
PLANETS: Venus and Mercury
QUOTE: *'Women won't let me stay single and I won't let me stay married.'* Errol Flynn

STRENGTHS: Lover of words, canny.
WEAKNESSES: Easily seduced, fickle.

June 21

You are a light-hearted and sociable person with an insatiable curiosity about life. You love words and expressing yourself whether through poetry or song. You have an eternally youthful air about you and are in touch with your inner child. You are a great conversationalist and have an excellent memory for names and remember the tiniest detail about people's lives. You genuinely like people – unless they are rude – and in return they like you. You are concerned for the welfare of others, which serves you well as a social worker. Relationships are a top priority in your life and you need to have a mental affinity with your partner. You can chat and joke at times to avoid your deeper feelings. You tend to scatter your energies, so a calming cup of herbal tea will soothe you.

TAROT CARD: The World
PLANETS: Moon and Mercury
QUOTE: *'Democracy is necessary to peace and to undermining the forces of terrorism.'* Benazir Bhutto

STRENGTHS: Gregarious – a people person.
WEAKNESSES: Of nervous disposition, scared of deep emotion.

BORN ON THIS DAY:
Benazir Bhutto
(Pakistani prime minister)
Ray Davies
(singer/songwriter – The Kinks)
Ron Ely
(actor)
Juliette Lewis
(actor)
Jane Russell
(actor)
Jean Paul Sartre
(writer)

MEDITATION:
When we sip tea, we are on our way to serenity.

TYPICAL GEMINI:
JOHN F. KENNEDY

'Change is the law of life. And those who look only to the past or present are certain to miss the future.'

GEMINI TRAITS:
Geminis are competitive and are able to talk themselves into and out of situations as necessary – a good quality that comes with a side effect – not being able to keep secrets. This is not done maliciously – you just have a constant love for communication!

4

Cancer

June 22 – July 22

TAROT CARD: The Chariot

ELEMENT: Water

QUALITY: Cardinal

NUMBER: 4

RULING PLANET: Moon

GEMSTONES: Pearl and moonstone

COLOURS: White and silver

DAY OF THE WEEK: Monday

COMPATIBLE SIGNS:
Capricorn, Taurus, Virgo

KEY WORDS: Sensitive to people's
feelings, caring and nurturing, moody,
nostalgic and sentimental

ANATOMY: Chest, breasts and womb,
stomach, alimentary canal

HERBS, PLANTS AND TREES: Cucumber,
squash, melons, all plants that grow in
water eg. water lilies

KEY PHRASE:
I feel

Cancer is the mother and nurturer of the zodiac and is the sign that corresponds with the chest, the breasts, the womb and the stomach. Cancerians are governed by their emotions and, like their symbol, the crab, they carry their homes on their backs. The crab has a protective shell which Cancerians often adopt in order to hide their vulnerable soft interior. Like the crab, you can take three steps forward and two back, but once committed you will eventually achieve your goals.

PLANETARY RULER AND QUALITIES
Cancer is a cardinal water sign. As the first water sign, it gives feeling to the ideas circulated by Gemini, so Cancerians are wonderful at mothering people. Cancer is governed by the moon, which guides us through the cold and darkness of the night, but is always waxing and waning.

The moon is the brightest and most fascinating object in the sky, because it constantly changes shape and moves through the entire zodiac in a month. The moon is the subject of poetry, songs and movies and we all know the effect that it can have on our emotions. The moon is the great mother, and there are 13 lunar months in the solar year. The moon in our astrological birth charts shows us how we were mothered and cared for and how we mother others.

RELATIONSHIPS
All relationships are personal to a Cancerian and it is not possible for you to play it cool. The Cancerian man is very fond of his mother and will compare all partners to her. The Cancerian woman is looking for a man to mother. You can appear shy, are very sensitive and take things personally; when hurt you withdraw into your shell. Cancerians need warmth – you need the light of the sun so you can absorb it and reflect it back to your partner. Cancerians need to care for people and to have that care recognized. You are loyal and faithful and have friends for life. Marriage was made for Cancerians. Your perfect mate is Capricorn, your opposite sign, who can offer you the structure and security you crave. There is potential for a beautiful and easy friendship with the earth signs, Taurus and Virgo. Aries is the masculine and Cancer the feminine, which makes for a hot combination. Leo is good as long as Leo is able to be the king. Scorpio can be too powerful a partner, but Pisceans are perfect – however, Cancer needs to be the decision-maker!

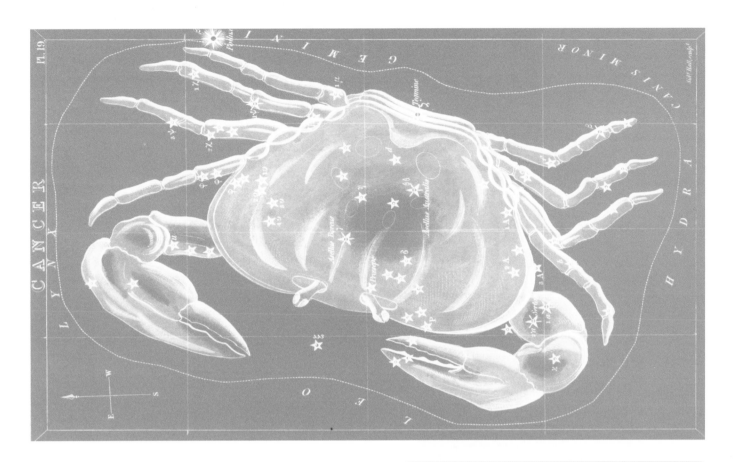

MYTH

Cancer was the crab sent to harass Hercules while he was on his second labour. As he battled the Hydra, Hera – the jealous wife of Zeus – sent a crab to bite his heels. Hercules crushed the crab under his feet, but Hera placed it in the heavens as a reward for its faithful service.

STRENGTHS AND WEAKNESSES

Cancer is the most maternal and nurturing of all the signs. Your softness and sensitivity is both an asset and a weakness. You are very receptive and sympathetic and wear your heart on your sleeve. You excel in taking care of people and are best suited to any profession that serves the public, so you make ideal counsellors, cooks and homemakers. However, you can be touchy and snap at people if offended. You are too easily hurt and your emotions can take over, giving you a reputation for being moody and unstable. You have a vivid imagination and are nostalgic, which means you make great writers and diarists, but you also have a tendency to cling too much to the past. You will defend friends and family to the end and value the security of your home above most things.

TYPICAL CANCER:
NELSON MANDELA

'Never, never and never again shall it be that this beautiful land will again experience the oppression of one by another.'

CANCERIAN POWERS: A true nurturer who always thinks of those around them. Great powers of perseverance – will reach their goal in the end.

CANCERIAN NEGATIVES: Take things personally, withdraw into self when hurt emotionally.

June 22

BORN ON THIS DAY:
John Dillinger
(American gangster)
Sir Henry Rider Haggard
(writer)
Eddie Kidd
(motorcycle stunt rider)
Kris Kristofferson
(singer/songwriter)
Meryl Streep
(actor)
Billy Wilder
(screenwriter and producer)

MEDITATION:

*In time of test,
family is best.*

You are a soft and perceptive person with an excellent memory, assets which serve you well in life. You retain information and have a shrewd mind for business. Devoted to your family and friends, you have a gift for making people feel included. You are imaginative, poetic and observant. You have an uncanny knack of being able to catch the tender and funny moments of family life with your camera or your pen. However, you are also thin-skinned and can hold onto past hurts. Learning to forgive and forget is a lifetime lesson. You value your relationships highly because you need a family of your own. Children give your life meaning. Since you are so emotional, tai 'chi or yoga, which strengthen the inner core, would help you to keep centred.

TAROT CARD: The Emperor
PLANETS: Moon and Moon
QUOTE: *'My family really does come first. It always did and always will.'* Meryl Streep

STRENGTHS: Strong family values, insightful.
WEAKNESSES: Unforgiving and over-sensitive.

June 23

BORN ON THIS DAY:
Selma Blair
(actor)
June Carter
(singer, wife of Johnny Cash)
King Edward VIII
(British monarch)
Johannes Gutenberg
(inventor of the first printing press)
Randy Jackson
(musician and TV personality)
Zinédine Zidane
(soccer player)

MEDITATION:

*There is no pillow so soft
as a clear conscience.*

You are a dramatic yet sensitive person with a shy exterior that hides your warm heart. You are caring and radiate such an extraordinary energy that others want to be near you. You were born to shine, are very talented with a powerful belief in yourself that comes from a happy childhood. You take the lead, whatever your gender. You are a natural performer and can be a bit of a prima donna, but people forgive you, as you truly are great at what you do. In romance you are extremely loving and attentive and give totally of yourself. You are a family person. You need a mate who is creative with a passionate nature to give you the adoration you expect. Unwind by playing games; these have immense appeal – especially those you remember from childhood, such as skipping.

TAROT CARD: The Hierophant
PLANETS: Sun and Moon
QUOTE: *'After you've listened, you'll feel like you know us a little bit better.'* June Carter

STRENGTHS: Self-confident and considerate to the needs of others.
WEAKNESSES: Egotistical and needy.

June 24

You are a delightfully imaginative person who is always kind and helpful to others. You are concerned for the well-being of people and offer practical support. You are thoughtful; a person who remembers birthdays and anniversaries. You are efficient; an asset nowadays since so many people lead busy lives. You could make a career from sorting out the mess in somebody's home or office – filing is your forté! Your clear head and natural concern for the feelings of others means you would never throw away what they might treasure. A happy and committed relationship is a priority for you, and you will work at making it last. At times you can be over-fussy and caught up in trivia. A massage is ideal for when your mind gets bogged down in the minutiae of life.

TAROT CARD: The Lovers
PLANETS: Mercury and Moon
QUOTE: *'I was a pretty good fighter. But it was the writers who made me great.'* Jack Dempsey

STRENGTHS: Considerate, organized.
WEAKNESSES: Fussy and uptight.

BORN ON THIS DAY:
Jeff Beck
(rock guitarist)
Billy Casper
(professional golfer)
Jack Dempsey
(champion boxer)
King Edward I
(British monarch)
Sam Jones
(basketball player)
Horatio Herbert Kitchener
(British field marshall
and statesman)

MEDITATION:
It's not what you look at that matters, it's what you see.

June 25

You are a gracious and likeable person with a strong need to be appreciated for your talents and beauty. You enjoy giving pleasure to people and take a genuine delight in making others happy. You have a social conscience and are patriotic, but can be overly defensive if anyone criticizes your family or your country. You enjoy being a part of a large organization and will be drawn to work in human resources. Your weakness is your tendency to indecision as you don't like to upset people. You settle into a loving relationship early and become a devoted parent. However, you also need to be adored and pampered. When you get down in the doldrums, a trip to the hairdresser will cheer you up and a new outfit will restore your self-esteem.

TAROT CARD: The Chariot
PLANETS: Venus and Moon
QUOTE: *'Serious sport is war minus the shooting.'* George Orwell

STRENGTHS: Charming and righteous.
WEAKNESSES: Hesitant with decision making, over-sensitive.

BORN ON THIS DAY:
Apo Gaga
(Tibetan religious figure)
Antoni Gaudí
(architect)
Ricky Gervais
(actor and comedian)
June Lockhart
(actor)
George Michael
(singer/songwriter)
George Orwell
(writer)

MEDITATION:
A wise man makes his own decisions, an ignorant man follows public opinion.

June 26

BORN ON THIS DAY:
Peter Lorre
(actor)
Willy Messerschmitt
(aeroplane designer)
Eleanor Parker
(actor)
Johannes Schultz
(composer)
William Thomson, 1st Baron Kelvin
(scientist)
Babe Zaharias
(sportswoman)

MEDITATION:
Make your judgement trustworthy by trusting it.

You are a charismatic and intensely emotional person who is unforgettable. There is an air of mystery about you and you can be a master of disguise. When hurt you sulk and can retreat into your shell for a long time until your wounds are healed. You delve into your emotions and love to investigate the dark side of life. You are a superb detective and you love to be entrusted with secrets. You are attracted to a career in the police force or forensics. You are tenacious and determined and have an inner core that can survive almost anything. You need to be adored and usually have many suitors. The one you choose understands that your defences hide a soft and sensitive underbelly. A family outing with a difference such as visiting underground caves will thrill and fascinate you.

TAROT CARD: Strength
PLANETS: Pluto and Moon
QUOTE: *'All of my life I have always had the urge to do things better than anybody else.'* Babe Zaharias

STRENGTHS: Memorable and trustworthy.
WEAKNESSES: Prone to moodiness, hard to read.

June 27

BORN ON THIS DAY:
J.J. Abrams
(film producer)
Bruce Johnston
(musician, songwriter –
The Beach Boys)
Helen Keller
(blind and deaf writer and educator)
Tobey Maguire
(actor)
Lewis Bernstein Namier
(historian)
Vera Wang
(fashion designer)

MEDITATION:
Be prepared to live with the consequences of a decision.

You are a colourful and dramatic person with a delicate and soothing touch that people love. You set yourself big juicy goals and dedicate yourself to fulfilling them. You have an inner faith that inspires you and others. Throughout your life you reach out to huge groups of people. There is a creative flair about everything you do, but you can be too hasty and overlook the details. In business you are the entrepreneur and need a backup team to support you. In a personal relationship you expect a lot of freedom and need someone who totally supports your endeavours. You relate well to people but have an introverted side and need private space to totally relax and recuperate. A desert island would suit you, but on a practical level going to the sauna or hot tub would be bliss.

TAROT CARD: The Hermit
PLANETS: Jupiter and Moon
QUOTE: *'A woman is never sexier than when she is comfortable in her clothes.'* Vera Wang

STRENGTHS: Calming and inspirational.
WEAKNESSES: Rash and over-reliant on others.

June 28

You are a person with an air of authority, whose strong leadership skills tend to overshadow your soft and caring centre. You are a pillar of strength in a crisis because you are solid and dependable. You are in touch with your feelings, which means you respond rather than react. You reach out to people in a maternal way, yet have the attributes of a wise father. At times you are over-controlling and treat people as if they were children. You are a romantic and seek a relationship where your mate is also your ally. The added bonus for you would be if you could work well together at a business. A laconic sense of humour is your biggest asset. You tend to contract your chest to protect yourself. Swimming, especially the breaststroke, would be tremendously beneficial for you.

TAROT CARD: The Wheel of Fortune
PLANETS: Saturn and Moon
QUOTE: *'People who know little are usually great talkers, while men who know much say little.'* Jean Jacques Rousseau

STRENGTHS: Trustworthy, with a dry sense of humour.
WEAKNESSES: Dominant and, at times, patronizing.

BORN ON THIS DAY:
Kathy Bates
(actor)
Mel Brooks
(filmmaker)
Alexis Carrel
(Nobel prize winning scientist)
John Cusack
(actor and screenwriter)
Richard Rodgers
(composer)
Jean Jacques Rousseau
(philosopher)

MEDITATION:

One never needs their humour as much as when they argue with a fool.

June 29

You are a kind hearted person, a progessive with a strong intellect. You are deeply concerned with the family of man, and you truly believe all people are created equally. You reach out to people and gather many friends in the course of your life. You are fascinated by radical ideas and love to debate with others. However, you can cling to your friends and family and become over-protective of them. Your people skills would serve you as a politician because you are keen to be involved with the public's welfare. In love you can be attracted to a bohemian lifestyle in your youth as you value freedom, but later on your emotional need for a home and nesting takes over. Playing a game of chess or practising an unconventional sport such as hang-gliding are great ways for you to unwind.

TAROT CARD: Justice
PLANETS: Uranus and Moon
QUOTE: *'I love being famous. It validates that I have something to say.'* Richard Lewis

STRENGTHS: Caring and communicative.
WEAKNESSES: Clingy and possessive.

BORN ON THIS DAY:
Gary Busey
(actor)
Nelson Eddy
(singer and actor)
Little Eva
(singer)
Richard Lewis
(comiedian and actor)
Slim Pickens
(actor and rodeo performer)
Antoine de Saint-Exupéry
(pilot and writer)

MEDITATION:

Learn to lead without being possessive.

June 30

MEDITATION:

The person who says it cannot be done should not interrupt the person doing it.

You are a colourful and expressive person who hides the fact they are a sensitive soul behind a façade of wit and practical jokes. You have a wonderful gift with comedy and your jokes lift people's spirits. You move quickly and gracefully and have a friendly and bubbly manner that is enchanting. You would do well in PR because you love to talk to new people. You enjoy circulating and networking and you mix in a wide circle. You speak from your heart. However, you remember past hurts – a trait which does not serve you well. In a relationship you value someone who is gentle and tender; you need to trust a person before you open up to them completely. A daily diary where you write down what brought you happiness that day would greatly promote a positive outlook.

TAROT CARD: The Empress
PLANETS: Mercury and Moon
QUOTE: *'I want to test my maximum and see how much I can do. And I want to change the world of swimming.'* Michael Phelps

STRENGTHS: Eloquent and lively.
WEAKNESSES: Find it hard to forgive and forget – which breeds negativity.

July 1

MEDITATION:

Insecurities are useless – get positive or get out of the situation.

You are a spontaneous and volatile person who has a strong sense of your individuality. You will fight for your rights and are also sensitive and protective of the rights of others. You have a lot to give but can be demanding and need a lot of affection and reassurance from others to feel secure. There is a certain childlike quality about you, and on occasions you can be highly temperamental if things don't go your way. You bounce back once your concerns are listened to. You can be forthright in your opinions and put your foot in your mouth when you speak before you think. Relationships fulfil you emotionally but can be a mix of tenderness and fights. A sport such as kickboxing or maybe playing table tennis with the family will allow you to release pent-up feelings in a fun way.

TAROT CARD: The Magician
PLANETS: Mars and Moon
QUOTE: *'Nothing gives me more happiness than to try to aid the most vulnerable of this society.'* Diana, Princess of Wales

STRENGTHS: Caring and uninhibited.
WEAKNESSES: Moody and insecure in relationships.

July 2

You are a caring and dependable person whose values are rooted in a love of the countryside and of nature. You have a strong artistic ability and musical talent. There is always a song in your head and you often hum softly to yourself. You are tenacious and hold onto friends, claiming them and their loyalty. You know what the public want and would do well in the restaurant or entertainment business. At work or at home you are quite happy to be second in command, rather than take the lead. Family life is your priority and you are a faithful partner. In love affairs your controlling streak can stifle your mate and ruin your relationship. You relax easily, and lethargy can take over. A daily routine of walking while listening to music will ground you and restore inner peace.

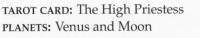

TAROT CARD: The High Priestess
PLANETS: Venus and Moon
QUOTE: *'I did not have three thousand pairs of shoes, I had one thousand and sixty.'*
Imelda Marcos

STRENGTHS: Creative and caring.
WEAKNESSES: Prone to sluggishness, possessive.

BORN ON THIS DAY:
Larry David
(film producer and actor)
Sir Alec Douglas-Home
(British prime minister)
Jerry Hall
(actor and model)
René Lacoste
(champion tennis player)
Lindsay Lohan
(actor)
Imelda Marcos
(first lady of the Philippines)

MEDITATION:
Idleness is the mother of all vices.

July 3

You are a person with a great variety of faces as you adapt brilliantly to whomever you are with. You can easily imitate others which is great fun for you and highly entertaining for them. You are sensitive and so can use this gift with skill and not offend anyone. NLP (Neuro-Linguistic Programing) is a perfect training and profession for you because connecting with people is what you do naturally. You are influenced by what others think of you and pick up on atmosphere, so can get unexpectedly depressed. In relationships you are quixotic which can be confusing for your partner. You care deeply one minute then are light and breezy the next. Balance is important for you to maintain; too much talking and empathizing wears you out, so escape for a while and read a good book.

TAROT CARD: The Empress
PLANETS: Mercury and Moon
QUOTE: *'A thing named is a thing tamed.'*
Joanne Harris

STRENGTHS: Versatile and understanding.
WEAKNESSES: Unrealistic and over-sensitive.

BORN ON THIS DAY:
Tom Cruise
(actor)
Joanne Harris
(writer)
King Louis XI
(French monarch)
Ken Russell
(film director)
Tom Stoppard
(playwright)
Edward Young
(poet)

MEDITATION:
It takes courage to grow up and become who you really are.

71

July 4

BORN ON THIS DAY:
Calvin Coolidge
(US president)
Ulysses S. Grant II
(American soldier)
Meyer Lansky
(American gangster)
Gina Lollobrigida
(actor)
Pam Shriver
(champion tennis player)
Bill Withers
(singer/songwriter)

MEDITATION:

*Fall seven times,
stand up eight.*

You are an emotional and sensitive person who cares deeply about how others feel. You are governed by your feelings and are influenced, probably without realizing it, by the moon's monthly cycles. Just as it waxes and wanes so you can feel joy one day and gloom the next. If you focus your energy on helping those around you, you can change your mood when feeling down. You work well in the public sector, assisting those in need of protection. You are just the person to represent them and this is where your tenacity becomes an asset. You can marry young; having a secure and stable home life is essential to your happiness. You are a bit of a worrier, which upsets your sensitive stomach, so take care to listen to what your body needs and avoid spicy foods.

TAROT CARD: The Emperor
PLANETS: Moon and Moon
QUOTE: *'It takes a great man to be a good listener.'* Calvin Coolidge

STRENGTHS: Determined and understanding.
WEAKNESSES: Anxious and prone to depression.

July 5

BORN ON THIS DAY:
P.T. Barnum
(circus owner)
Jean Cocteau
(writer)
Huey Lewis
(singer/songwriter –
Huey Lewis and the News)
Georges Pompidou
(French prime minister)
Cecil Rhodes
(South African politician)
Bill Watterson
(cartoonist – *Calvin and Hobbes*)

MEDITATION:

*No man is an island,
entire of itself; every man
is a piece of the continent.*

You are an affectionate and devoted person who has high aspirations to fulfil your creative potential. You have an imperious, almost regal, air about you and naturally take a leadership position. You work well with both sexes as you are well balanced. You can be a little conceited at times. Your weakness reveals itself when others don't do what you say – you then cut off from them until they obey you. However, you eventually learn to laugh at yourself which helps bring people back on side; with age you should learn how to resist the urge to control. You are the star in the show and amateur dramatics will delight you if you're not a professional actor – you see life as production. In relationships you jump in heart first and love the idea of love. You respond to romantic gestures and any gift from a child melts you.

TAROT CARD: The Hierophant
PLANETS: Sun and Moon
QUOTE: *'Every crowd has a silver lining.'* P.T. Barnum

STRENGTHS: Loving and tender.
WEAKNESSES: Bossy and unable to take orders from others.

July 6

You are a sympathetic and loyal person with enormous integrity. You have a strong sense of duty which was instilled at an early age. You have a desire to serve and dedicate yourself to that purpose. However, you are tremendously sensitive to criticism and get hurt easily by an unkind word. The result is you become extremely self-protective and you can appear to hold yourself back. When stressed you get nervous and can find yourself mumbling. You have sound common sense and old-fashioned values with a close family to support you. Your relationship is your safe haven; a place where you receive the nurturing you deserve. You can get caught in worry and suffer from nervous complaints. A relaxing stroll in beautiful surroundings with a congenial companion is good for your well-being.

TAROT CARD: The Lovers
PLANETS: Mercury and Moon
QUOTE: *'Playing polo is like trying to play golf during an earthquake.'*
Sylvester Stallone

STRENGTHS: Dutiful, honest.
WEAKNESSES: Anxious and restrained.

BORN ON THIS DAY:
George W. Bush
(US president)
Frida Kahlo
(artist)
Bill Haley
(singer)
50 Cent
(rapper)
Sylvester Stallone
(actor)
Lhamo Thondup
(Dalai Lama)

MEDITATION:
See each day as a blank canvas and make it a masterpiece.

July 7

You are a perceptive and kind-hearted person with a fine intellect. You have original and progressive ideas. Someone who takes action, you push through your concepts with eloquence and determination. You can be a bit of an intellectual snob and struggle to mix with people of a lower class or intellect. You have an innate talent for beauty and harmony and are gifted at interior design as you have natural homemaking skills. Feng shui or vastu would appeal to you. You are a perfectionist and complain when people aren't up to your high standards of excellence. Relationships suit you because you need someone to create a balance in your life, but they need to be your intellectual equal. Love poetry, soft romantic music and a bunch of scented flowers are the perfect gifts to give yourself and share with your beloved.

TAROT CARD: The Chariot
PLANETS: Venus and Moon
QUOTE: *'All that is not perfect down to the smallest detail is doomed to perish.'*
Gustav Mahler

STRENGTHS: Well-read and resolute.
WEAKNESSES: Elitist with impossibly high standards.

BORN ON THIS DAY:
Pierre Cardin
(fashion designer)
Shelley Duvall
(actor)
King Henry VIII
(English monarch)
Tony Jacklin
(professional golfer)
Gustav Mahler
(composer)
Ringo Starr
(singer/songwriter, drummer –
one quarter of The Beatles)

MEDITATION:
A book is like a garden carried in the pocket.

July 8

You are a magnetic and entrancing person. You are sensual and very attractive. You are highly subjective and respond by what you feel at the time rather than with logic. You can be fretful and it is difficult to get you out of a bad mood once you sink into one. You are perceptive and your radar for how others are feeling is superb. You do well in the fields of psychoanalysis and child welfare. You can handle death and birth so midwifery is also ideal. You have a satirical sense of humour and you love busting taboos, but this is not to everyone's tastes! Your relationship is intense and your partner needs to give constant reassurance if you are not to be irrationally jealous. When emotions take over, moving your body by cycling or walking near a river will restore you.

BORN ON THIS DAY:
Ernst Bloch
(philosopher)
Billy Eckstine
(singer and bandleader)
Marty Feldman
(comedian and actor)
Anjelica Huston
(actor)
Nelson A. Rockefeller
(US vice president)
Ferdinand Graf von Zeppelin
(German general and
aircraft manufacturer)

MEDITATION:
*See things as you would
have them be instead
of as they are.*

TAROT CARD: Strength
PLANETS: Pluto and Moon
QUOTE: *'The pen is mightier than the sword, and considerably easier to write with.'* Marty Feldman

STRENGTHS: Bewitching and insightful.
WEAKNESSES: Insecure and prone to anxiety attacks.

July 9

You are a good humoured, affable and utterly honest person. You have an enthusiasm and optimistic outlook on life that gets you through the darkest of times – you will always take the positive from a situation. For you, life has to have meaning, and you can be religious or spiritual. You are restless and impatient; a doer rather than a thinker, you can't abide time wasters. Your greatness comes from a combination of being in touch with people's feelings and your vision of a positive future. You can be outspoken yet charming, so people are beguiled. You are vulnerable. A close relationship is important for you. You need someone who loves to talk as much as you do and shares your philosophy. You need to let off steam so watching an exciting sport where you can cheer your heart out is excellent.

BORN ON THIS DAY:
Tom Hanks
(actor and filmmaker)
Sir Edward Heath
(British prime minister)
David Hockney
(artist)
Donald Rumsfeld
(US secretary of defense)
O. J. Simpson
(NFL player and actor)
Jack White
(musician – White Stripes front man)

MEDITATION:
*If you don't get lost,
there's a chance you
may never be found.*

TAROT CARD: The Hermit
PLANETS: Jupiter and Moon
QUOTE: *'If you have to have a job in this world, a high-priced movie star is a pretty good gig.'* Tom Hanks

STRENGTHS: Ethical and cordial.
WEAKNESSES: Fidgety, unguarded.

July 10

You are a loyal and responsible person with good listening skills which makes you a well-liked and trusted confidant. You have old-fashioned values and love tradition. You are ambitious and work hard in life to get to the top. A true patriot, you work out of love, for your kin and your country. You have a protective instinct which is admirable. You will always keep to the letter of the law. You are shrewd at business, especially as you mature. You need to be respected. You have an air of gravitas about you and people often comment that you are too serious. The single life is not for you; you yearn for a secure and stable relationship and for someone to be waiting for you when you get home. Swimming is a perfect antidote to all the hard work you do.

TAROT CARD: The Wheel of Fortune
PLANETS: Saturn and Moon
QUOTE: *'Success is a journey, not a destination. The doing is often more important than the outcome.'* Arthur Ashe

STRENGTHS: Attentive and dependable.
WEAKNESSES: Sombre with orthodox views.

BORN ON THIS DAY:
Arthur Ashe
(champion tennis player)
Camille Pissarro
(artist)
Marcel Proust
(writer)
Neil Tennant
(singer – Pet Shop Boys)
Virginia Wade
(champion tennis player)
James McNeill Whistler
(artist)

MEDITATION:
Loneliness can be conquered only by those who can bear solitude.

July 11

You are a loving and compassionate person with a fine intellect. You are generous and charitable – a humanitarian who can communicate your ideas with a heartfelt conviction that encourages others to take action. You are attracted to societies and groups that support human rights. You love symbols and metaphors and learning how to decipher dreams. You are naturally gifted as an astrologer or tarot reader. Social work is also a good profession for you. You are unpredictable and change your mind depending on how you are feeling. Your weakness is that you can go into yourself to avoid emotional upsets, preferring to sort out the world's problems rather than your own. A partner who shares your convictions is essential, and with a light touch who can cajole you to lighten up when you get too heavy.

TAROT CARD: Justice
PLANETS: Uranus and Moon
QUOTE: *'Jeans represent democracy in fashion.'* Georgio Armani

STRENGTHS: Generous and compassionate.
WEAKNESSES: Erratic, unpredictable.

BORN ON THIS DAY:
John Quincy Adams
(US president)
Giorgio Armani
(fashion designer)
Robert the Bruce
(Scottish monarch)
Yul Brynner
(actor)
Tokugawa Mitsukuni
(Japanese warlord)
Richie Sambora
(guitarist – Bon Jovi)

MEDITATION:
If you can't feed a hundred people, then feed just one.

July 12

MEDITATION:

To grow up is to accept vulnerability and move on.

You are an imaginative person with brilliant creative gifts to give to the world. You can touch the souls of people with what you express because you are connected to the divine. At times you can feel overwhelmed by the suffering in the world and watching scenes of starvation or victims of state violence can be too much for your tender heart. Assisting humankind is second nature to you. However, you need to learn to say no to requests for help or you will fall into a pattern of sacrifice. You also need to take care of yourself emotionally and physically. You are easily misled in romance and can try and rescue people, so reflect before you commit to one person. Laughter is the best medicine for lifting your mood. A partner and friends who are grounded and practical are best for you.

TAROT CARD: The Hanged Man
PLANETS: Neptune and Moon
QUOTE: *'Human beings are the only creatures on earth that allow their children to come back home.'* Bill Cosby

STRENGTHS: Highly creative, solicitous.
WEAKNESSES: Unable to say no, vulnerable.

July 13

MEDITATION:

If you never fail, you will never succeed.

You are a highly subjective person with radar for how other people are feeling. You give compassion, affection and understanding and in return you expect the same. People feel an immediate rapport with you. However, at times you can overflow with feeling and get very needy, which can be smothering. You adore history and love acquiring valuables and antiques. You have many collections and hold onto things for sentimental reasons. This results in you being a hoarder so periodic clear outs are essential. Being the faithful type there's a strong chance you'll marry your childhood sweetheart. Your relationship gives you the stability you crave. You require an earthy and practical person to balance you. If you get caught up with negative feelings, reach out for help. You respond well to flower essences or homeopathy.

TAROT CARD: Death
PLANETS: Moon and Moon
QUOTE: *'I do not truly consider myself an icon, but the Cube has been quite successful.'* Ernö Rubik

STRENGTHS: Sympathetic and kind-hearted.
WEAKNESSES: Overwhelming, a hoarder.

July 14

A demonstrative and imaginative person, you inspire others by your courage and leadership. You are kind and open-hearted, and have a real gift of hospitality, always making others welcome. You are great at promoting a person or cause you believe in, and your endorsement makes a world of difference. This could be a good career choice for you as people take you seriously. You have an artistic streak and are an avid collector of fine and precious artefacts, especially gold jewellery. You know the value of things. In relationships you are an ardent lover and want to impress and dazzle your partner, but you also want to rule the roost. They will be more than satisfied basking in the glow of your love. A family barbecue with you at the helm will always be a success and please others as much as yourself.

TAROT CARD: Temperance
PLANETS: Sun and Moon
QUOTE: *'We are here not because we are law-breakers; we are here in our efforts to become law-makers.'* Emmeline Pankhurst

STRENGTHS: Accommodating, valiant.
WEAKNESSES: An exhibitionist, controlling.

BORN ON THIS DAY:
Ingmar Bergman
(film director)
Gerald Ford
(US President)
Woody Guthrie
(singer/songwriter and musician)
William Hanna
(animator, director and producer)
Gustav Klimt
(artist)
Emmeline Pankhurst
(suffragette)

MEDITATION:
Don't show off every day, or you will stop surprising people.

July 15

You are a responsive and attentive person with excellent powers of observation. These qualities enable you to make pertinent and witty remarks about people and the human condition. You are gifted at writing – especially scripts for soap operas or composing a daily journal or blog. The rush of daily life can throw you off balance and you can get caught in attending to everyone's needs. You are reflective and need time alone to commune with your inner world. You are naturally dexterous, so a hobby such as knitting brings you joy as you love to create something useful. There is an essential purity about you and you thrive in a relationship where your partner is faithful and enjoys pottering around chatting with you. Asian-style cooking which involves a lot of chopping is very therapeutic.

TAROT CARD: The Devil
PLANETS: Mercury and Moon
QUOTE: *'I daresay anything can be made holy by being sincerely worshipped.'* Iris Murdoch

STRENGTHS: Perceptive and thoughtful.
WEAKNESSES: Hurried, prone to self-neglect.

BORN ON THIS DAY:
Ian Curtis
(lead singer – Joy Division)
Clive Cussler
(writer)
Inigo Jones
(architect)
Iris Murdoch
(writer)
Rembrandt van Rijn
(artist)
Forest Whitaker
(actor)

MEDITATION:
A ruffled mind makes a restless pillow.

July 16

You are a graceful and sophisticated person with immense style about all you do. You are both compassionate and caring. You have good powers of observation and have artistic gifts and refined taste. You want to be part of the fashionable set – the in-crowd – and have a powerful need to be recognized. You love being the public face of a company, so working in show business or public relations would suit you. You take pride in your image and can appear vain when in public, but can be perfectly happy in old and comfortable clothes at home. In love you are affectionate and dote on your partner, and in return they provide the security you cherish. You also need and value friends and won't put up with a possessive partner. Dancing cheek to cheek with a partner is your idea of heaven.

MEDITATION:
No truly great person ever thought themselves so.

TAROT CARD: The Tower
PLANETS: Venus and Moon
QUOTE: *'When two people love each other, they don't look at each other, they look in the same direction.'* Ginger Rogers

STRENGTHS: Elegant and tender.
WEAKNESSES: Vain, self-aggrandizing.

July 17

You are a compelling and seductive person with natural dignity. You are attracted to danger and can be quite daring, taking big risks. People never quite know you, because you guard your private life. In turn you respect the privacy of others. You can come across as proud and haughty, but this is just your outer shell. You have a soft and sentimental side which shows itself when you are with your family. You are a born researcher and investigator and revel in a career that tests you emotionally and intellectually. You could work as a counsellor and adviser to powerful people because you can keep their secrets. Your relationships are complex; anything straightforward bores you. Once committed you are in for the long term. A murder-mystery play or movie is a real treat for you.

MEDITATION:
The shell must break before the bird can fly.

TAROT CARD: The Star
PLANETS: Pluto and Moon
QUOTE: *'I'm six foot four, an all-American guy, and handsome and talented as well!'* David Hasselhoff

STRENGTHS: Captivating and alluring.
WEAKNESSES: Reserved and enigmatic.

July 18

You are an expansive and generous person with strong moral integrity. You have two aspects to you. Your public persona is open and good humoured but in private you are shy and sensitive. You seek justice for others and can talk convincingly about a pet cause. You are drawn towards a career as a charity worker or as an explorer. You are a born romantic and adore symphonic music and operas that sweep you away. You thrive in a personal relationship. You enjoy making expensive gestures – a weekend away with your partner somewhere lavish is typical. You are prone to mood swings because you have such high expectations about people and get crushed if they don't live up to your ideal. Hiking and camping are activities that suit your style – you live for adventure.

TAROT CARD: The Moon
PLANETS: Jupiter and Moon
QUOTE: *'I will always dance in the street.'* Martha Reeves

STRENGTHS: Loving, fair.
WEAKNESSES: Temperamental, over idealistic.

BORN ON THIS DAY:
Sir Richard Branson
(entrepreneur)
James Brolin
(actor)
Vin Diesel
(actor)
Nelson Mandela
(first South African president)
Martha Reeves
(singer)
William Makepeace Thackeray
(writer)

MEDITATION:
Make sure you have more than just ideals.

July 19

You are a considerate person who is very self aware. Work is important to you and you are professional through and through. Everything you do is planned to last for the long term. You are self-reflective and understanding of your own – and other people's – emotions. Training is a priority for you. You could become a family therapist or work in a children's home. Although you are well-mannered, you are no pushover and can stand your ground with an writerity way beyond your years. In a relationship you need time to decide if they are 'the one' and won't be forced into making a hasty decision. They, in turn, feel you are being elusive. When upset you can close down and sulk for days. Rowing is an excellent exercise that strengthens you physically and, being on water, soothes you emotionally.

TAROT CARD: The Sun
PLANETS: Saturn and Moon
QUOTE: *'Art is not what you see, but what you make others see.'* Edgar Degas

STRENGTHS: Assertive and mindful.
WEAKNESSES: Evasive, prone to moodiness.

BORN ON THIS DAY:
Vikki Carr
(singer)
Samuel Colt
(inventor of the revolver)
A. J. Cronin
(writer)
Edgar Degas
(painter)
Brian May
(astrophysicist and guitarist – Queen)
Ilie Nastase
(champion tennis player)

MEDITATION:
Even if happiness forgets you a little bit, never completely forget about it.

79

4

July 20

BORN ON THIS DAY:
Gisele Bundchen
(supermodel and actor)
Frantz Fanon
(philosopher, revolutionary and writer)
Sir Edmund Hillary
(adventurer and writer)
Dame Diana Rigg
(actor)
Carlos Santana
(singer and guitarist)
Natalie Wood
(actor)

You are a down-to-earth, sensual person with a deep connection to the place where you were born. You have luxurious tastes and appreciate things that are tactile and beautiful to look at. Good design matters to you and you are able to make a career out of it. You are kind and helpful in what you say and do, and always offer practical advice. You are a capable organizer and take a methodical approach to tasks. A long-term relationship gives you the stability you seek, and you love taking care of your family. You love to be cosy and are content to stay at home with your beloved. Nevertheless, you can be stubborn and get irritable when tired, or if you haven't eaten for a while. Watch your blood sugar levels and carry a snack with you to keep your energy levels up.

MEDITATION:
Remember to eat – the belly rules the mind.

TAROT CARD: Judgement
PLANETS: Venus and Moon
QUOTE: *'There is precious little in civilization to appeal to a Yeti.'*
Sir Edmund Hillary

STRENGTHS: Kindhearted, pragmatic.
WEAKNESSES: Obstinate and tetchy.

July 21

BORN ON THIS DAY:
Josh Hartnett
(actor and film producer)
Ernest Hemingway
(writer)
Yusuf Islam – Cat Stevens
(singer/songwriter)
Sir Walter Raleigh
(courtier and explorer)
Tony Scott
(film director)
Robin Williams
(actor and comedian)

You are a witty and kind-hearted person who has a gift of empathy; you truly understand what it is to walk in someone else's shoes. This uncanny knack of identifying with other people's emotions makes you a natural counsellor. Even if this isn't your chosen profession people feel comfortable pouring their hearts out to you. This can be tiring because you have the tendency to neglect yourself while you take on everyone else's problems. You need some time to yourself in order to unwind – and a confidant of your own to share what's going on in your life. Relationships are essential as you are always communicating. You need a partner who is fun-loving because you can be quite childish at times. Keeping a daily journal is an excellent way to contact your inner world.

MEDITATION:
Maturity is knowing when to be immature.

TAROT CARD: The World
PLANETS: Mercury and Moon
QUOTE: *'Do you think God gets stoned? I think so... look at the platypus.'*
Robin Williams

STRENGTHS: Entertaining and understanding.
WEAKNESSES: Manic and immature.

July 22

You are a nurturing and motherly person who is incredibly receptive to the emotions of others around you. It is as if you have no skin and can be prone to catch any bug that is going around. Early in life you have to acquire a protective shell or you would not survive. Everyone turns to you for help and you can end up taking care of every waif and stray in the neighbourhood. By getting too absorbed with others you sometimes neglect your own considerable talents as a writer or musician. You tend to live close to your birth place, but water is your element, so you're happiest living by the sea or a river. An intimate relationship supports your growth and allows you to blossom. You can stagnate, so a detox would be an effective way to clear you energetically.

TAROT CARD: The Emperor
PLANETS: Moon and Moon
QUOTE: *'Life is a game and true love is a trophy.'* Rufus Wainwright

STRENGTHS: Protective, open-minded.
WEAKNESSES: Sluggish, prone to self-neglect.

BORN ON THIS DAY:
Willem Dafoe
(actor)
Don Henley
(musician – founding member of the Eagles)
Edward Hopper
(artist)
Mireille Mathieu
(singer)
Terence Stamp
(actor)
Rufus Wainwright
(musician)

MEDITATION:
Bad habits are easier to abandon today than tomorrow.

TYPICAL CANCER:
THE DALAI LAMA

'If you want others to be happy, practise compassion. If you want to be happy, practise compassion.'

CANCER TRAITS:
Inner peace is extremely important to Cancerians, and they do everything they can to keep trouble as far away as possible – retreating into their crab-like shell if necessary.

Emotionally, Cancer is a very up-and-down sign, but despite this they have a lot of love to give and cannot bear to see anyone suffering.

5

Leo
July 23 – August 23

TAROT CARD: Strength

ELEMENT: Fire

QUALITY: Fixed

NUMBER: 5

RULING PLANET: Sun

GEMSTONES: Ruby and garnet

COLOURS: Gold

DAY OF THE WEEK: Sunday

COMPATIBLE SIGNS: Aries, Sagittarius, Pisces

KEY WORDS: Wholehearted, powerful leadership skills, warm and sincere, protective and affectionate, vain, self-seeking, a show-off

ANATOMY: Heart, chest, spine and upper back

HERBS, PLANTS AND TREES: Anise, camomile, daffodil, fennel, lavender, poppy, marigold, mistletoe and parsley

KEY PHRASE:
I create

Leo is the lion, the king – or queen – of the zodiac, commanding and hard to miss. This sign governs the heart, and as such, Leo is born to be at the centre of the action, pointing the way. Leo is the pilot, the superstar, the lead role or conductor of the orchestra and the focal point of the whole zodiac. The glyph is like the lion's mane, so Leos often have a strong hairline and, like a cat, they need to be stroked. Leo is the height of summer, the time of year when children are on holiday, and Leos, too, can be childlike and the most playful of all the signs.

PLANETARY RULER AND QUALITIES
Leo is governed by the sun, which is not a planet but a star. Leo is here to shine and also to pass on its warmth. It is a fixed fire sign, so the energy of fire is most stable, like the eternal flame. The sun is at the centre of the zodiac and follows a steady path along the ecliptic. It brings both light and warmth, and without it we would die. Apollo, the sun god, was the beautiful youth who rode in his chariot across the sky. He represented qualities of truth, light and prophecy.

RELATIONSHIPS
Leo is a passionate and extremely romantic sign. You love the theatrical and adore the stages of courtship. You are warm and bear no grudges and you love the idea of love – for a Leo, life isn't worth living without it. You can be extremely depressed when a relationship doesn't work out, especially if it is the other person that ends it – you will lick your wounds and then come back emotionally stronger than ever.

The Leo male is confident and self-assured which is very attractive and the Leo female is regal with an innate grace. However, both need to be the leader in their relationships, so there is conflict with Capricorns, who also like to be the boss, and Aquarians, who value equality. Your most suitable signs are the other fire signs: Aries and Sagittarius. Interestingly, marriage can also work out with Pisceans. Geminis are light-hearted and fun, qualities which Leos adore. Leos and Librans get on well, but need the money to sustain the extravagant lifestyle they both love.

MYTH
Leo is the constellation of the Lion, with the Royal Star Regulus at its heart. Leo was the cave-dwelling Nemean lion, with the impenetrable skin that Hercules had to kill as his first labour. Hercules wrestled the Nemean lion and finally strangled it to death – realizing that

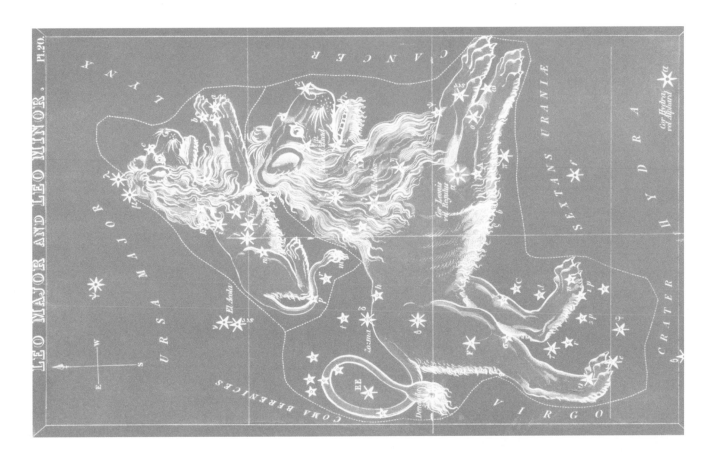

a sword or spear were useless. He skinned the lion with its own claw and from that day on used it as a protective cloak in battle.

STRENGTHS AND WEAKNESSES

Due to the sun being such a focal point for Leos, they can be hot-headed and hot-tempered at times, especially when things do not go their way.

Leos, although strong and proud, deep down are all heart. This warm-heartedness can be endearing, especially when it comes across as pure and unconditional. Generally with Leos, as long as they are stroked they will respond with love. They need to be appreciated and given a lot of praise for what they do, and are sensitive to teasing. Just like the lion, nothing is sadder than when a Leo's pride is hurt and they hide away to lick their wounds. However, Leo is the king, and can turn into an autocrat at the drop of a hat. Leos hate to come across as needy or reliant, therefore rarely ask for a helping hand, even when they really need it. Leos have to be at the centre of things, and their craving of the spotlight can result in others being pushed aside. Like the lion of the sign, they can be lazy and dismiss new ideas, until they are ready to pounce.

TYPICAL LEO:
MADONNA

'I have the same goal I've had ever since I was a girl. I want to rule the world.'

LEO POWERS: Powerful and strong-minded with a massive heart. If you have made it into a Leo's life you will be adored by them.

LEO NEGATIVES: Hot-headed, with a constant need to lead others. Unable to be on the sidelines.

83

July 23

MEDITATION:
*Don't underestimate
the power of the
understatement.*

You are an enthusiastic person, exuberant and full of life. You exude confidence and have a convincing manner about you. You can dazzle people with your brilliance and always need to command centre stage. You take the lead without being asked – it just seems right. You have an almost mythic life with wonderful opportunities falling into your lap, which can make others envious as you seem to be successful without even trying. In relationships you need an enormous amount of affection and admiration. You can dominate your environment and are not always that easy to live with. At times you are just too hot to handle and you need to cool down and learn to appreciate others more. You are an exhibitionist, so entertaining others will give them pleasure and help you let off some of your excess energy.

TAROT CARD: The Hierophant
PLANETS: Sun and Sun
QUOTE: *'I never was disillusioned with acting because I love acting.'* Woody Harrelson

STRENGTHS: Cheerful and full of positivity.
WEAKNESSES: A constant need for attention and a showoff.

July 24

MEDITATION:
*When what you think, say
and do are in harmony –
happiness will come.*

You are a dedicated and articulate person who inspires others with your desire for excellence. You are kind and warm and you come across to people as supremely self-confident. However, there is an inner voice which is less sure and is always criticizing whatever you do or say. Your biggest weakness is that you tend to over-analyse yourself and others. Professionally you work best alone or freelance – you can contribute to a team but groups do not interest you much. You work well with detail and can spend hours perfecting your creations. You are very fussy when it comes to relationships; you need someone who is willing to shower you with affection, and put up with your idiosyncrasies. You can get edgy, so watch your diet and avoid too many spicy foods.

TAROT CARD: The Lovers
PLANETS: Mercury and Sun
QUOTE: *'I want to do it because I want to do it.'* Amelia Earhart

STRENGTHS: Eloquent and committed.
WEAKNESSES: Fastidious, tense.

July 25

You are a soft and loving person with innate qualities of the diplomat. You see the world – maybe a little naively – as a place of harmony and you bring sweetness and sparkle just by your presence. You cannot help but win attention from others as you have an aura that glows with a deep sense of peace and happiness. You were well brought up and your manners are impeccable. You like things to be in the right place and have a strong sense of design and artistic talent. You can succeed in the areas of illustration, interior design and floristry. Your home always looks beautiful with your impeccable good taste. You long for romance and seek a partner who has a strong sense of identity. Sugary foods can be your downfall – your need for sweetness is really a need for love.

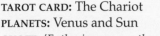

TAROT CARD: The Chariot
PLANETS: Venus and Sun
QUOTE: *'Enthusiasm moves the world.'*
Arthur James Balfour

STRENGTHS: Affectionate, creative.
WEAKNESSES: Mawkish and sweet-toothed.

BORN ON THIS DAY:
Arthur James Balfour
(British prime minister)
David Belasco
(playwright)
Louise Brown
(first test tube baby)
Thomas Eakins
(artist)
Matt LeBlanc
(actor)
Maxfield Parrish
(artist)

MEDITATION:
We're fools whether we dance or not, so we might as well dance.

July 26

You are a magnetic and attractive person with a powerful presence. You have a true star quality, a strong sense of purpose and the determination to win at all costs. You never give up on yourself and your ambition has no limits. You have tremendous willpower and once at the top you can beat off all competition. Relationships are vital for you and you will often have more than one true love. The aura of mystery emanating from you is extremely seductive. You are fiercely loyal to your loved ones and yet your partners feel they never really understand you. Your need for secrecy holds you back from real intimacy. Learn to trust more and open up. You love murder mysteries and thrillers, so time out for you at the theatre or movies is a favourite way to relax.

TAROT CARD: Strength
PLANETS: Pluto and Sun
QUOTE: *'Thank you for leaving us alone but giving us enough attention to boost our egos.'*
Mick Jagger

STRENGTHS: Devoted, enthusiastic when interested.
WEAKNESSES: Ruthless and secretive.

BORN ON THIS DAY:
Aldous Huxley
(writer)
Mick Jagger
(singer/songwriter – Rolling Stones, producer and actor)
Carl Jung
(psychiatrist)
Stanley Kubrick
(film director)
Roger Taylor
(drummer – Queen)
(writer)
Kevin Spacey
(actor)

MEDITATION:
Try not to become a person of success, but rather try to become a person of value.

July 27

MEDITATION:
*Travel for fulfilment,
not distraction.*

You are a person with a positive outlook on all that life has to offer; someone who has an immense belief deep inside that life is meant to be an adventure and lived to the full. You explore the world, either literally or in your imagination. You have a wanderlust that lasts all your life and you can take a long time to settle down, if indeed you do. You are incredibly warm and generous – a real party person – and offer kindness to everyone you meet. You have high moral standards and defend the truth, so are naturally attracted to the legal professions. The courtroom suits your large personality. You are a rolling stone so a full-time relationship can be difficult, but you value your partner's friendships highly. You love to learn, so home study will keep you occupied and satisfy your restless spirit.

TAROT CARD: The Hermit
PLANETS: Jupiter and Sun
QUOTE: *'We wander for distraction, but we travel for fulfilment.'* Hilaire Belloc

STRENGTHS: Adventurous and generous.
WEAKNESSES: Nomadic and consumed by wanderlust.

July 28

MEDITATION:
*What soap is to the body,
laughter is to the soul.*

You are a formidable and ambitious person with a positive manner yet you are basically quite shy. The support of older people helps you throughout your life. You develop a self-controlled polish as you get older and you love formality and grand functions. You long for a bygone era when good manners and traditions were valued. You are always respected but can remain dazzlingly aloof to some, so developing compassion would behove you. You get to the top, whether on your own or with a partner. It is a position that you are well suited to. You also make a loyal partner and marriage flatters you, as you crave material security and a stable home. Working fulfils you, but you also need to laugh and have fun more often or you'll get old before your time.

TAROT CARD: The Wheel of Fortune
PLANETS: Saturn and Sun
QUOTE: *'If you bungle raising your children, I don't think whatever else you do matters very much.'* Jackie Kennedy Onassis

STRENGTHS: Determined, optimistic.
WEAKNESSES: Timid and serious.

July 29

You are an innovative leader who does things in your own inimitable style. You are resourceful and are willing to try out new methods, the more whacky the better, and are never put off if things don't go according to plan! You are truly inventive and can go to extremes in what you are prepared to do. The problem is your lack of perspective and you can be very resistant to change once you have decided on a course of action. You aim to include people and, as long as you are the boss, you work well in a team. In relationships you want both a best friend and someone to look up to you. You have a love/hate affair with technology and need to switch off at night as your mind gets over-active. Going for a walk – without your mobile phone – will help you unwind.

TAROT CARD: Justice
PLANETS: Uranus and Sun
QUOTE: *'A negative judgement gives you more satisfaction than praise, provided it smacks of jealousy.'* Jean Baudrillard

STRENGTHS: Original, enterprising.
WEAKNESSES: Stubborn and domineering.

BORN ON THIS DAY:
Jean Baudrillard
(sociologist)
Baron Marcel Bich
(founder of the Bic company)
Clara Bow
(actor)
Nelli Kim
(champion Olympic gymnast)
Benito Mussolini
(Italian dictator)
William Powell
(actor)

MEDITATION:
The best remedy for a short temper is a long walk.

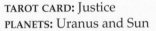

July 30

You are a strong and lively person with a gift of humour. You have a warm spontaneity about you and a playful way with words which means that you can come out with the perfect one liner at exactly the right time. You can be the clown, and yet never look foolish or lose your innate self-confidence. Your quick wit and intelligence is engaging and you are a popular leader. You are the perfect host or dinner party guest as you keep peple entertained with the latest gossip. You are well-meaning and honourable, and speak from the heart. Although you like to be in charge you never take yourself too seriously. In romance you have a penchant for variety and are inclined to make sure you are always very busy to avoid relating on a deep level. Your temperament is fire/air so avoid icy drinks as they can upset you.

TAROT CARD: The Empress
PLANETS: Mercury and Sun
QUOTE: *'Milk is for babies. When you grow up you have to drink beer.'* Arnold Schwarzenegger

STRENGTHS: Light-hearted and quick-witted.
WEAKNESSES: Unemotional, a tattler.

BORN ON THIS DAY:
Peter Bogdanovich
(film director)
Emily Brontë
(writer)
Henry Ford
(automobile entrepreneur)
Henry Moore
(sculptor)
Arnold Schwarzenegger
(actor and governor of California)
Hilary Swank
(actor)

MEDITATION:
A problem shared is a problem halved.

July 31

MEDITATION:

Without criticism there will be no succeess.

You are a person with a big heart who deeply cares for your family and home life. You express yourself dramatically and playfully. You have natural charisma and are good at promoting yourself to others in a genuine way. You do well in the world of show business where you shine brightly. You had a close relationship with your mother / mother-figure and needed a lot of care and affection. Later in life you carry that inner security within you and create a home wherever you go. You tend to settle down early, are a dependable partner and provide emotional security to those you love. On the negative side, you can be too self-absorbed and over-react when criticized, although your natural warm-heartedness means you never sulk for long. Playing with your children is always a solution to going within yourself.

TAROT CARD: The Emperor
PLANETS: Moon and Sun
QUOTE: *'If you want to see the true measure of a man, watch how he treats his inferiors, not his equals.'* J.K. Rowling

STRENGTHS: Faithful, sympathetic.
WEAKNESSES: Egotistical and unable to take criticism.

August 1

MEDITATION:

Too much time spent on yourself means you will miss the greatness of others.

You are a passionate and creative person with strong and vibrant leadership qualities. You are intuitive and fiery, with a lot to express and give to the world. Your self-confidence is such that you know – not believe – you are the centre of the universe and have a group of adoring followers who simply love you and everything you have to offer. You are talented, love drama and are well suited to the stage. You have innate courage and will risk all for what you believe in. You also have a very tender side and are relationship orientated. You give wholeheartedly to your partner and, male or female, are very chivalrous. You can be too self-centred and need to have someone by your side to bring you back down to earth. You can easily burn yourself out and need someone around to remind you to take better care of yourself.

TAROT CARD: The Magician
PLANETS: Mars and Sun
QUOTE: *'Fashions fade, style is eternal.'* Yves Saint Laurent

STRENGTHS: Brave and romantic.
WEAKNESSES: Self-absorbed, an exhibitionist.

August 2

You are a charismatic and magnetic person with a love for splendour and magnificence. You take great delight in creating a lifestyle in which you can enjoy the good things in life. You have a touch of the showman about you. Your flamboyant and glamorous personality are reflected in your taste at home – gilded mirrors, thick metallic blankets, flowers and fur. Gold is your favourite colour – and you love real gold, too. You are a creative person who can produce things that people want, whether that's an artistic experience or an exquisitely hand-made chocolate. You need a reliable mate, someone beautiful and who always matches your style. You can be stubborn and tend to see things from your point of view so need to learn to be more flexible. You love perfume – a deliciously scented bath is ideal to relax you.

TAROT CARD: The High Priestess
PLANETS: Venus and Sun
QUOTE: *'I'm the most gregarious of men and love good company, but never less alone when alone.'* Peter O'Toole

STRENGTHS: Captivating and stylish.
WEAKNESSES: Obstinate and narcissistic.

BORN ON THIS DAY:
Wes Craven
(film director)
Myrna Loy
(actor)
Nell Irvin Painter
(historian)
Kevin Smith
(film director)
Peter O'Toole
(actor)
Jorge Rafael Videla
(Argentinian dictator)

MEDITATION:
Be strong-minded, but listen to the other side too.

August 3

You are a youthful and optimistic person out of whom a message of hope and positivity shines. You are persuasive and believe in causes with all of your heart. You can be a political activist and you like to move in influential circles. You need to be admired for the work you do. You are a perennial student in the sense that you love to try out new things. However, you can find it hard to focus on one thing at a time. You need a partner to be your ally and loyal supporter as opposed to someone who will challenge you. At times you can appear naive and childlike, and this emotional immaturity can play havoc with your relationships. Humour is your saving grace and can lift you up when things get tough. When the blues descend, keep to yourself and watch a comedy until your mood changes.

TAROT CARD: The Empress
PLANETS: Mercury and Sun
QUOTE: *'I don't think that people in America are really given enough information about the Third World.'* Martin Sheen

STRENGTHS: Sanguine, compelling.
WEAKNESSES: Emotionally naive, jejune.

BORN ON THIS DAY:
Stanley Baldwin
(British prime minister)
Tony Bennett
(singer)
Rupert Brooke
(poet)
P. D. James
(writer)
Martin Sheen
(actor)
Martha Stewart
(entrepreneur)

MEDITATION:
It is better to have loved and lost than never to have loved at all.

89

August 4

BORN ON THIS DAY:
Louis Armstrong
(singer and trumpeter)
Elizabeth Bowes-Lyon
(the Queen Mother)
Barack Obama
(US president)
Percy Bysshe Shelley
(poet)
Louis Vuitton
(designer)
José Luis Rodríguez Zapatero
(Spanish prime minister)

MEDITATION:

*Patience is the
companion
of wisdom.*

You are a big personality with enormous presence and a strong sense of purpose. You have an aristocratic bearing but also the rare gift of being able to reach out to others. Everyone you meet feels your warmth and included in your circle of influence. You make a truly excellent leader because imbued in you are the protective qualities of a good father as well as the emotional depth of a good mother. On the debit side you can get moody if things do not go your way. In early life you may cling to your mother and need her physical presence to feel safe. You view a loving relationship as something to commit to for life, and you are perfectly content to relax at home with the family. You can get irritable and impatient if your creativity isn't expressed. Singing helps you to let off steam.

> **TAROT CARD:** The Emperor
> **PLANETS:** Moon and Sun
> **QUOTE:** *'We need to internalize this idea of excellence. Not many folks spend a lot of time trying to be excellent.'* Barack Obama
>
> **STRENGTHS:** Good-natured and purposeful.
> **WEAKNESSES:** Changeable, irritable.

August 5

BORN ON THIS DAY:
Neil Armstrong
(astronaut)
Patrick Ewing
(basketball player)
Edward John Eyre
(explorer)
John Huston
(film director)
Guy de Maupassant
(writer)
Robert Taylor
(actor)

MEDITATION:

*Let others make their
own mistakes and
their own successes.*

You are a magnetic and warm-hearted person whose life is a journey of self-discovery. You are an inspiration and give yourself totally to whatever endeavour you get involved with. You are best suited to being in a managerial or executive role and do not take kindly to being in a menial position. You are hopeless at detail – it just doesn't interest you. You radiate out into the world and to be successful you need others to appreciate you. Be mindful that your ego can be overwhelming and you need to give other people some time in the limelight. Your passionate nature can lead to temptation in relationships; if your partner doesn't adore you constantly, you'll swap them for someone who does. The theatre is a wonderful arena for you, and amateur dramatics is a way to get your needs met.

> **TAROT CARD:** The Hierophant
> **PLANETS:** Sun and Sun
> **QUOTE:** *'The one thing I regret was that my work required an enormous amount of my time, and a lot of travel.'* Neil Armstrong
>
> **STRENGTHS:** Captivating and inspirational.
> **WEAKNESSES:** Self-important, overbearing.

August 6

You are an ethical and rigorous person with strongly held ideals. However, even though you know deep down what you think, you have a tendency to hesitate and procrastinate. You notice all the flaws in a project and want to remedy them – you need an external deadline otherwise nothing would ever be finished. Once you focus, though, you go for it and produce an excellent end result. You are benevolent and find true fulfilment when in service to others. You make a good teacher and researcher, in particular in the health industry, and you are happy to work alone. In relationships you are choosy; you want someone who cares about their health and watches what they eat. A detox you could do together would be beneficial for you both and also help satisfy your need for self-discipline.

TAROT CARD: The Lovers
PLANETS: Mercury and Sun
QUOTE: *'It would be very glamorous to be reincarnated as a great big ring on Liz Taylor's finger.'* Andy Warhol

STRENGTHS: Kind-hearted and virtuous.
WEAKNESSES: Time-wasting, perfectionist.

BORN ON THIS DAY:
Geri Halliwell
(singer – Spice Girls, author and activist)
Alexander Fleming
(scientist – discovered penicillin)
Robert Mitchum
(actor)
Alfred, Lord Tennyson
(writer)
Andy Warhol
(artist and filmmaker)
Barbara Windsor
(actor)

MEDITATION:
Better to do something imperfectly than to do nothing flawlessly.

August 7

You have immense charm and grace. You love luxury and the finer things in life. You could have a successful career in selling or PR; your warm and engaging personality could easily sway people into buying whatever you offered them. A genuine desire to see others happy makes you a perfect hostess. In return they give you the recognition you need. There is a danger of you getting too wrapped up in yourself when alone, so spending time with others is important. You need a partner, and your ideal mate would appreciate entertaining as much as you do. You are not a loner, so could run a business in partnership with your spouse. If ignored, you soon send out distress signals. Rather than having to keep asking for attention, give your love and energy to a partner who shares your fear of neglect.

TAROT CARD: The Chariot
PLANETS: Venus and Sun
QUOTE: *'I am a woman who enjoys herself very much; sometimes I lose, sometimes I win.'* Mata Hari

STRENGTHS: Elegant and lovable.
WEAKNESSES: An attention seeker, extravagant.

BORN ON THIS DAY:
Ralph Bunche
(politician and diplomat)
David Duchovny
(actor)
Mata Hari
(dancer and infamous Dutch spy)
Wayne Knight
(actor)
Vladimir Sorokin
(writer)
Charlize Theron
(actor, film producer and director)

MEDITATION:
Sticks in a bundle are unbreakable.

August 8

You are a highly competitive person who needs a sense of danger to feel really alive. You are entranced by challenge and constantly creating life and death dramas that you have to overcome. You are incredibly passionate with strong desires and ideals. You automatically take command in a crisis and people respect you as the number one. You do, however, have the tendency to be stubborn and possessive and won't let go of a project even when others advise you to do so. You bring intensity to all your relationships; they are never dull. Even if you stray you expect your mate to give you unquestioning loyalty. You can remain an elusive, enigmatic personality; it would take a lifetime to unravel your complexity. Your emotions can take over, so the tranquillity of water, especially the ocean, calms you.

BORN ON THIS DAY:
Ronnie Biggs
(great train robber)
Chris Eubank
(champion boxer)
Roger Federer
(champion tennis player)
Dustin Hoffman
(actor)
Dino De Laurentiis
(film producer)
Nigel Mansell
(champion F1 and CART racing driver)

MEDITATION:
Don't make a mountain out of a molehill, there' are enough real peaks to climb.

TAROT CARD: Strength
PLANETS: Pluto and Sun
QUOTE: *'I feel cheated never being able to know what it's like to get pregnant, carry a child and breast feed.'* Dustin Hoffman

STRENGTHS: Commanding and enthusiastic.
WEAKNESSES: Overdramatic, obstinate.

August 9

You are an enthusiastic person with strong opinions and a love of storytelling. You travel a great deal and prefer going on expeditions to regular holidays. You are never still for a minute and are always seeking new and wonderful experiences. Your aim is to lead a life of mythical proportions – one that people remember. You take huge risks and love to gamble. You enjoy living on the edge and you are very exciting to be around – you could have an excellent career teaching dangerous sports. In relationships your demands and excessive energy constantly test the patience of your partner. You can't bear to be ordinary which makes you a challenging person to live with. You need to learn to reflect. Tuning into your body with yoga would be hugely relaxing.

BORN ON THIS DAY:
Gillian Anderson
(actor)
Johann Michael Bach
(composer)
Melanie Griffith
(actor)
Whitney Houston
(singer and actor)
Philip Larkin
(poet)
Audrey Tautou
(actor)

MEDITATION:
By all means take risks, but sprinkle them with sense.

TAROT CARD: The Hermit
PLANETS: Jupiter and Sun
QUOTE: *'I decided long ago never to walk in anyone's shadow; if I fail, or if I succeed, at least I did as I believe.'* Whitney Houston

STRENGTHS: Dynamic and ebullient.
WEAKNESSES: Insistent, a risk-taker.

August 10

You are a highly gifted person, a professional with unique capabilities. You have a natural lust for life and take a bold approach to all you do. Proud of your achievements, you need to be honoured with certificates, a university degree or a seat on the board. Although you enjoy parties, you are also perfectly happy with your own company. You possess enormous dignity but your pride can be hurt if people don't show you respect or – even worse – if they laugh at you. You won't show your hurt; your self-control sees to that. You adore romance and are extravagant with your partner, showering affection on them. Looks matter, and you need someone who is both attractive and worthy of your respect. You need to let your defences down so playing silly games is an antidote to your seriousness.

TAROT CARD: The Wheel of Fortune
PLANETS: Saturn and Sun
QUOTE: *'I just want to get on stage and sing and be happy.'* Ronnie Spector

STRENGTHS: Talented and tender.
WEAKNESSES: Sombre and uptight.

BORN ON THIS DAY:
Antonio Banderas
(actor, director and singer)
Laurence Binyon
(poet)
Leo Fender
(inventor of the Fender electric guitar)
Herbert Hoover
(US president)
Jean-François Lyotard
(philosopher)
Ronnie Spector
(singer)

MEDITATION:
Happiness is the key to success.

August 11

You are an original, a person with a delicious sense of the ridiculous and whimsy. You have a fertile imagination and will experiment with unusual, yet inspired, combinations. You stand out in a group as the one with creative flair and will naturally be elected to lead. In politics you are a radical and will rebel against the status quo. But, however far you are from the majority, you still want people to respect you and treat you like a king/queen. You can be infuriating when you are unwilling to listen to other people's points of view. In relationships you need closeness and affection but also space and personal freedom. Travelling with your work, so you are not constantly at home, keeps your relationship alive and stops boredom setting in. However, be aware of overworking; let others care for you.

TAROT CARD: Justice
PLANETS: Uranus and Sun
QUOTE: *'Every dream I've ever had in life has come true ten times over.'* Steve Wozniak

STRENGTHS: Unique and playful.
WEAKNESSES: Obstinate and domineering.

BORN ON THIS DAY:
Enid Blyton
(writer)
Alex Haley
(historian and writer)
Hulk Hogan
(professional wrestler)
Shidehara Kijuro
(Japanese prime minister)
Jean Parker
(actor)
Steve Wozniak
(co-founder of Apple Inc)

MEDITATION:
What you do today matters most.

August 12

MEDITATION:

*Trust only movement.
Life happens at the level
of events, not of words.*

You are a poetic person with an extraordinary imagination. You are in touch with the highest inspiration and express it through art, music or writing. You are intensely romantic, possibly a creative genius, and can be totally absorbed and lost for hours when the muse takes over. You are deeply touched and delighted when your art is appreciated. You enjoy partying with fellow artistic types and you need to exhibit what you produce. Your biggest joy is when others understand and share your vision. But you can fall in love with unsuitable people, because you are gullible and can be taken in by a sob story. At times you can be despondent and oversensitive to the moods of others. That is when meditation and time alone is essential for your soul. Sitting near water restores your equilibrium.

TAROT CARD: The Hanged Man
PLANETS: Neptune and Sun
QUOTE: *'Every guitar I own gets used and has its purpose.'* Mark Knopfler

STRENGTHS: Creative and compassionate.
WEAKNESSES: Prone to dejection, overtrustful.

August 13

MEDITATION:

*Looking at the mirror
distracts one's attention
from the problem.*

You are a congenial and confident person with an immense sense of fun. You are determined to produce and create things that everyone enjoys. This ability means you can connect with adults and children alike. You have a strong sense of identity and often follow in your father's footsteps. You are approachable and welcome people into your inner circle where you love to be the centre of attention. You seek a partner who is equal in status to you, because you like to show them off. In a relationship you can share your feelings and yet still be strong. You are a devoted partner and parent. You can exhaust yourself because you feel you have to entertain people all the time. Let them know when you need time out. An appetizing dinner at a good restaurant will help you to bounce back fast.

TAROT CARD: Death
PLANETS: Moon and Sun
QUOTE: *'Blondes make the best victims. They're like virgin snow that shows up the bloody footprints.'* Alfred Hitchcock

STRENGTHS: Friendly and personable.
WEAKNESSES: Egotistical and a bit of a show-off.

August 14

You are a giving person with a huge personality that lights up the world. Full of sunshine and love, you share yourself with all and sundry – however, you are easily flattered and so find it hard to see when people are trying to use you. You are an individualist and treat life as a play with you in the leading role; as long as you are in the spotlight all is well in your world. This contradiction in your nature can confuse those around you. In relationships you need to be the star, so do well with a partner who is willing to be back stage but hugely supportive. You can be too self-centred and if you don't get what you want you can indulge in a temper tantrum. Your fiery energy needs expression. One way for you to lighten up is by playing charades, where everyone gets a chance to shine.

TAROT CARD: Temperance
PLANETS: Sun and Sun
QUOTE: *'I think it's always best to be who you are.'* Halle Berry

STRENGTHS: Magnanimous, caring.
WEAKNESSES: Self-obsessed and short-tempered.

BORN ON THIS DAY:
Halle Berry
(actor)
Magic Johnson
(basketball player)
Gary Larson
(cartoonist)
Steve Martin
(comedian and actor)
Danielle Steel
(writer)
Sir Walter Scott
(writer and poet)

MEDITATION:
If you kick a stone in anger, you'll hurt your own foot.

August 15

You are a radiant and hearty person with a robust sense of humour. You are self-contained to the point where you can appear aloof at times. You need a stage and will patiently work towards a position of being in the centre. People look up to you and admire your perseverance and integrity. Constant seeking to improve yourself can make you too analytical. You are very moral and have a prudent side. In your relationships you need to be in charge; your household can appear to be run like a well-oiled machine. The overly critical side of your nature can block your creativity. Nevertheless, you are still a superb artisan and fine craftsman, which is where your attention to detail is an asset. A sport – such as golf – which allows you to demonstrate your skill will help steady your sometimes skittish temperament.

TAROT CARD: The Devil
PLANETS: Mercury and Sun
QUOTE: *'You must not fight too often with one enemy, or you will teach him all your art of war.'* Napoleon Bonaparte

STRENGTHS: Joyful and honest.
WEAKNESSES: Jittery, a nit-picker.

BORN ON THIS DAY:
Ben Affleck
(actor)
Princess Anne
(British royal)
Napoleon Bonaparte
(French emperor)
Dame Wendy Hiller
(actor)
Oscar Peterson
(pianist)
Samuel Coleridge-Taylor
(composer)

MEDITATION:
Nothing in life is to be feared. It is only to be understood.

August 16

MEDITATION:

Like nature, develop power and success from a calm centre.

You are an expressive and outgoing person with a compelling and noble presence. Generally, you have a very positive outlook on your own life and on the lives of others, and always see the best in people. You have a unique style and a luminous quality, with a boundless zest for life. People gravitate towards you and choose you to lead the way. You can come across as imperious; you will always delegate unpleasant tasks to others. At times you are controversial and provocative. You can deliberately stir things up as you enjoy a heated debate of opposing views. You revel in relationships and will choose a partner who likes to spar with you; you enjoy the making up after a fight, but don't overdo the rows. If you give back to others the flattery you so love to receive, the resulting tenderness will reward you.

TAROT CARD: The Tower
PLANETS: Venus and Sun
QUOTE: *'What happens in the heart simply happens.'* Ted Hughes

STRENGTHS: Demonstrative, with unlimited energy.
WEAKNESSES: Feisty, overbearing.

August 17

MEDITATION:

Being a fair player makes the only real winner.

You are a dramatic and mysterious person with a quiet yet commanding demeanour. You are brilliantly creative and can trigger deep emotions in people. You are fascinating to watch – you move with a sexual tension that is hypnotic. You are dynamic and forceful yet can't be rushed or pushed by others. Your need to win makes you a poor loser, and you will often resort to manipulative temper tantrums to get your way. People can be in awe of you and sense that you need to be given space. Your relationships can be tumultuous because of your excessive jealousy. The big scenes you create can become very tiring for partners – give them a break and learn to master your emotions. Your stress levels can be high and drumming would be a fabulous way to release your energy.

TAROT CARD: The Star
PLANETS: Pluto and Sun
QUOTE: *'I generally avoid temptation unless I can't resist it.'* Mae West

STRENGTHS: Quietly confident and imaginative.
WEAKNESSES: Unsporting, distrustful.

August 18

You are an expressive and outspoken person who has a strong desire to use the example of their own life to teach people how to expand their minds and explore what the world has to offer. You cannot be limited and have to give full rein to your creativity and vision – which is big. You love horses and the wildness of the outback, and feel most alive when roaming across wide open spaces. A brilliant raconteur, your stories have a moral to them. You love with a passion and are very dramatic, but your tendency not to commit to a long-term relationship suggests that you avoid deep emotions. You could have many romances until you meet your intellectual equal, who will keep you on your toes. Staying still is difficult for you, and burn out is a real danger if you neglect to eat and rest. Superfoods and vitamins will support you.

BORN ON THIS DAY:
Felipé Calderón
(president of Mexico)
Max Factor
(cosmetics entrepreneur)
Edward Norton
(actor and filmmaker)
Roman Polanski
(film director)
Robert Redford
(actor and film director)
Patrick Swayze
(actor, dancer, singer/songwriter)

TAROT CARD: The Moon
PLANETS: Jupiter and Sun
QUOTE: *'When people are away from home, they do things they might not normally do.'* Patrick Swayze

STRENGTHS: An adventurer, a true visionary.
WEAKNESSES: A roamer, outspoken.

MEDITATION:
Silence is the true friend that never betrays.

August 19

You are a bright star, someone who will make a mark on the world for a long time and from a very early age. You have a natural charisma and charm that both men and women adore; you make them feel special and in turn they respond by giving you whatever you want. You desire power and status and will work long hours to achieve success. You exude an aura of confidence but in your youth can be self-questioning and doubt your ability. You have very high standards of excellence and set tests for others. You view relationships as serious and enduring, and whatever happens between you and a partner you'll stay and sort it out. You can be vain and seduced by flattery. Your gifts of leadership are well used when you donate time to helping others. A social sport such as golf would help you unwind.

BORN ON THIS DAY:
Coco Chanel
(fashion designer)
Bill Clinton
(US president)
John Dryden
(poet)
John Deacon
(bassist – Queen)
Matthew Perry
(actor)
Orville Wright
(aviation pioneer)

TAROT CARD: The Sun
PLANETS: Saturn and Sun
QUOTE: *'A girl should be two things: classy and fabulous.'* Coco Chanel

STRENGTHS: Charming and faithful.
WEAKNESSES: Self-admiring, power hungry.

MEDITATION:
Power only follows respect for others and for oneself.

August 20

BORN ON THIS DAY:
Rajiv Gandhi
(Indian prime minister)
Benjamin Harrison
(US president)
Isaac Hayes
(singer/songwriter)
Don King
(boxing promoter)
Slobodan Milosevic
(first Serbian president)
Jim Reeves
(singer)

MEDITATION:

It is just as important not to waste time as it is not to waste money.

You are a generous and sincere person with an expressive, almost theatrical, personality. You know what you want in life and set yourself a series of goals in order to achieve it. You have good financial common sense and in business you know what makes sense commercially. You have a large appetite for life and are very talented. You can achieve success in whatever you turn your hand to. You would do well in the fashion business when it is your name on the label. You can, however, be quite scathing and forthright in your opinions yet people still love you. You need to shine and be adored. You don't take criticism well. Your relationships matter to you. You are an intensely amorous lover with a tactile nature. Keeping a pet you can stroke is a lovely way to keep you relaxed.

TAROT CARD: Judgement
PLANETS: Venus and Sun
QUOTE: *'You go for the quality of the performance, not the longevity of it.'* Don King

STRENGTHS: Thrifty, passionate.
WEAKNESSES: Critical and opinionated.

August 21

BORN ON THIS DAY:
William 'Count' Basie
(bandleader)
Aubrey Beardsley
(illustrator)
Usain Bolt
(champion Olympic sprinter)
Kim Cattrall
(actor)
Princess Margaret
(British royal)
Kenny Rogers
(singer and actor)

MEDITATION:

The smallest good deed is better than the grandest intention.

You are a light-hearted inquisitive person who is very adaptable and ambitious. You have well developed communication skills and are both resourceful and a quick learner. You have a strong sense of honour combined with flexibility. Although you like to be in the leadership position, you don't care for hierarchy. You excel at creative writing. You appeal to children and the young at heart. In romance it is hard to pin you down; you can be like a butterfly, always moving around. You are a born narcissist and need many people to adore you. Your partner can nudge you if you get too pompous. Your biggest asset is the ability to laugh at yourself. You love the sun and don't do well in a damp climate. Hot saunas would give you the tonic you need in the depths of winter.

TAROT CARD: The Empress
PLANETS: Mercury and Sun
QUOTE: *'I just blew my mind and blew the world's mind.'* Usain Bolt

STRENGTHS: Carefree and determined.
WEAKNESSES: An attention seeker, imperious.

August 22

You are an imaginative and single-minded person with a colourful personality. You are very receptive to people. You have a fertile imagination and create vivid pictures with words or images of the world you see. You translate your impressions into an art form that has the capacity to touch people's hearts. You are very sociable and possess the gift of creating a warm and vibrant atmosphere around you. You care for people deeply and keep in close contact with your family. You need to have a mate, because without one you feel incomplete. You make a devoted partner and parent. But because you express yourself with your whole heart, you are emotionally vulnerable. If you feel attacked, you are prone to stomach upsets. Camomile or peppermint teas are better for you than caffeine.

TAROT CARD: The Emperor
PLANETS: Moon and Sun
QUOTE: *'Art is the most beautiful of all lies.'*
Claude Debussy

STRENGTHS: Creative, strong-minded.
WEAKNESSES: Insecure and over-sensitive.

BORN ON THIS DAY:
Henri Cartier-Bresson
(photographer)
Gerri Carr
(astronaut)
Claude Debussy
(composer)
Beenie Man
(rapper)
Dorothy Parker
(writer and critic)
Norman Schwarzkopf
(US general)

MEDITATION:
Put your future in good hands – your own.

August 23

You are a hard-working person with a playful child inside you that just has to be expressed. With your innate artistic flair you are dedicated to being the best at what you do, and will practise laboriously to perfect any weakness. Your nature is to be useful but there is also a part of you that loves showing off – although this is just a mask for your self-consciousness. In relationships you crave appreciation and to be recognized for your talent. If your partner neglects to do this, you can sulk. However, you cannot be pushed into the spotlight and at times you can be shy and excessively modest. This ambivalence can make it difficult for people to know where they stand. Winter isn't a good time for you. You need sunshine. Taking a short break somewhere hot will restore your spirits at this time of year.

TAROT CARD: The Hierophant
PLANETS: Mercury and Sun
QUOTE: *'I have a lot of chameleon qualities. I get very absorbed in my surroundings.'*
River Phoenix

STRENGTHS: Mischievous, helpful.
WEAKNESSES: Moody and insecure.

BORN ON THIS DAY:
Baron Georges Cuvier
(scientist, founder of paleontology)
Gene Kelly
(dancer, actor, singer and filmmaker)
Louis XVI
(French monarch)
Keith Moon
(drummer – The Who)
River Phoenix
(actor)
Willy Russell
(playwright)

MEDITATION:
Nobody can make you feel inferior without your consent.

99

Virgo

August 24 – September 23

Virgo is the helper of the zodiac and it governs the intestines. People born under this sign are prone to worry, which can result in tummy upsets. Virgos digest and analyse, breaking everything down and examining it, before using what they can for the benefit of others. They don't waste anything and they do things properly and well. Virgos love systems for filing; organizing wardrobes, tool kits, beauty kits, filofaxes etc.

The Sun passes through Virgo when the harvest is gathered in, and this is manifested in the wealth of talents and skills that Virgos possess. They are practical and good with their hands and apply high standards to their work. Virgos are often craftspeople and technicians: the weavers, potters, dressmakers, carpenters and IT experts of the zodiac.

PLANETARY RULER AND QUALITIES

Virgo is a mutable earth sign. Traditionally it is ruled by the planet Mercury, the messenger god. It is now also associated with Chiron, the Wounded Healer, and Ceres (a new planet upgraded from an asteroid), the goddess of the Harvest. Mercury is exalted in the sign of Virgo. As an earth sign Mercury is both analytical and practical; it sorts the wheat from the chaff and is discriminating with information. Mercury is the messenger and you use the information you learn for the benefit of others.

RELATIONSHIPS

Virgo is emotionally cool and always looking for a perfect mate. This is of course not possible so you need to learn to accept people as they are and not try to improve them. Marriage is best approached as a friendship with common goals. The best kind of relationship is one where there is sympathy and understanding, which you can find with Capricorn and Taurus the other earth signs, and the caring water sign Cancer. Aries can be good for business and Gemini keeps you on your toes with lively mental debates. You can adapt well to another Virgo, and Sagittarius has the optimism and spontaneity that lightens you up.

MYTH

Virgo lies in a very bountiful area of the heavens with over 500 nebulas. She forms the constellation of The Virgin, a goddess holding a wheatsheaf represented by the star Spica. Virgo is connected with many goddess myths, of which the most prevalent is the story of Demeter (Ceres) the Greek goddess of grain and fertility. Demeter's daughter Persephone was abducted by Pluto, god of the Underworld. In her anguish Demeter left her temple to

TAROT CARD: The Hermit

ELEMENT: Earth

QUALITY: Mutable

NUMBER: 6

RULING PLANET: Mercury

GEMSTONES: Emerald, peridot

COLOURS: Navy blue, dark brown, green

DAY OF THE WEEK: Wednesday

COMPATIBLE SIGNS: Capricorn, Taurus

KEY WORDS: Practical, resourceful, modest, shy, unassuming, versatile, meticulous, calm, self-reliant, critical, fussy

ANATOMY: Intestines

HERBS, PLANTS AND TREES: All bright, small flowers like anemones, and nut-bearing trees

KEY PHRASE:
I serve

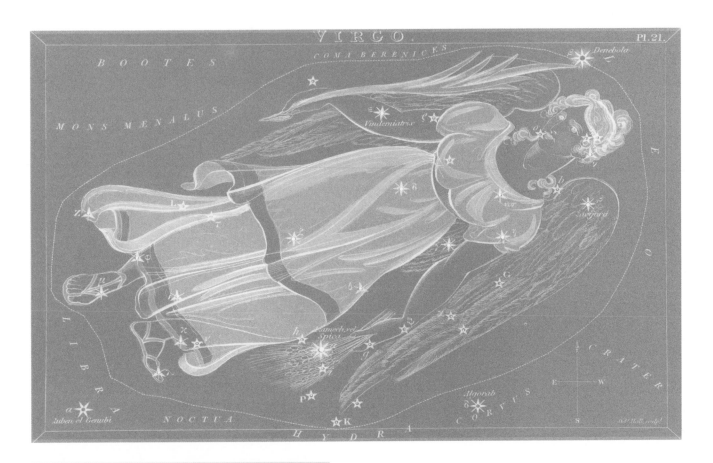

TYPICAL VIRGO:

LANCE ARMSTRONG

'Winning is about heart, not just legs. It's got to be in the right place.'

VIRGO POWERS: Skilled in whatever they set their minds to and a master of detail.

VIRGO NEGATIVES: Prone to exhaustion due to overwork, bogged down by inessentials.

search for her, and the crops died. The gods took pity and decided to reunite mother and daughter. However Persephone, forbidden by Pluto to eat while in the Underworld, had disobeyed and eaten some pomegranate seeds, so each year she has to return for six months to join her consort Pluto and the earth becomes barren. This story explains the seasons of the year.

STRENGTHS AND WEAKNESSES

Virgo is a master of detail, skilled in techniques. You are an excellent critic and notice what others might overlook. Virgos ability to take care of others brings you into the health professions as a nurse, doctor, healer, herbalist, nutritionalist, social worker or teacher. You also thrive in the media and investigative journalism. Your perfectionism gives you the reputation of being fussy, however you can be very messy. This mess gets to a point where you have to clear it up, which gives you immense satisfaction. Virgos are always busy and prone to overwork, as you often do more than you need to in order to get results. This is because you are easily distracted and sometimes focus too much on the nitty-gritty as opposed to looking at the bigger picture.

August 24

MEDITATION:

There is more to life than increasing its speed.

You are a meticulous and disciplined person who takes great care over the smallest details. Your mind is superb and you apply your knowledge in a practical, down-to-earth way. Researching and getting the facts right fascinates you and gives you inordinate satisfaction. You can get obsessed with your own health and with the well-being of others, and you sometimes worry unnecessarily. Work can become the be all and end all for you, and your problem is that you never stop! You tend to see flaws in everything and so you aren't always the best person to be in charge. Your relationships matter to you and you are quite sentimental and soft-hearted. You keep your private life private and really need a partner who gets you to laugh at yourself and lighten up a little.

TAROT CARD: The Lovers
PLANETS: Mercury and Mercury
QUOTE: *'It is a cliché that most clichés are true, but then like most clichés, that cliché is untrue.'* Stephen Fry

STRENGTHS: Compassionate and conscientious.
WEAKNESSES: Workaholic, neurotic.

August 25

MEDITATION:

Please all, and you will please none.

You are a charming and gracious person with a gift for using the right words at the right time. You carefully measure what you say and are always courteous, so are popular and well-liked. Integrity matters to you and you live by a high moral code – which you expect everyone else to follow too. You also have a love of justice and fair play, so you are attracted to the legal professions. Your worst trait is your habit of sitting on the fence, dissecting every nuance of a question in your mind, so that you lose impetus and spontaneity. You enjoy one-to-one relationships with many friends and your lover has to be your intellectual equal. You avoid conflict and can be too 'nice' which infuriates your partner. A sport such as tennis where you get into healthy competition would help you express your passion.

TAROT CARD: The Chariot
PLANETS: Venus and Mercury
QUOTE: *'More than anything else, I'd like to be an old man with a good face, like Alfred Hitchcock or Pablo Picasso.'* Sean Connery

STRENGTHS: Thoughtful and enchanting.
WEAKNESSES: Non-committal, a pushover.

August 26

You are a powerful person who is a meticulous and dedicated worker. You have a strong sense of duty and once you begin a project that you are passionate about, you never give up. You rise to challenges and can endure many setbacks. This capacity for an enormous amount of hard work gains you the respect of your superiors and peers. You like being of service, whether to friends or colleagues, and you are not fazed by difficult issues and the darker side of life. This makes you a reliable and valuable friend. Your relationships are emotional and deep but you can be controlling and manipulative. You can get obsessive about diet, either by over-indulging or being very restrictive. Learning moderation and relaxing your control will benefit both you and your relationships.

TAROT CARD: Strength
PLANETS: Pluto and Mercury
QUOTE: *'Do not wait for leaders; do it alone, person-to-person'* Mother Teresa

STRENGTHS: Ardent, diligent.
WEAKNESSES: Crafty and dominating.

BORN ON THIS DAY:
Prince Albert
(husband of Queen Victoria)
Guillaume Apollinaire
(poet and art critic)
Macaulay Culkin
(actor)
Peggy Guggenheim
(art collector)
Antoine Lavoisier
(pioneer of modern chemistry)
Mother Teresa
(Albanian missionary)

MEDITATION:
Remember to listen — our best thoughts come from others.

August 27

You are a person with impeccable morals and integrity, and set yourself high standards. You admire the hierarchical system and have a deep respect for justice and the law. Your life is all about being of service and you have a genuine concern for your fellow human beings, but you can be judgemental of others for their lack of charity. A deep-seated love of learning attracts you to the educational professions. You adore travelling to far-flung places, and with your eye for detail and appreciation of factual information, you would also be a superb tour guide or travel writer. In relationships you are restless and find it hard to settle down. Your partner needs to give you the freedom to stretch your wings and also have their own exploits to share with you. An impromptu picnic is the perfect antidote for all your worthwhile work.

TAROT CARD: The Hermit
PLANETS: Jupiter and Mercury
QUOTE: *'A President's hardest task is not to do what is right, but to know what is right.'* Lyndon B. Johnson

STRENGTHS: Honest, law-abiding.
WEAKNESSES: Unsettled, judgemental.

BORN ON THIS DAY:
Tom Ford
(fashion designer)
Georg Wilhelm Friedrich Hegel
(philosopher)
Lyndon B. Johnson
(US president)
Bernhard Langer
(professional golfer)
Giuseppe Peano
(mathematician)
Man Ray
(photographer)

MEDITATION:
Be curious, not judgemental.

August 28

MEDITATION:

Never bend your head.
Always hold it high.

You are a methodical and efficient person who is caring and concerned about genuinely contributing to making the world a better place. You always give your best and will spend years training to improve your capabilities. You can appear older than you actually are as you are often solemn, with a pensive expression. Your saving grace is your earthy sense of humour which borders on the ridiculous. You are ambitious but not hasty and will spend a long time taking slow, steady steps to get to the top. You tend to become frustrated if you are not promoted and this causes you huge amounts of self-doubt – you can be far too hard on yourself. When you focus instead on your relationship as a journey where you can open up and be truly understood, you feel far more fulfilled.

TAROT CARD: The Wheel of Fortune
PLANETS: Saturn and Mercury
QUOTE: *'You must never underestimate the power of the eyebrow.'* Jack Black

STRENGTHS: Thoughtful, droll.
WEAKNESSES: Self-critical, lacking in confidence.

August 29

MEDITATION:

Friends can make you
laugh like no one else can.

You are an extraordinary and reliable person with a deft touch. You have a superb mind and your intellect can border on genius. You can get obsessed with detail but then come up with inventive and inspired ideas. You can be rebellious and are not by nature a conformist. You have progressive ideals that concern large groups of people, so politics or social work are eminently suitable for you. You enjoy observing other people's behaviour, so a favourite activity is to hang out at a pavement cafe watching the world go by. You have a quirky sense of humour and there is a humility about you. In relationships it's not easy for you to trust, so you can come across as overly detached, missing out on deeper emotions. Friends matter to you and being in a support group, learning about emotional intelligence, will greatly reward you.

TAROT CARD: Justice
PLANETS: Uranus and Mercury
QUOTE: *'I was the shyest human ever invented, but I had a lion inside me that wouldn't shut up!'* Ingrid Bergman

STRENGTHS: Unconventional, dependable.
WEAKNESSES: Distrustful and aloof.

August 30

You are a light-hearted and witty person with a natural flair for comedy as your timing is superb. You have many strings to your bow – you are musical, artistic and, when you put your mind to it, skilled at writing. You have a talent for quick repartee and love to chat, as you enjoy observing and analyzing people. You dabble with ideas and can be easily side-tracked and seduced by the latest trend. Variety is your life-blood and your ever-changing personality is both youthful and entertaining. However you can be fickle and in relationships you need a partner to help you explore your emotional side. You are curious so self-improvement courses would interest you. You can get swamped by too much information, so having a really good spring clean on a regular basis does wonders for clearing your head.

TAROT CARD: The Empress
PLANETS: Mercury and Mercury
QUOTE: *'French fries. I love them. Some people are chocolate and sweets people. I love French fries. That and caviar.'* Cameron Diaz

STRENGTHS: Carefree, witty.
WEAKNESSES: Volatile and easily distracted.

BORN ON THIS DAY:
Jonathan Aitken
(British politician)
Elizabeth Ashley
(actor)
Cameron Diaz
(actor and model)
Théophile Gautier
(artist, poet and critic)
John Peel
(radio DJ and journalist)
Andy Roddick
(champion tennis player)

MEDITATION:
Concentration is the secret of strength.

August 31

You are a sensitive and affectionate person with a winning way of connecting with people. You appear shy and can be uncomfortable in social situations, preferring to keep the company of a few close friends. You can be content with a quiet life of introspection and are happy in your own company. One thing that brings you out into the world is a strong concern for the welfare of others. Once you've found a cause you believe in you'll put your heart and your considerable mental focus into it. Your solitary and cloistered life is best shared by a soulmate who gently coaxes and supports you into gaining the recognition you deserve. You need to take care of your health as you run on nervous energy. Make a balanced diet with plenty of vitamins and superfoods part of your daily routine.

TAROT CARD: The Emperor
PLANETS: Moon and Mercury
QUOTE: *'Meditation is such a more substantial reality than what we normally take to be reality.'* Richard Gere

STRENGTHS: Compassionate, loving.
WEAKNESSES: Farouche, reclusive.

BORN ON THIS DAY:
Gaius Caligula
(Roman emperor)
Richard Gere
(actor)
Maria Montessori
(educator)
Van Morrison
(musician)
Chris Tucker
(actor and comedian)
Yoshihito
(Japanese emperor)

MEDITATION:
Take care of your body. It's the only place you have to live.

September 1

MEDITATION:

Don't be afraid of growing slowly, only be afraid of standing still.

You are a no-nonsense, self-motivated person who is immensely practical. You have an exuberant approach to life and are always busy. You are best suited to working on your own as your pace is fast and you have a strong sense of direction. You get on and do things and dislike hanging around for others as you feel like you are wasting precious time. Your temperament is fiery, so you need to be active in your daily life and your work is your number one priority. Your greatest asset is your zany sense of humour and you are known as a practical joker, however, you can lack refinement and be blunt with your style of delivery. In relationships you need a partner who is able to accept your busy life and share your hobbies. Hot saunas would help you detox, unwind and force you to slow down.

TAROT CARD: The Magician
PLANETS: Mars and Mercury
QUOTE: *'As long as you're having fun, that's the key. The moment it becomes a grind, it's over.'* Barry Gibb

STRENGTHS: Cheerful and quirky.
WEAKNESSES: Impatient and at times cutting.

September 2

MEDITATION:

To wish you were someone else is to deny the person you are.

You are a passionate and artistic person who is highly practical and down-to-earth. You make a very loyal and reliable friend and keep your word. You are kind-hearted and have a great affinity with nature and the land. You are also skilled with your hands and enjoy giving massage. You would make an excellent carpenter or jeweller as you appreciate beautiful, well-designed things. In relationships you adore being touched and show your affection physically – you need your partner to respond or you can feel unloved. You have a tendency to be a stickler for routines, so now and again need to lighten up with a bit of chaotic mess – if you have children they will help you! Face or body painting would be great fun for you and a good old-fashioned pillow fight would also do the trick!

TAROT CARD: The High Priestess
PLANETS: Venus and Mercury
QUOTE: *'It's fun to be hopelessly in love. It's dangerous, but it's fun.'* Keanu Reeves

STRENGTHS: Sensual with an artistic flair.
WEAKNESSES: Needy and inhibited.

September 3

You are a spontaneous and playful person who is highly adaptable. You can be serious and are dedicated to your work, but the genial, friendly side of you is always there. You're a great organizer and conscientious about your job, yet you always find time to play. You are very funny and can easily make people laugh with your imitations. Playing word games and dry intellectual debates interest you equally. You are could become skilled or even professional at many sports as you have good eye and hand coordination. Partly because of your skill, you can appear aloof and snobby to some, but in time they realize this is not the case. In love you are attracted to a younger person – or certainly someone who is young at heart. You lighten up with games such as Scrabble™ and remember to also allocate time for peace and quiet or you'll burn out.

TAROT CARD: The Empress
PLANETS: Mercury and Mercury
QUOTE: *'I've always been pretty old-fashioned. I'm kind of a missionary guy.'* Charlie Sheen

STRENGTHS: Bright and affable.
WEAKNESSES: Snobbish at times, hectic.

BORN ON THIS DAY:
Frank Macfarlane Burnet
(Nobel prize-winning scientist)
Steve Jones
(guitarist and singer – Sex Pistols)
Charlie Sheen
(actor)
Louis H. Sullivan
(architect)
Al Jardine
(guitarist – The Beach Boys)
Shaun White
(champion Olympic snowboarder)

MEDITATION:
Every person has something to offer, whether you understand it or not.

September 4

You are a warm, tender and approachable person. You are quiet and not at all showy and people may not realize just how generous you are. You are conscientious and take care over the smallest details but can be pedantic and finicky. However, at times you can get muddled which is endearingly human. You like to offer help in a practical way and are incredibly supportive of your friends and family. You listen to what people say and this would make you a great therapist or counsellor. In relationships you are loyal and fuss over your loved ones. You appear, on the outside, to be self-sufficient, however, you are easily wounded if overlooked. At times you get moody and need your own space and time to recover. A stretching exercise such as yoga may get you back into emotional equilibrium.

TAROT CARD: The Emperor
PLANETS: Moon and Mercury
QUOTE: *'I'm a human being and I fall in love and sometimes I don't have control of every situation.'* Beyoncé Knowles

STRENGTHS: Unselfish, helpful.
WEAKNESSES: Fussy and demanding.

BORN ON THIS DAY:
Anton Bruckner
(composer)
Daniel H. Burnham
(architect)
Mitzi Gaynor
(singer, dancer and actor)
Beyoncé Knowles
(singer and actor)
Mark Ronson
(music producer)
Ivan the Terrible
(Russian tsar)

MEDITATION:
If you want to be happy, practise compassion.

107

September 5

MEDITATION:

All the riches do not bring happiness – positivity does.

You are a shy and obliging person who has an innate quality that radiates warmth. You are very talented, take your work seriously and have exceptionally high standards. You seem to know that you are privileged to be able to share your skills for the benefit of others, and at times this may come across as being elitist. You have a good sense of your own worth, but when you're not out in the world, you're less confident than you appear. In relationships you are passionate yet modest. You adore your lover yet also need a lot of affection and hugs to feel loved. If you haven't had enough attention you have a tendency to be rather self-indulgent and childish. Playing a sport where you excel you will get the praise you desire but you also need to learn the importance of losing graciously.

TAROT CARD: The Hierophant
PLANETS: Sun and Mercury
QUOTE: *'The reason we're successful, darling? My overall charisma, of course.'* Freddie Mercury

STRENGTHS: Skilled, meticulous.
WEAKNESSES: Extravagant, and at times, pretentious.

September 6

MEDITATION:

Do not waste time worrying about what has not yet happened.

You are a conscientious and helpful person with an eye for detail and an innate skill for handling intricate work. You are hyper-efficient and superb at organizing. You are both honest and kind, and always offer impartial advice. You can get weighed down with the imperfections you see in your creations – you are your own worst critic and need to learn to be less hard on yourself. Worry can result in digestive problems and rather than taking medicine you would be better off learning to let go of your compulsive need for perfection. Your relationships tend to be conventional and you are devoted to your family. You adore home improvements but can have too many jobs on the go at once. A messy but creative hobby such as pottery would go a long way to loosening you up.

TAROT CARD: The Lovers
PLANETS: Mercury and Mercury
QUOTE: *'Look into the nature of things. Search out the grounds of your opinions, the for and against.'* Frances Wright

STRENGTHS: Co-operative, methodical.
WEAKNESSES: Prone to anxiety attacks, self-critical.

September 7

You are an idealist with strong organizational skills and practical abilities which you utilize in everything that you do. You are naturally well-mannered and polite, and know how to turn on the charm to please people. You are very critical and love order and it gives you immense pleasure when the house or office is clean and tidy. You could be an excellent interior designer or architect as you notice and care about the smallest details. You are very discerning with objects and people and tend to avoid situations that are distasteful to you. You attract beautiful and cultured people into your world and move in particular social circles. In relationships you can be overly rational and controlling, so a partner that gets you in touch with the deeper emotions will stretch you in a good way.

TAROT CARD: The Chariot
PLANETS: Venus and Mercury
QUOTE: *'Without Elvis none of us could have made it.'* Buddy Holly

STRENGTHS: Courteous, astute.
WEAKNESSES: Dictatorial, fault-finding.

BORN ON THIS DAY:
Elizabeth I
(English monarch)
Gloria Gaynor
(singer)
Matthäus Günther
(artist)
Buddy Holly
(singer/songwriter)
Chrissie Hynde
(singer/songwriter and guitarist –
The Pretenders)
Evan Rachel Wood
(actor)

MEDITATION:
Many hands make light work.

September 8

You are a magnetic and intense person who can become very emotional. At times you get carried away with your feelings and lose sight of rational logic. You are not shocked by any aspects of life and have a probing mind, so you could flourish as a psychoanalyst or detective. You are comfortable handling power and large amounts of money so the world of high finance also beckons. You have a sexual aura that is entrancing and a compelling presence, but you are incredibly self-sufficient, so relationships can be a struggle. You can be accused of loving your work more than your partner and they may become jealous. A personal development course would be a transformative experience for you as once you learn how to understand your emotions, you could become an extraordinary intuitive healer.

TAROT CARD: Strength
PLANETS: Pluto and Mercury
QUOTE: *'Practise meditation regularly. Meditation leads to eternal bliss. Therefore meditate, meditate.'* Swami Sivananda

STRENGTHS: Instinctive, enchanting.
WEAKNESSES: Overly independent, absorbed by your work.

BORN ON THIS DAY:
David Arquette
(actor)
Patsy Cline
(singer/songwriter)
Antony Dvořák
(composer)
Pink
(singer/songwriter, dancer
and record producer)
Peter Sellers
(actor and comedian)
Swami Sivananda
(Indian guru and holy man)

MEDITATION:
Follow your instincts. That's where true wisdom manifests itself.

September 9

MEDITATION:

Have ideals, but keep them within grasp.

You are an enthusiastic and friendly person and a superb raconteur, which makes you immensely popular. You are a free spirit and will explore many religions and cultures in your quest for truth. You have a vivid imagination and are gifted at improvization and sharp, comic one-liners. You are the eternal optimist and this quality, combined with a practical realism, ensures your ventures are successful. When under stress you can lack empathy and become quite snappy. In relationships you are an idealist and put your partner on a pedestal, although of course they are only human so you can end up disappointed. Recognizing that people aren't perfect will be a useful life lesson for you. You would love to go up in a hot air balloon as views inspire you, and the experience will help you to keep things in perspective.

TAROT CARD: The Hermit
PLANETS: Jupiter and Mercury
QUOTE: *'I'm a laugh tart. I make no secret of that fact.'* Hugh Grant

STRENGTHS: A great storyteller, uninhibited.
WEAKNESSES: Too idealistic, irritable.

September 10

MEDITATION:

All cruelty springs from weakness.

You are a serious, single-minded person who is determined to achieve success and will work extremely hard to get it. You are disciplined and focused with tremendous amounts of stamina. You are a welcome addition to any business and are suited to positions of responsibility. As a professional, you are well respected in your field, and as a friend you can be totally relied upon. You are down-to-earth and practical and when you offer help, you roll up your sleeves and get on with it. In relationships you are attracted to someone older than yourself, and you may even marry to enhance your career. You can become too serious and critical of yourself, so playing a child's game will help you lighten up. Build a sand castle, or splash in puddles – just for the sheer fun of it!

TAROT CARD: The Wheel of Fortune
PLANETS: Saturn and Mercury
QUOTE: *'Success in golf depends less on strength of body than upon strength of mind and character.'* Arnold Palmer

STRENGTHS: Superb concentration skills, trustworthy.
WEAKNESSES: Sombre, ruthless.

September 11

You are a friendly and quietly dignified person with a brilliant and original mind. You can grasp complex concepts with ease and would be well suited to a scientific or academic profession. Human rights matter immensely to you and you are broad-minded and tolerant. You adore watching people and the drama of their passions and conflicts, but you try to avoid fights in your own life, tendencies that would make you a good clinical psychologist or writer. You form intellectual friendships and your partner has to be your equal and share your philosophy. You tend to be controlling as you are emotionally vulnerable and find it hard to trust, so you take your time in forming intimate relationships. You can suffer from mental overload, so half an hour enjoying the fresh air clears your mind ready for the next exciting idea to pop in.

TAROT CARD: Justice
PLANETS: Uranus and Mercury
QUOTE: *'The cruelest thing a man can do to a woman is to portray her as perfection.'* D.H. Lawrence

STRENGTHS: Distinguished and a deep thinker.
WEAKNESSES: Untrusting, an authoritarian.

BORN ON THIS DAY:
Harry Connick Jr
(singer, pianist and composer)
D.H. Lawrence
(writer and poet)
Chantal Mauduit
(mountaineer)
Jessica Mitford
(writer)
Moby
(DJ, singer/songwriter)
Brian De Palma
(film director)

MEDITATION:
Love all, trust a few, do wrong to none.

September 12

You are an inspired and compassionate person with the ability to express poetry from your soul. You could be a gifted songwriter or artist. You have great wisdom and healing ability as you truly understand people's concerns and hidden needs. You would be an ideal counsellor or therapist, as you are happy working with just one person at a time. You are intuitive and respond to people emotionally rather than reacting impulsively. You are naturally shy and introverted and when under pressure you can get nervous and anxious. You are highly sensitive to atmosphere and are easily hurt by a sharp comment. You need a tender and gentle lover – someone who is a soulmate and a confidant and listens to your musings. Lying in a floatation tank would be a wonderful way for you to reconnect with the tranquillity of the womb.

TAROT CARD: The Hanged Man
PLANETS: Neptune and Mercury
QUOTE: *'I'll come to you with gifts of knowledge, wisdom and truth.'* Barry White

STRENGTHS: Empathic towards others, creative.
WEAKNESSES: A born worrier, easily hurt.

BORN ON THIS DAY:
Bertie Ahern
(Irish prime minister)
Francis I
(French monarch)
Sir Ian Holm
(actor)
Jennifer Hudson
(actor and singer)
Jesse Owens
(champion Olympic athlete)
Barry White
(singer/songwriter)

MEDITATION:
Worry never robs tomorrow of its sorrow, it only saps today of its joy.

September 13

You are a helpful and practical person who delights in taking care of others. A domestic maestro, you are likely to be knowledgeable about nutrition and a great cook. These talents would make you perfect for the restaurant industry or the nursing profession as you balance efficiency with a warm heart. You can get stuck in old habits and become disheartened if challenged. Your relationship is likely to be long-lasting and your family life is what brings you the most joy. You are the one – male or female – who tends to the wellbeing of your family and you are genuinely concerned that their daily lives operate smoothly. You can get uptight if anything goes wrong so you need to let yourself have a day off from time to time. Jazz dance or a game of tennis will release any pent-up stress.

BORN ON THIS DAY:
Stella McCartney
(fashion designer)
Roald Dahl
(writer)
Alain Ducasse
(chef and restaurateur)
Milton Hershey
(industrialist and philanthropist)
J.B. Priestley
(writer)
Arnold Schoenberg
(composer)

MEDITATION:
Better than a thousand hollow words, is one word that brings peace.

TAROT CARD: Death
PLANETS: Moon and Mercury
QUOTE: *'A little nonsense now and then, is cherished by the wisest men.'* Roald Dahl

STRENGTHS: Family orientated, warm-hearted.
WEAKNESSES: Too much a creature of habit, prone to tension.

September 14

You are a kind-hearted and deeply honourable person who has a powerful intellect and is highly articulate. You are skilled at choosing the right words to say, and most importantly, you say them at the right time. You can appear to others to be quiet and unassuming but on the inside you have a courageous, proud and fiery nature. There are two sides to you – the sensible adult and the irrepressible child. Combining them is quite a challenge but a career in acting would suit you, or a leadership role in the nursing profession. On a bad day you are prone to wallowing in self-pity and dwelling on what other people think of you. In relationships you need a partner who allows you to lead yet also showers you with affection and treats you to indulgent presents. You needn't feel guilty if you are a little vain at times.

BORN ON THIS DAY:
Tom Cora
(cellist)
Mary Crosby
(actor)
Renzo Piano
(architect)
Margaret Sanger
(nurse and birth control activist)
Amy Winehouse
(singer/songwriter)
David Wojnarowicz
(artist)

MEDITATION:
Self-pity is humankind's worst enemy – rise above it.

TAROT CARD: Temperance
PLANETS: Sun and Mercury
QUOTE: *'Girls talk to each other like men talk to each other. But girls have an eye for detail.'* Amy Winehouse

STRENGTHS: Expressive, forthright.
WEAKNESSES: Explosive, prone to self-pity.

September 15

You are a focussed, industrious and discerning person. You have an excellent brain and love sifting through information, analysing and sorting out what is most vital. You worship intellect and seek out like-minded people, so would be attracted to debating societies or internet forums. You would make a talented writer as you take careful note of conversations and observe the minutiae of life. You are extremely careful and thoughtful about the welfare of others, but you can be too fastidious and end up nannying people. In relationships you are incredibly loyal and aim to serve your partner. However, you need to be aware of being too servile and ending up in a position of inferiority. You need to assert yourself so a sport such as fencing would be good for your self-development and confidence.

TAROT CARD: The Devil
PLANETS: Mercury and Mercury
QUOTE: *'Good advice is always certain to be ignored, but that's no reason not to give it.'*
Agatha Christie

STRENGTHS: Intellectual, meticulous.
WEAKNESSES: Over-particular, smothering.

BORN ON THIS DAY:
Agatha Christie
(writer)
Prince Harry
(British royal)
Tommy Lee Jones
(actor and film director)
Marco Polo
(explorer)
Richard I
(English monarch)
Oliver Stone
(film director)

MEDITATION:
What we think, we become.

September 16

You are a kind-hearted and honest person who enjoys the good things in life. You have excellent powers of observation and can sense when anything is out of place. You think and listen carefully, assessing all the options before making a move. Your consideration for others and reasonable nature make you easy to be around. A career in the diplomatic service would suit you as you are a good arbitrator. You are critical but able to be honest about your fallibility and can laugh at yourself – which is an invaluable quality. In relationships you spend a lot of time talking and discussing the affairs of the day, but you can hide behind a veneer of niceness, so others don't really know who you are. You can get caught up with your appearance and what people think about you, so getting dirty and messy would do you the world of good once in a while.

TAROT CARD: The Tower
PLANETS: Venus and Mercury
QUOTE: *'The beautiful thing about learning is nobody can take it away from you.'*
B.B. King

STRENGTHS: Honourable, easy-going.
WEAKNESSES: Hard to read, vain.

BORN ON THIS DAY:
Lauren Bacall
(actor)
David Copperfield
(illusionist)
Peter Falk
(actor)
Henry V
(English monarch)
B.B. King
(singer/songwriter and guitarist)
Alexander Korda
(film director)

MEDITATION:
Vanity is often the unseen spur.

September 17

BORN ON THIS DAY:
Anne Bancroft
(actor)
Césare Borgia
(Italian politician)
Robert Dudley
(Earl of Leicester and favourite
of Elizabeth I)
Baz Luhrmann
(film director)
Bryan Singer
(film director)
Hank Williams
(musician)

MEDITATION:

Fill your paper with the breathings of your heart.

You are a loyal and supportive person who is secretive and loves intrigue. You are extremely perceptive, with an ability to see beneath the surface of people's words and actions. You are skilled with language and excel at detailed mental work. Working as a politician or as a critic would be the perfect arena for your talents, as you also understand the power of propaganda. You are faithful and make a valuable confidant. You have a close circle of friends and they tend to be people you meet through work. In relationships you need to take your time to get to know your partner. You are so used to keeping a tight rein on your feelings that you find it hard to trust. You love to renovate as you get a buzz from transforming things, so knocking down walls is your idea of fun.

TAROT CARD: The Star
PLANETS: Pluto and Mercury
QUOTE: *'We don't live in the world of reality, we live in the world of how we perceive reality.'* Baz Luhrmann

STRENGTHS: Insightful and a keen wordsmith.
WEAKNESSES: Reticent, untrusting.

September 18

BORN ON THIS DAY:
Lance Armstrong
(world champion cyclist and activist)
Rossano Brazzi
(actor)
Greta Garbo
(actor)
Samuel Johnson
(writer)
Dee Dee Ramone
(bassist and songwriter –
The Ramones)
Paul J. Zimmer
(poet)

MEDITATION:

You are never too old to set another goal or to dream a new dream.

You are an ingenious and visionary person who is incredibly kind with good intentions. You love talking and analysing the meaning of life with fellow philosophers. You are a deep thinker and a communicator so the realms of academia may beckon, as could the Church or the law. You are sensible yet also eager for adventure and are tempted to leave everyday life to travel the world. Even though you respect the rules you can throw caution aside and act impulsively and you may be prone to gambling. You live for the future and want to improve your life, so often take up higher education long after you leave school. In your relationships you can be too sentimental rather than romantic, and you need a strong mental affinity with your partner. A visit to the theatre is a wonderful treat for you.

TAROT CARD: The Moon
PLANETS: Jupiter and Mercury
QUOTE: *'I never said, "I want to be alone." I only said, "I want to be left alone." There is all the difference.'* Greta Garbo

STRENGTHS: Intrepid, a visionary.
WEAKNESSES: Compulsive, unsettled.

September 19

You are a capable and helpful person with refined taste. You know what you want and set your mind to get it. For you work is not just about making a living; it is your vocation, and you will make personal sacrifices to pursue long-term goals. You can be frugal and manage limited resources well, so being in charge of a budget is your forté. You are used to doing things on your own, your own way, however, you can end up taking over other people's roles and risk offending them as a result. You need tangible proof of your achievements and place a high value on material possessions. In relationships you need a mate who offers you security. You love culture and can become obsessed by work so taking regular city breaks would be a source of pleasure and relaxation.

TAROT CARD: The Sun
PLANETS: Saturn and Mercury
QUOTE: *'If a person is treated like a patient, they are apt to act like one.'* Frances Farmer

STRENGTHS: Good business skills, refined.
WEAKNESSES: A workoholic, tendency to take over.

BORN ON THIS DAY:
Cass Elliot
(singer – The Mamas and the Papas)
Brian Epstein
(manager of The Beatles)
Frances Farmer
(actor)
Jeremy Irons
(actor)
Twiggy
(model)
Emil Zatopek
(champion Olympic athlete)

MEDITATION:
None of us is as smart as all of us.

September 20

You are a caring and thoughtful person with an innate modesty about your talents and personal appearance. You enjoy helping others and being useful is vitally important. You are concerned with the real world, what you can touch and see, rather than the intuitive realm. You have good financial acumen and a large dose of common sense so you are well-suited to business. Your vocation is to assist others and provide a tangible service for them. At times you can get quite lazy and can spend hours loafing on the sofa or sitting in the garden. Your relationships are steady and enduring but can get dull. Your weaknesses are your overwhelming desire for security and possessiveness. You need to make an effort to let go of your busy schedule for some frivolous fun with your loved one.

TAROT CARD: Judgement
PLANETS: Venus and Mercury
QUOTE: *'The two big advantages I had at birth were to have been born wise and to have been born in poverty.'* Sophia Loren

STRENGTHS: Unpretentious, levelheaded.
WEAKNESSES: Lethargic, jealous.

BORN ON THIS DAY:
Taro Aso
(Japanese prime minister)
Joyce Brothers
(psychologist, writer and actor)
Steve Gerber
(comic book writer)
Sophia Loren
(actor)
Upton Sinclair
(writer)
Leo Strauss
(philosopher)

MEDITATION:
The jealous are troublesome to others, but a torment to themselves.

September 21

You are an articulate and highly sociable person, the proverbial butterfly. You play a lot and believe that life is fun. You have an exceptional mind and are able to grasp details and analyse facts. However you can be too intellectual and risk making the subject at hand as dry as dust. You are a wordsmith so a career as a songwriter or linguist would be right up your street. You need to keep your nimble hands busy, so a hobby such as knitting or macramé is ideal. Computers were made for you and typing is an essential skill in your repertoire. In relationships you are restless and your social calendar is usually full well in advance. Your partner needs to balance you and should be clever or you will get bored. A spontaneous style of dancing is perfect for you to loosen up.

BORN ON THIS DAY:
Leonard Cohen
(singer/songwriter)
Stephen King
(writer)
Ricki Lake
(talk-show host and actor)
Bill Murray
(actor and comedian)
Nicole Richie
(socialite daughter of Lionel Richie)
H.G. Wells
(writer)

MEDITATION:
Act the way you'd like to be and soon you'll be the way you act.

TAROT CARD: The World
PLANETS: Mercury and Mercury
QUOTE: *'Only enemies speak the truth; friends and lovers lie endlessly, caught in the web of duty.'* Stephen King

STRENGTHS: Articulate and affable.
WEAKNESSES: Too highbrow at times, tense.

September 22

You are a charismatic and self-reflective person. You are intuitive and imaginative with an ear for music and the tone of a person's communication. Education interests you and the academic life appeals to you. You are also drawn to work in the area of mental health as you understand the human condition. You can spot the faults in a system and sometimes you can be too critical. However, you do adapt easily and are able to accommodate other people's wishes at the expense of your own preferences. You give a lot of your energy away and can get cranky when you neglect yourself. In relationships, you need a partner to adore and pet you as physical touch makes you feel loved and cherished. Let yourself go and join a dance exercise group. Being in a nurturing atmosphere is especially beneficial for you.

BORN ON THIS DAY:
Scott Baio
(actor)
Andrea Bocelli
(tenor)
Nick Cave
(singer/songwriter)
Anne of Cleves
(fourth wife of King Henry VIII)
Joan Jett
(singer/songwriter and guitarist)
Ronaldo
(soccer player)

MEDITATION:
When the sun rises it rises for everyone.

TAROT CARD: The Emperor
PLANETS: Moon and Mercury
QUOTE: *'I am very ambitious. I want to enjoy this and then really go for it.'* Ronaldo

STRENGTHS: Charming and sympathetic.
WEAKNESSES: Scathing, a whiner.

September 23

You are a radiant and magnetic person with a charismatic presence. You are light-hearted and playful; a gregarious party person who is fond of practical jokes. Immensely popular for your ability to have fun and see the comedy in every situation, you have many friends and are well-connected. You are artistic and have excellent taste. A career in the theatre as a director or costume designer would appeal to you. Your extravagance is a weakness and you have a penchant for anything shiny and expensive. Romance is your reason for living, and being in love brings out the best in you. However, as a result you find it difficult to commit to one partner as you want your love life to be one long honeymoon. Attending seminars on relationships would be an excellent way to help you understand the real art of love.

TAROT CARD: The Hierophant
PLANETS: Sun and Mercury
QUOTE: *'I never wanted to be famous. I only wanted to be great.'* Ray Charles

STRENGTHS: Charming and fun.
WEAKNESSES: Scared of commitment, lavish.

BORN ON THIS DAY:
Augustus Caesar
(Roman emperor)
Ray Charles
(singer/songwriter, musician, composer and bandleader)
John Coltrane
(saxophonist)
Euripides
(Ancient Greek playwright)
Aldo Moro
(Italian prime minister)
Bruce Springsteen
(singer/songwriter and musician)

MEDITATION:
No road is long with good company.

TYPICAL VIRGO:
MICHAEL JACKSON

'I'm never pleased with anything, I'm a perfectionist, it's part of who I am.'

VIRGO TRAITS:
The perfectionist side of Virgos can lead to self-criticism and shyness. This can be misrepresented as stand-offish behaviour, whereas in reality, Virgo is a kind and loyal sign and the most modest of the zodiac.

Virgos need to be aware of burning themselves out due to overworking and consant striving for perfection. Once they learn that no one is perfect life will be more positive and less complicated.

Libra

September 24 – October 23

TAROT CARD: Justice

ELEMENT: Air

QUALITY: Cardinal

NUMBER: 7

RULING PLANET: Venus

GEMSTONES: Diamond and quartz crystal

COLOURS: White and multi-colours

DAY OF THE WEEK: Friday

COMPATIBLE SIGNS:
Gemini, Leo and Sagittarius

KEY WORDS: Impartial and balanced mind, perfect partner, sociable and gregarious, graceful, indecisive, extravagant, pleasure-seeking, superficial

ANATOMY: Kidneys, skin, lumbar region and buttocks

HERBS, PLANTS AND TREES: Watercress, strawberry, vines, violets, pansy and primrose

KEY PHRASE:
I unite

Libra is the diplomat of the twelve signs. It is the seventh sign of the zodiac, beginning at the Autumn Equinox – when day and night are exactly equal. Libra is the sign of harmony and balance and Librans always weigh up all their options before commiting to anything. It is not easy being Libran, always fighting hard to balance but rarely winning, and instead, you tend to veer from one extreme to the other.

Librans ardently believe in justice and in peaceful solutions against all odds. You are well known for your superb dress sense and artistic taste. Your home is full of designer items – you could not bear to buy something that was not pleasing to the eye. Librans are huge fans of the art world, the opera and good restaurants. For you the experience of dining has to be done in elegant and refined surroundings.

PLANETARY RULER AND QUALITIES
Libra is a cardinal air sign. It is ruled by Venus in her role as patron of the arts. Venus attracts people because of her charm and grace. Librans like to create a harmonious and peaceful environment. The glyph is a symbol of the setting Sun and sunsets are breathtaking in their beauty. However, the Sun is weak in Libra as it is setting and losing energy. Also the Sun is a king, and in Libra it always has to take into account the needs of others. Saturn is exalted in this sign which lends business acumen to those born under it.

RELATIONSHIPS
Librans make the perfect partners as you will always complement the person you are with. You look to find affinity with everyone you meet and also admire and seek out beauty. You love to socialize and air your views with friends. Partnering is essential, and you use it as a way to gain knowledge about yourself and to attain balance in your life.

Libran's opposite sign is Aries and this pairing results in the classic Venus/Mars magnetic, passionate attraction. In a business relationship Aries will take the lead, but the Libran is best at talking. You get on well with Taureans as you are both ruled by Venus, but you have more in common with Gemini. Your relationships with Aquarians are a meeting of minds and you form good social bonds with them, however they prefer group situations whereas you prefer an intimate dinner for two. Usually you will find that fire signs have more going for you if you want to achieve something. You adore Leo and you are compatible as long as you let them be boss. Sagittarius is a true friend who joins in enthusiastically with your social life.

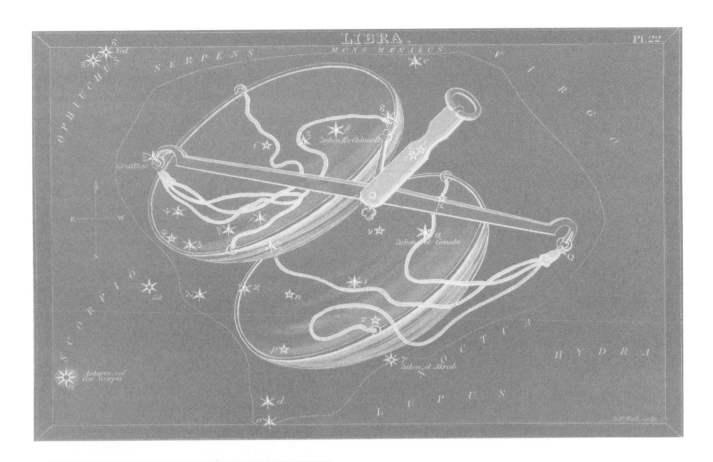

TYPICAL LIBRA:

LUCIANO PAVAROTTI

'In opera, as with any performing art, to be in great demand and to command high fees you must be good of course, but you must also be famous. The two are different things.'

LIBRAN POWERS: Graceful and charming, a wonderful friend.

LIBRAN NEGATIVES: A fiery side, an attention seeker.

MYTH

Represented by the constellation of the scales, Libra is the youngest of the zodiac signs and the only one not to be represented by a living creature. The symbol relates to the ancient Egyptian goddess Maat who personified the concepts of truth, balance, order, law, morality and justice. Her role was in upholding the laws of the Creator. It was believed that after death, she weighed the human soul (thought to reside in the heart) on one scale and a feather on the other. If the soul was heavier than the feather it had to reincarnate – if lighter – the soul would go to paradise.

STRENGTHS AND WEAKNESSES

Librans are charming and soothing and people feel good around you. Your social life is very important to you, so you need to find a balance between personal and social time, and this can result in many ups and downs. When you find the stillness at the centre of the scales, the point of true balance, you will be truly peaceful and contented with life.

September 24

You are a self-sufficient and practical person with an artistic eye. Highly civilized, you are rational, articulate and graceful. You make a superb craftsperson as you have both artistic and technical skills. An attentive listener, you are a great manager as you are genuinely interested in serving people and would be well suited to the retail or restaurant trades. Your weakness is being finicky and over-analysing people and situations. However, when you let your hair down you have a whacky sense of humour. In a relationship you are an affectionate and devoted partner. You need to be able to share the same interests. You delight in domestic life and find joy in keeping the household running smoothly. Relaxing in a playful manner will balance you, so children's games are perfect.

BORN ON THIS DAY:
Linda McCartney
(ex-wife of Paul McCartney)
F. Scott Fitzgerald
(writer)
E. Franklin Frazier
(sociologist)
Sir Arthur Guinness
(Irish brewer)
Henry V
(English monarch)
Jim Henson
(puppeteer)

MEDITATION:
Failure teaches success.

TAROT CARD: The Lovers
PLANETS: Mercury and Venus
QUOTE: *'The most sophisticated people I know – inside they are all children.'* Jim Henson

STRENGTHS: Funny and independent.
WEAKNESSES: Overly meticulous, picky.

September 25

You are a beautiful and loving person with immense charm. The epitome of gracefulness and elegance, you are able to blend into any social situation with ease. You adore being around people and have a wide social circle. Whether professional, personal or family, relationships play a vital part in your life and you rely on them to help you understand who you are. This makes you very dependent on others for your well-being and you can be thrown off centre if you think someone doesn't like you. As a people person Public Relations would be an obvious choice of profession, as would a musical, modelling or acting career. In love you have a tendency to idealize your partner until you recognize they are only human. You can get lazy so exercise with a social aspect is an incentive – cricket or baseball fit the bill.

BORN ON THIS DAY:
Michael Douglas
(actor and producer)
Mark Hamill
(actor)
Catherine Zeta Jones
(actor)
Jodie Kidd
(supermodel)
Christopher Reeve
(actor and filmmaker)
Will Smith
(actor, rapper, film/TV and record producer)

MEDITATION:
When there is no enemy within, the enemies outside cannot hurt you.

TAROT CARD: The Chariot
PLANETS: Venus and Venus
QUOTE: *'In my mind, I've always been an A-list Hollywood superstar. Y'all just didn't know yet.'* Will Smith

STRENGTHS: Endearing and caring.
WEAKNESSES: Easily hurt, dependent.

September 26

You are a suave and magnetic person with great allure and mysticism. You can be mesmerizing to watch as you move with sensuality and grace. You have a combination of a sharp intellect and emotional strength, you are both charming and debonair so are popular with many people. Money and power are very attractive to you and a career in business or politics is likely. Show business is also appealing as you can handle the adulation and fame. With your courage and tenacity you can get to the very top of your profession. You are renowned for your willpower and can be a formidable enemy. If thwarted you can manipulate to get what you want. Your intimate relationships are intense and stormy as you relish drama. The opera or heavy rock music are your kind of relaxation because you love the passion in them.

TAROT CARD: Strength
PLANETS: Pluto and Venus
QUOTE: *'Only those who will risk going too far can possibly find out how far one can go.'* T.S. Eliot

STRENGTHS: Refined and captivating.
WEAKNESSES: Unscrupulous, overly ostentatious at times.

BORN ON THIS DAY:
T. S Eliot
(writer)
Bryan Ferry
(singer/songwriter, musician – Roxy Music)
George Gershwin
(composer)
Olivia Newton-John
(actor and singer)
Moses Mendelssohn
(philosopher)
Serena Williams
(champion tennis player)

MEDITATION:
The real measure of wealth: how much you'd be worth if you lost all your money.

September 27

You are an idealistic and persuasive person with a burning desire to share your vision with people. You believe in a better future for the world and that all people can have wonderful, loving relationships. With your flair and great organizational skills, you are the perfect campaigner for whichever pet cause you adopt. You are likely to be a spiritual person and have a missionary zeal that could take you into the ministry. You love to help people but you can overestimate your capabilities, taking on too many projects and thus spreading yourself too thin. You need a great deal of freedom in your intimate relationships so look for a partner who shares the same passion as you do for your projects. A weekend trip with your lover to explore a foreign culture would be an inspirational experience for you.

TAROT CARD: The Hermit
PLANETS: Jupiter and Venus
QUOTE: *'Beauty, to me, is about being comfortable in your own skin. That, or a kick-ass red lipstick'* Gwyneth Paltrow

STRENGTHS: Great coordination skills, obliging.
WEAKNESSES: Over-stretching yourself, prone to burning out.

BORN ON THIS DAY:
Avril Lavigne
(singer/songwriter)
Meat Loaf
(singer/songwriter)
Gwyneth Paltrow
(actor)
Jim Thompson
(writer)
Lil' Wayne
(rapper)
Irvine Welsh
(writer)

MEDITATION:
Take rest; a field that has rested gives a bountiful crop.

121

September 28

MEDITATION:

We must never confuse elegance with snobbery.

You are a courteous and tactful person who is worldly-wise. Purposeful and ambitious, you can cultivate influential people to help you succeed. You enjoy being part of a team, have great organizational skills and make a superb manager. People respect your leadership and natural writerity. You have impeccable taste and extremely high standards, which are exemplified by the designer-label clothes you wear. However, you can also have impossible expectations of people and need to learn to be more tolerant. To some you can appear snobbish, to others you are a steadfast friend. In your intimate relationships you need to be able to respect your partner and to feel adored. Physical affection is vitally important for you to open up your heart to another. Aromatherapy massage is a wonderful way for you to feel total relaxation.

TAROT CARD: The Wheel of Fortune
PLANETS: Saturn and Venus
QUOTE: *'Wheresoever you go, go with all your heart.'* Confucius

STRENGTHS: Well-mannered and enlightened.
WEAKNESSES: Supercilious with impossibly high standards.

September 29

MEDITATION:

He who sings, frightens away all his ills.

You are a freewheeling individual who seeks the ideal romantic relationship. Very friendly and sociable, you are a lively and witty companion. You adore discussing new ideas and solutions for the injustices in the world. With clear logic and a rational mind, you are a thinker and would be well suited to intellectual careers in technology and engineering. You want to know how things work and love solving problems. In your intimate relationships you can over-analyse as a defence against feeling your own deep emotions. You have impossibly high standards for how a partner should behave and are frequently disappointed. This keeps you independent and you can remain single for a long time. You need to discover a spiritual path which will fulfil you. Singing can help you open up and connect with your heart's desire.

TAROT CARD: Justice
PLANETS: Uranus and Venus
QUOTE: *'Time is everything; five minutes make the difference between victory and defeat.'* Horatio Lord Nelson

STRENGTHS: Self-reliant, well-reasoned.
WEAKNESSES: Scared of emotion, prone to despondency.

September 30

You are a lively and intelligent person with a bright and breezy manner. You are ever-youthful and have a childlike innocence. Immensely curious, you are always asking questions, so you would be a natural journalist or writer. With a friendly style, you are skilled at putting people at their ease so they open up to you. Being an interviewer could be a rewarding profession. In relationships you get bored easily, always moving on to pastures new. Some say that you skim the surface and are afraid to go deep into your feelings, however, your significant other is very important to you, so slowing down to reflect on your emotional world helps you enormously. You are so easily distracted that giving your lover your undivided attention by turning off your gadgets, means more than words can say.

TAROT CARD: The Empress
PLANETS: Mercury and Venus
QUOTE: *'Failure is the condiment that gives success its flavour.'* Truman Capote

STRENGTHS: Inquisitive and full of life.
WEAKNESSES: Undemonstrative, and at times, naive.

BORN ON THIS DAY:
Cecelia Ahern
(writer and television producer)
Marc Bolan
(singer/songwriter
and guitarist –
T. Rex)
Truman Capote
(writer)
Marion Cotillard
(actor)
Mireille Hartuch
(composer and child prodigy)
Johnny Mathis
(singer/songwriter)

MEDITATION:
Do not to stop questioning – curiosity has its own reason for existing.

October 1

You are a convivial and lively person with a restless spirit who needs to experience new things on a regular basis. With high energy levels and plenty of drive and courage, you love taking the initiative and leading people. Your mind races ahead and you will try anything new. A natural champion of the underdog, you have a persuasive and direct style of talking which is hard to resist. As such you are a skilled negotiator and would flourish as a diplomat. You are more sensitive than you appear and react badly to criticism, which can throw you off course. At times you make rash judgements. Love is what you live for, and all the rituals of courtship thrill you. However, you bore easily when the passion cools and will start a fight just to liven things up. Competitive sport is essential for you to let off steam.

TAROT CARD: The Magician
PLANETS: Mars and Venus
QUOTE: *'All love shifts and changes. I don't know if you can be wholeheartedly in love all the time.'* Julie Andrews

STRENGTHS: Jovial, ambitious.
WEAKNESSES: Easily offended, a short attention span.

BORN ON THIS DAY:
Julie Andrews
(actor and singer)
Sir Peter Blake
(explorer, scientist and yachtsman)
William Boeing
(engineer)
Jimmy Carter
(US president)
Walter Matthau
(actor)
Bonnie Parker
(American outlaw)

MEDITATION:
Restlessness and discontent are the first necessities of progress.

123

October 2

MEDITATION:
*Collect as precious pearls
the words of the wise
and virtuous.*

You are a charming and delightful person with a great sense of style. Very classy and with aesthetically good taste, you are one of the beautiful set. A lover of beauty and art, you are a creative and naturally drawn to work in the fashion or music business. You also possess good business acumen and can handle large amounts of money with ease. Relationships are essential for you and you are a keen lover. The problem is that you are extremely flirtatious and even if you do not mean anything by it, people are very attracted to you as you can make them feel special. You can also be tempted by a hedonistic lifestyle, which can cause your partner to be jealous. As a tactile and sensual person an aromatherapy massage is what you need, and what you can give to demonstrate your love.

TAROT CARD: The High Priestess
PLANETS: Venus and Venus
QUOTE: *'If I had no sense of humour, I would long ago have committed suicide.'* Mohandas Gandhi

STRENGTHS: Elegant and financially competent.
WEAKNESSES: A thrill-seeker, coquettish.

October 3

MEDITATION:
*There is a time for many
words, and there is also a
time for sleep.*

You are a sophisticated and engaging person with a lively wit. A gifted raconteur, you can charm almost everyone, but you can also be provocative and have a mischievous side to you. In a debate you love to take the opposite side just to stir things up. You manage to wriggle out of awkward situations through quick thinking and humour. The communications industry would be a good field for you, whether as a copywriter in advertising, or as a gossip columnist for a glossy magazine. At times you can be overly flippant and come across as emotionally immature. In relationships you need to keep it light and you can spend a long time playing the field before you settle down. Insomnia can be a problem as you are so mentally active – yoga in the evening and avoiding caffeine can help.

TAROT CARD: The Empress
PLANETS: Mercury and Venus
QUOTE: *'I really don't care what people say. It's not like it discourages me from doing something I want to do.'* Gwen Stefani

STRENGTHS: Droll, a raconteur.
WEAKNESSES: Facetious, a tattler.

October 4

You are a warm and hospitable person with a caring, sensitive nature. A great friend and an excellent host, you love entertaining and making people feel welcome. The hotel and entertainment industries are areas in which you could excel. You have artistic gifts and need to express yourself in order to feel fulfilled. Your weakness is that you can be emotionally unstable and easily hurt by the slightest negative comment. A close support network of family and friends is essential for your confidence. An intimate relationship plays an important role on your life and it is rare for you to be on your own. Very affectionate, you need to be appreciated and respond quickly to a hug. You are naturally nostalgic and food is close to your heart, so a family picnic by the seaside makes a wonderfully soothing trip down memory lane.

TAROT CARD: The Emperor
PLANETS: Moon and Venus
QUOTE: *'I want to fight poverty and ignorance and give opportunity to those people who are locked out.'* Russell Simmons

STRENGTHS: A born entertainer, tender.
WEAKNESSES: Emotionally unstable, easily upset.

BORN ON THIS DAY:
Jackie Collins
(writer)
Rutherford B. Hayes
(US president)
Charlton Heston
(actor)
Jacqueline Pascal
(child prodigy)
Anne Rice
(writer)
Russell Simmons
(co-founder of Def Jam records)

MEDITATION:
A hug is a handshake from the heart.

October 5

You are a vivacious, generous person with a warm and open heart. Your kindness and playfulness are very attractive and people love to be in your company. Leadership positions in the fields of politics, music or the theatre are appealing as career paths. You are self-confident and adore being the centre of attention. However, if people fail to recognize and appreciate your talents, you can get very upset and become quite temperamental. Your lifestyle is important and you often live beyond your means for the sake of keeping up appearances. Romance keeps your inspiration flowing and is an essential part of your life. The only problem is your tendency to worship your lover and keep them on a pedestal. Creativity is your strength so when your emotions overcome you, it's time to express yourself through your art.

TAROT CARD: The Hierophant
PLANETS: Sun and Venus
QUOTE: *'Music is what I must do, business is what I need to do and politics is what I have to do.'* Bob Geldof

STRENGTHS: Self-assured, with a sympathetic nature.
WEAKNESSES: Highly-strung, and at times, needy.

BORN ON THIS DAY:
Denis Diderot
(philosopher and encyclopaedist)
Sir Bob Geldof
(musician – Boomtown Rats and political activist)
Ray Kroc
(entrepreneur)
Joshua Logan
(film director and writer)
Louis Lumière
(film pioneer)
Kate Winslet
(actor)

MEDITATION:
Don't smother your loved one. No one can grow in the shade.

October 6

You are an articulate and peace-loving person with fine reasoning abilities. You have a love of justice and are concerned with what people think. A natural advocate and campaigner, you are charming and diplomatic in what you say, nevertheless you can put your point across powerfully. You enjoy opening people's minds to new concepts, are patient and thorough, so make an excellent teacher. With your quick mind and cleverness you can appear to some to be aloof and cool. In your personal relationships you are faithful, devoted and enjoy the daily routines of family life. A problem of yours is that you can't bear mess, so can be obsessed with tidiness and cleanliness. You enjoy taking care of others and also need to be pampered. A day at a spa or on the golf course with a close friend would restore your equilibrium.

BORN ON THIS DAY:
Gerry Adams
(Irish Republican politician)
Le Corbusier
(architect)
Britt Ekland
(actor)
Reginald Aubrey Fessenden
(inventor and radio pioneer)
Fannie Lou Hamer
(civil rights activist)
George Westinghouse Jr
(entrepreneur and engineer)

MEDITATION:
Make sure your house is a home.

TAROT CARD: The Lovers
PLANETS: Mercury and Venus
QUOTE: *'The home should be the treasure chest of living.'* Le Corbusier

STRENGTHS: Forbearing, prudent.
WEAKNESSES: Neurotic and unapproachable to some.

October 7

You are an idealistic and refined person with a courteous and graceful manner. A born diplomat, your ability to put people at ease works well for you whatever career you follow. You are concerned with fairness and justice for all and are impartial and rational; so careers as a judge, lawyer or negotiator are all suitable. A lover of peace, you are also more than happy to fight for what you believe in and can be disarmingly outspoken. However, you express yourself with such impish charm that most people warm to you. Narcissism can be a problem as you are overly concerned with your appearance and are always stylish. Relationships are vital as you feel incomplete without a partner. You adore romance and a sport which is glamorous that involves your partner – such as skiing – is ideal for you.

BORN ON THIS DAY:
Niels Bohr
(physicist)
Tony Braxton
(singer)
Simon Cowell
(recording executive and entrepreneur)
Vladimir Putin
(Russian prime minister)
Desmond Tutu
(activist and SA archbishop)
Thom Yorke
(singer/songwriter musician –
Radiohead)

MEDITATION:
Preconceived notions are the locks on the door to wisdom.

TAROT CARD: The Chariot
PLANETS: Venus and Venus
QUOTE: *'If you are neutral in situations of injustice, you have chosen the side of the oppressor.'* Desmond Tutu

STRENGTHS: Alluring, a peacemaker.
WEAKNESSES: Vain, dependent in love.

October 8

You are an astute and self-possessed person with good instincts. You can weigh people up and are an excellent judge of character and situations. Although you promote peace and harmony you are not afraid of conflict and can provoke a fight as you enjoy the intense emotions involved. Debating is one of your skills and you will gladly support the underdog. Politics is a natural arena for your talents, as is the law – you are incredibly effective as your enthusiasm and positive approach disarms any opposition. In your personal relationships you need depth – a light-hearted affair will bore you. Once committed, you can develop into a faithful and passionate lover, as long as your partner retains an air of mystery. Your weakness is that you can be insecure and suspicious. You need to express your raw emotions so martial arts appeal.

TAROT CARD: Strength
PLANETS: Pluto and Venus
QUOTE: *'If you come back from the dead, you don't have the same value system, I think.'* Sigourney Weaver

STRENGTHS: Wholehearted, fervent.
WEAKNESSES: Self-conscious, untrusting.

BORN ON THIS DAY:
Matt Damon
(actor)
Jesse Jackson Sr
(civil rights activist)
Juan Perón
(Argentinian president)
Fred Stolle
(champion tennis player)
Sigourney Weaver
(actor)
Edward Zwick
(film director and producer)

MEDITATION:
The only way to make someone trustworthy is to trust them.

October 9

You are a witty, humourous person, with a lively, original mind. You are diplomatic and unafraid of expressing the truth with compelling charm. You have strong convictions and are incredibly enthusiastic and vocal about your beliefs. People listen and take note as you speak from your heart. You would make an inspiring teacher, lecturer or educationalist as you truly desire to help and motivate others. A weakness is that you can appear proud and aloof and turn to work to hide from your personal problems. An intimate relationship supports your emotional growth if you can commit yourself and not get side-tracked by work and your many projects. Being spontaneous with your lover and suggesting a romantic weekend away somewhere warm and exotic can reignite your passion and give you the adventure you adore.

TAROT CARD: The Hermit
PLANETS: Jupiter and Venus
QUOTE: *'Avant-garde is French for bullshit'* John Lennon

STRENGTHS: Adventure-seeker, waggish.
WEAKNESSES: Unable to relax, and at times, unforthcoming.

BORN ON THIS DAY:
Brian Blessed
(actor)
John Entwistle
(singer/songwriter and bassist – The Who)
Joseph Friedman
(inventor)
John Lennon
(singer/songwriter – member of the Beatles, artist and activist)
Sharon Osbourne
(music manager – wife of Ozzy)
Sayyid Qutb
(philosopher and writer)

MEDITATION:
One should count each day a separate life.

October 10

BORN ON THIS DAY:
Anne Mather
(writer)
Anita Mui
(singer)
Harold Pinter
(playwright)
Rumiko Takahashi
(comic book artist)
Midge Ure
(singer/songwriter and musician –
Ultravox)
Ed Wood
(filmmaker)

MEDITATION:
*He that will not reflect
is a ruined man.*

You are sophisticated, sociable and skilled in many areas. You have the confidence of an older person even when young and people choose you as their protector and leader. You are sensitive to others and make friends for life. Totally responsible and with a reverence for hierarchy, you are well suited to a traditional career in a large corporation, easily working your way up to management level. You love justice and could train for the Bar as you have the discipline for lengthy study. Some people can feel you are too controlling and writeritarian, but those who know you find you a sympathetic and witty companion. In your love life you are a devoted partner once you feel you have met your intellectual equal. To relax you need fun and something that loosens you up – dancing is excellent for you.

TAROT CARD: The Wheel of Fortune
PLANETS: Saturn and Venus
QUOTE: *'We are going to finish this picture just the way I want it... because you cannot compromise an artist's vision.'* Ed Wood

STRENGTHS: Wise, looked up to.
WEAKNESSES: Dominant and over-bearing.

October 11

BORN ON THIS DAY:
Sir Bobby Charlton
(soccer player)
Dawn French
(comedian)
Henry Heinz
(businessman)
King Richard III
(English monarch)
Eleanor Roosevelt
(US first lady)
Michelle Wie
(professional golfer)

MEDITATION:
*Friendship isn't a big
thing – it's a million
little things.*

You are a creative thinker with innovative ideas and a gift of clarity to disseminate them. Your diplomatic skills, combined with a social conscience and a desire to be truly helpful to your fellow man, would make you a gifted reformer or politician. Plus your persuasive logic and impartiality are assets for a brilliant negotiator. At times you can be impractical and live in your head, dreaming your life away. Your love life can be up and down as you yearn for the ideal relationship. You hold a vision of utopia and can feel extreme discomfort in dealing with deep emotions such as hate and jealousy. A good friendship can compensate for lack of intimacy and is a priority with your lover. You would come into your own at a debating society and a cocktail party gives you a buzz.

TAROT CARD: Justice
PLANETS: Uranus and Venus
QUOTE: *'I'm not really interested in sports psychology. It makes me feel like a crazy person.'* Michelle Wie

STRENGTHS: Expressive and tactful.
WEAKNESSES: An idealist, unrealistic.

October 12

You are a gentle and sensitive person who is a romantic dreamer. With your almost childlike innocence you can be endearingly sweet. You are very versatile and can easily adapt to situations. Artistic, musical and good with words, you inspire others with your vision of transcendent beauty. Your ability to understand and feel what others feel makes you a superb counsellor and group facilitator. A big weakness is in romance. You long for the ideal lover and have huge expectations which are impossible for a mere mortal to fulfil. Despite this, in your desire to keep a mate you have a tendency to become a doormat. Expressing your creativity is essential for you to feel valued. You enjoy relaxing with close friends and being by the sea touches your soul, so sailing can bring you deep contentment.

TAROT CARD: The Hanged Man
PLANETS: Neptune and Venus
QUOTE: *'I'm a big goofball, you know. Don't tell anyone that, but I'm a big goofball. In Australia we call it a dag.'* Hugh Jackman

STRENGTHS: Likeable, compassionate.
WEAKNESSES: Unrealistic, a walkover.

BORN ON THIS DAY:
Susan Anton
(singer and actor)
Joe Cronin
(baseball player)
Hugh Jackman
(actor)
Luciano Pavarotti
(opera singer)
Hiroyuki Sanada
(actor)
Elmer Ambrose Sperry
(inventor and entrepreneur)

MEDITATION:
The cure for anything is salt water – sweat, tears, or the sea.

October 13

You are an adaptable and ambitious person with a shrewd mind. You are both logical and sentimental, a fascinating and sometimes difficult combination. In your career you aim high and use your feminine intuition – whether male or female – with great aplomb. You have a natural empathy and people respond positively to you, as they feel that you understand them. Your family life is of equal importance and it is only when you create your own nest that you feel supported and secure. Managing people is a talent of yours and this can be used in business or politics. A weakness is your moodiness which leads you to withdraw and brood. An intimate relationship is essential and you tend to marry young. Cooking for a dinner party of close friends is your idea of a treat as you truly enjoy making people happy.

TAROT CARD: Death
PLANETS: Moon and Venus
QUOTE: *'It's a big error to think that because you like somebody's work, you're going to like him.'* Paul Simon

STRENGTHS: Determined and kind-hearted.
WEAKNESSES: Capricious, a sulker.

BORN ON THIS DAY:
Sacha Baron Cohen
(screenwriter and comic actor)
Bob Hunter
(co-founder of Greenpeace)
Lillie Langtry
(actor)
Paul Simon
(singer/songwriter and musician – Simon & Garfunkel)
Art Tatum
(jazz pianist)
Margaret Thatcher
(British prime minister)

MEDITATION:
The real leader has no need to lead – he is content to point the way.

October 14

BORN ON THIS DAY:
BORN ON THIS DAY:
Steve Coogan
(screenwriter and comic actor)
E. E. Cummings
(poet)
Dwight D. Eisenhower
(US president)
Lilian Gish
(actor and silent film star)
Ralph Lauren
(fashion designer)
Roger Moore
(actor)

MEDITATION:

*Dancing is a short-cut
to happiness.*

You are a flamboyant and romantic person with great style and finesse. A quick wit, great sense of humour and sophistication make you an accomplished socialite. You enjoy being in the centre of the action and give of your best in a leadership position. Fashion and the media are just two arenas for your talents, just as long as you are in the spotlight. Wounded pride is your weakness as you tend to wilt if people say anything that you perceive as criticism, however, you have resilience and bounce back quickly. In love you can idealize your partner and get very disappointed when you discover their flaws – remember that no one is perfect! You are romantic by nature so old-fashioned ballroom dancing where you can strut your stuff together with your loved one could be a great way to exercise.

TAROT CARD: Temperance
PLANETS: Sun and Venus
QUOTE: *'Ankles are nearly always neat and good-looking, but knees are nearly always not.'* Dwight D. Eisenhower

STRENGTHS: Fashionable and a great people person.
WEAKNESSES: Wishful-thinker, unable to take criticism.

October 15

BORN ON THIS DAY:
Chris de Burgh
(singer/songwriter)
Richard Carpenter
(musician – half of The Carpenters)
Michel Foucault
(philosopher)
Friedrich Nietzsche
(philosopher)
Marie Stopes
(scientist and reformer)
P.G. Wodehouse
(writer)

MEDITATION:

*We are all full of errors, let
us mutually pardon each
other our follies.*

You are a kind and caring person with a fine intellect. You are immensely practical and interested in people's health and welfare. Incredibly patient, with the ability to attend to every detail, you are able to work through the nitty-gritty of any project. The health and healing professions appeal to you, especially alternative medicine. Your strength is your clever mind, but your weakness is a tendency to be over-critical and controlling of others. Learning to overlook people's little or unimportant mistakes will increase your popularity. In love you relax and a committed relationship brings you the deep peace you yearn for. You need to be able to share your hobbies and artistic interests with your partner. Time spent detoxing and relaxing in a sauna or steam room together is wonderful for you both.

TAROT CARD: The Devil
PLANETS: Mercury and Venus
QUOTE: *'He was white and shaken, like a dry martini.'* P.G. Wodehouse

STRENGTHS: Solicitous, intelligent.
WEAKNESSES: Fault-finding, forceful.

October 16

You are an elegant and cultured person who is charm personified. You have a strong sense of chivalry and are incredibly romantic. People see you as their knight in shining armour – whatever your sex. You will wage war on what you view as injustices and yet you are a lover of peace. Artistically gifted, you are a musician, artist, writer or actor – or maybe all of these. You abhor crudeness and vulgarity and your surroundings are harmonious and tasteful. Your worst trait is your indecisiveness and tendency to change your stance which can be very frustrating for others. You discover yourself through your intimate relationships, so your choice of partner is crucial. Once committed you are a gem of a lover. A competitive sport which involves your lover such as mixed doubles would be a wonderful way to add spark to your love life!

TAROT CARD: The Tower
PLANETS: Venus and Venus
QUOTE: *'I have the simplest tastes. I am always satisfied with the best.'* Oscar Wilde

STRENGTHS: Ravishing and artistically gifted.
WEAKNESSES: Vague and indecisive.

BORN ON THIS DAY:
Flea
(bassist – Red Hot Chili Peppers)
Angela Lansbury
(actor)
Nico
(model, actor, singer /songwriter)
Tim Robbins
(actor, film director and writer)
Oscar Wilde
(playwright and writer)
David Zucker
(film director and actor)

MEDITATION:
Good decisions come from experience, and experience comes from bad decisions.

October 17

You are a hypnotic and sensual person with a powerful intellect. You love the good life and have an appetite for comfort and luxury. Your career has to challenge you and stimulate your strong intellect. Acting and the music business both fit this description. You are frank and honest in your dealings and can spot hypocrisy in people. You like to be in a position of power and cannot bear to take second place. You revel in deep emotions so need a relationship to fulfil your high standards and keep you intrigued. You can, however, be very moody and jealous, and need a lot of physical affection to feel loved. If your partner takes you for granted you are capable of having an affair just to get their attention. Deep tissue massage is excellent for soothing your body and easing your mind.

TAROT CARD: The Star
PLANETS: Pluto and Venus
QUOTE: *'I don't hate women – they just sometimes make me mad.'* Eminem

STRENGTHS: Outspoken and sultry.
WEAKNESSES: Impossible standards, distrustful in love.

BORN ON THIS DAY:
Montgomery Clift
(actor)
Eminem
(rapper and record producer)
Rita Hayworth
(actor)
Evel Knievel
(daredevil)
Arthur Miller
(playwright)
Michael McKean
(actor, comedian, composer and musician)

MEDITATION:
The only way to make someone trustworthy is to trust them.

October 18

You are an adventurous person with amazing energy and passion. You have strong convictions and high morals and will express your opinions on a wide variety of topics to anyone who'll listen. Your enthusiasm, combined with your attractive and congenial manner, means that people respond favourably to you. You can charm the birds off the trees if you set your mind to it. You are naturally generous and, at times, over-extravagant in your desire to help people. Your popularity brings you a great deal of good fortune and once you gain wealth you are a born philanthropist. In your intimate relationships you need a warm and tender partner who inspires you and can keep up with your fast pace of living. Active sports which stretch and energize your body such as karate or ashtanga yoga are ideal.

BORN ON THIS DAY:
Chuck Berry
(musician)
Jean-Claude Van Damme
(martial artist and actor)
Zac Efron
(actor)
Martina Navratilova
(champion tennis player)
Frieda Pinto
(actor and model)
Om Puri
(actor)

MEDITATION:
A man who has attained mastery of an art reveals it in his every action.

TAROT CARD: The Moon
PLANETS: Jupiter and Venus
QUOTE: *'It is easier to do a job right than to explain why you didn't.'*
Martina Navratilova

STRENGTHS: A born benefactor, ardent.
WEAKNESSES: Dogmatic, unable to relax.

October 19

You are a disciplined and self-assured person with a strong determination to succeed. A great planner, you make decisions based on rational logic. You have a love of beauty and a harmonious, well-designed environment is vital for your peace of mind. Recognition is important and you work hard to get the top job in business or the arts. Your material possessions represent your achievements and you will save up to buy the most expensive items. A loving relationship is the foundation of your life. However, you can be too controlling and rational when it comes to emotions and you need to accept that you cannot be in charge all the time. Although you adore being with your lover you need time alone, so an early morning walk when the world is still asleep is a great time for you to gather your thoughts for the day.

BORN ON THIS DAY:
Umberto Boccioni
(artist)
John le Carré
(writer)
Jon Favreau
(actor, writer and film director)
Fannie Hurst
(writer)
John Lithgow
(actor)
Trey Parker
(cartoonist – co-creator of *South Park*)

MEDITATION:
Loneliness can be conquered only by those who can bear solitude.

TAROT CARD: The Sun
PLANETS: Saturn and Venus
QUOTE: *'I never get tired of hearing compliments.'* John Lithgow

STRENGTHS: Confident and well-reasoned.
WEAKNESSES: Bourgeois, domineering.

October 20

You are a likeable, attractive person who is very charming and easy-going, however, you do have a gullible side. You are a connoisseur of food, music and art and a sought-after member of many a social circle. People adore being in your company and want to please you. You need to live in a harmonious and beautiful environment, so a career in interior design is very appealing. You are sensitive to what people want and can interpret their ideas with flair and style. In your intimate relationships you are a wonderfully attentive lover and once committed, you are faithful. You can be too passive and if pushed too far will become stubborn to show your displeasure. Being out and about in nature is deeply relaxing and a sport – like golf – with its great social life has immense appeal for you.

TAROT CARD: Judgement
PLANETS: Venus and Venus
QUOTE: *'I love huge movies. Not sure I am the guy to make them, but you can rely on me being there watching them.'* Danny Boyle

STRENGTHS: Captivating, beautiful.
WEAKNESSES: Overtrusting and headstrong.

BORN ON THIS DAY:
Danny Boyle
(film director)
William the Conqueror
(English monarch)
Snoop Dog
(rapper)
Bela Lugosi
(actor)
Viggo Mortensen
(actor, poet and artist)
Tom Petty
(singer/songwriter and musician)

MEDITATION:
Adopt the pace of nature: her secret is patience.

October 21

You are an articulate and chatty person who is genuinely interested in what people think and feel. A keen observer, you know how to connect with and advise others, so work in retail or PR is an excellent choice. You are constantly on the move and often on the phone. As an information junkie you love collecting details to pass on. Committing to one thing is extremely difficult for you and you can often break promises simply because you cannot say no to anyone. This carefree nature of yours is very appealing and attractive, however, in a long-term relationship your partner can find your excuses wear a bit thin. Learning about emotional intelligence will enable you to become happier. You benefit from an exercise such as t'ai chi or yoga which discipline and increase your mental focus.

TAROT CARD: The World
PLANETS: Mercury and Venus
QUOTE: *'People of humour are always in some degree people of genius.'* Samuel Taylor Coleridge

STRENGTHS: Expressive and understanding.
WEAKNESSES: Break promises, tendency to be unfaithful.

BORN ON THIS DAY:
Samuel Taylor Coleridge
(poet and philosopher)
Carrie Fisher
(actor)
Dizzy Gillespie
(trumpeter, singer, bandleader and composer)
Benjamin Netanyahu
(Israeli prime minister)
Alfred Nobel
(inventor and founder of Nobel Prize)
Nick Oliver
(bassist – Queens of the Stoneage)

MEDITATION:
Learn to say 'no' to the good so you can say 'yes' to the best.

October 22

MEDITATION:

Be positive – see the invisible and achieve the impossible.

You are an emotional and artistic person with a soft heart. The arts, history and culture all interest you and your career can follow many paths as long as you feel a strong connection with the group of people you work with. You are sensitive to the needs of others and care about the 'little things' that actually matter a great deal – you are the one who remembers birthdays and anniversaries. Your relationship is a priority in your life and you will settle down early. You adore domesticity and taking care of your family, but by being the nurturer you have a tendency to neglect your own needs. You are affected by negativity and can sense the mood of a room when you walk into it. Jacuzzis and steam baths are wonderful – as is swimming – for totally reenergizing you and lifting your mood.

TAROT CARD: The Emperor
PLANETS: Moon and Venus
QUOTE: *'You can always pick up your needle and move to another groove.'* Timothy Leary

STRENGTHS: Compassionate, emotionally aware.
weaknesses: Prone to self-neglect, feisty.

TYPICAL LIBRAN:
SIMON COWELL

'The object of this competition is not to be mean to the losers but to find a winner. The process makes you mean because you get frustrated.'

LIBRAN TRAITS:
Librans are genuinely kind, generous and caring. However, being the sign of the scale, there is always a flip side to their personality. Librans want nothing more that to find equlibrium, but instead usually spend ther lives verring from one extreme to the other.

October 23

You are a flamboyant and charismatic person with a huge appetite for life. In public you shine, you are a star and love to be in the limelight. However, in private you can be a recluse, preferring your own company or that of a few close and trusted friends. You constantly visualize yourself at the pinnacle of your career, as success is of utmost importance to you – you feel like an under-achiever until you're at the top of your profession. You can be ruthless in the pursuit of your goals and unaware of how you use others to get there. You have a strong sense of drama and are enamoured of the theatrical life. You need a relationship where you are adored, yet a partner who can gently remind you of the need to compromise. Organizing fund-raising events for a charity would be the ideal outlet for your passions.

TAROT CARD: The Hierophant
PLANETS: Pluto and Venus
QUOTE: *'I don't like shows, I don't like to put on a show, I just really want to work intimately with my actors.'* Sam Raimi

STRENGTHS: Captivating, a born celebrity.
WEAKNESSES: Hard-hearted, manipulative.

BORN ON THIS DAY:
Pelé
(soccer player)
Michael Crichton
(writer)
Diana Dors
(actor)
Martin Luther King III
(human rights advocate)
Ang Lee
(film director)
Sam Raimi
(film director)

MEDITATION:
Never look down on anybody unless you're helping them up.

TYPICAL LIBRAN:
SERENA WILLIAMS

'I've always been a beauty junkie. I've tried every product. I'm addicted to products. I can't go into the mall without buying everything. I said to my manager, 'I should get a beauty deal, I'm going to go broke buying all these products.'

LIBRAN TRAITS:
Librans love to be in the limelight and will always dress up for an occassion, no matter how small – they always want to look as glamorous as possible.

8

Scorpio

October 24 – November 22

DEATH.

TAROT CARD: Death

ELEMENT: Water

QUALITY: Fixed

NUMBER: 8

RULING PLANETS: Mars and Pluto

GEMSTONE: Coral bloodstone

COLOURS: Red and black

DAY OF THE WEEK: Tuesday

COMPATIBLE SIGNS:
Cancer, Pisces and Taurus

KEY WORDS: Secretive, mysterious, emotional and intense, powerful, strong, a loyal friend, inspires faith, unshockable, obsessive and vengeful, refusal to change

ANATOMY: Reproductive system, sexual organs, bowels, excretory system

HERBS, PLANTS AND TREES: Aloe, geranium, holly, honey-suckle and bushy trees

KEY PHRASE:
I desire

Scorpio is the healer of the zodiac and it has three symbols, the scorpion, the eagle and the phoenix. Most people have heard of the sting in the Scorpio's tail, but as well as this, the eagle gives vision and the phoenix the ability to die and rise again from the ashes. In this way Scorpios can regenerate and reinvent themselves. Scorpio is dark and mysterious and is associated with death and rebirth. It rules the sexual and excretory organs which explains the secrecy of Scorpio.

PLANETARY RULER AND QUALITIES

Scorpio is ruled by Mars and Pluto and it is a fixed water sign. It is like the deep water of an underground cavern. The reputation of being the sexiest sign comes from the association with Mars who was originally a God of fertility. But there is more depth to Scorpio, so Pluto, which is on the outer reaches of the solar system farthest from the Sun, is more suited as the ruler of this sign. In classical mythology Pluto is the god of the Underworld and the only god that had no statues built for him. He was faceless and unknown, much like the character of Darth Vader in *Star Wars*. The dwarf planet Pluto was discovered in 1930 and plutonium was named after it, so it relates to nuclear power. In this way it can be harnessed for good or evil. Pluto also governs volcanoes – a power that can destroy but can also produce rich, fertile soil.

RELATIONSHIPS

Scorpio is emotionally intense and has an attractive, magnetic quality. The male can hypnotize with his gaze and the woman is the archetype of the seductress. Scorpio has to be in control and you can be suspicious of others' motives. You fall deeply in love, but if hurt can nurse your wounds and withdraw into your private world. Fellow water signs Cancer and Pisces are your soul mates, but the strongest attraction is to your opposite sign – Taurus. Virgo is a wonderful friend for you as they are so helpful, Capricorns are well suited to you especially as business partners. There are power struggles galore with fiery Leo and Aries. Aquarians can offer plenty of surprises.

MYTH

In Greek mythology Scorpius is the scorpion who killed Orion. The two constellations are placed at the opposite sides of the sky to prevent conflict. Scorpio is one of the two zodiac signs that cross over the Milky Way, and was thought to be where souls departed after death. Scorpius holds the bright red Antares, one of the Royal stars of Persia, at its centre. The ancient Chinese referred to it as 'the Great Fire at the heart of the Dragon'.

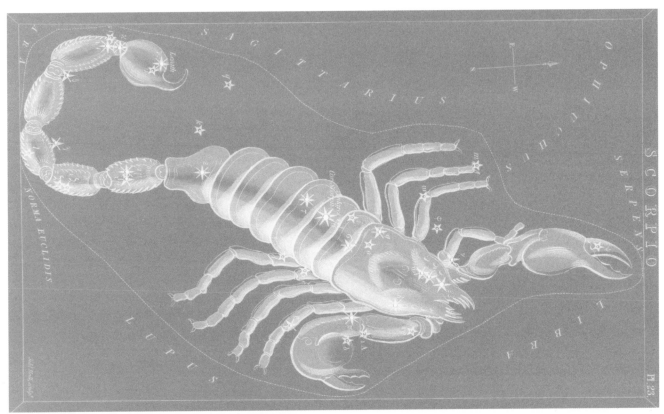

Another legend related to Scorpio is Hercules and the hydra. The hydra was an eight-headed monster who lived in a cave by a swamp. Hercules was charged to kill the beast as one of his twelve labours, but as he cut off one head many more grew. Finally he used a torch to cauterize the wound so the Hydra was killed. The moral is that Scorpio has the courage to face the monsters and taboos, and by exposing them to the light they lose their power.

STRENGTHS AND WEAKNESSES

Scorpios are imaginative, intensely emotional and loyal and devoted friends who offer strong support to others. You are there at the darkest times and nothing shocks you. You are a great listener, have the ability to empathize and offer profound wisdom, so you make an ideal therapist or priest. You are a brilliant researcher, as Scorpios love to investigate and find out how things work. Your secretive nature can make you suspicious, you are capable of plotting, scheming and manipulating and have the tendency to seek revenge if crossed.

Like the other fixed signs you find it hard to let go of grudges. You forgive but never forget. Your greatest weakness is inflexibility and your reluctance to change. Your greatest strength is that once committed you are in it for the long haul.

TYPICAL SCORPIO:

WILMA MANKILLER

'I don't think anybody anywhere can talk about the future of their people or of an organization without talking about education. Whoever controls the education of our children controls our future.'

LIBRAN POWERS: Ability to understand the feelings of others, resourceful and devoted.

LIBRAN NEGATIVES: Secretive and vengeful.

October 24

MEDITATION:

*It's okay to let yourself go,
as long as you can
get yourself back.*

You are a practical and passionate person with a strong sense of duty. You can cheerfully do the most routine and repetitive tasks – if you are in love with what you do, and if you feel it offers value to others. There is an aura of quiet dedication about you and you are more than happy to work alone. You are the archetypal planner; you love systems and calculate everything down to the last detail. This creates a lack of spontaneity and drives your impatient friends crazy! You can be stubborn and certainly won't be pushed around. The first impression you give potential lovers is of a self-controlled and modest person, but in private you are a very romantic and tactile lover. Fitness is a priority and running while listening to a self-improvement audio book combines your two loves.

TAROT CARD: The Lovers
PLANETS: Mercury and Pluto
QUOTE: *'I have very interesting hobbies like archeology and photography.'* Bill Wyman

STRENGTHS: Grounded, amorous.
WEAKNESSES: Obstinate and, at times, inhibited.

October 25

MEDITATION:

*Promise little and
do much.*

You are a charismatic showman, a person with immense panache and passion. You have a vivid imagination and an artistic fervour that you need to express through a creative medium. This could be through drama or another intense art form which becomes your career. People and relationships govern your entire life and you have a huge need to be liked. This can hinder you, since pleasing people is not possible all of the time. You sometimes say yes when you mean no, and then don't deliver on a promise, so you end up – inadvertently – upsetting people. Romance and love take priority, and you are happiest being with just one person. With your innate sense of style and grace, ballroom dancing with your partner is the ideal exercise and a great way to spend quality time with them.

TAROT CARD: The Chariot
PLANETS: Venus and Pluto
QUOTE: *'What a beautiful art, but what a wretched profession.'* George Bizet

STRENGTHS: Inventive, captivating.
WEAKNESSES: Sycophantic tendencies, unable to say no.

October 26

You are a dynamic and powerful person with strong convictions. You are self-possessed and confident, with a formidable determination to succeed. In your life you have been tested and can face situations that others shrink from. You will gladly fight on behalf of the underdog and make a resolute campaigner on social issues. You have entrenched opinions on most subjects and can be incredibly stubborn. Committed to your purpose from a young age, your focus is on analysing and investigating any subject in depth. Superficiality annoys you immensely and you cannot tolerate fools. Your relationships are intense and you are fiercely loyal. Once committed, you are unshakeable and rarely give up on your partner. Shiatsu, deep tissue massage or acupressure would be highly beneficial as you hold a lot of tension in your body.

TAROT CARD: Strength
PLANETS: Pluto and Pluto
QUOTE: 'You gotta keep the funny intact.'
Seth MacFarlane

STRENGTHS: Supportive, devoted.
WEAKNESSES: Obstinate, impatient.

BORN ON THIS DAY:
Hillary Clinton
(politician)
Seth MacFarlane
(animator, writer, producer
and creator of Family Guy)
Bob Hoskins
(actor)
Francois Mitterand
(French president)
Karl Leonhard Reinhold
(philosopher)
Rita Wilson
(actor)

MEDITATION:
A little learning is a dangerous thing, but a lot of ignorance is just as bad.

October 27

You are a passionate and outspoken person who needs a mission in life. Once found, your vision propels you forward and your commitment is strong. You are a philosopher, someone who adores discussing the meaning of life. Nothing shocks you and your natural optimism and good humour buoys others up in the face of trouble. You are a born psychologist and can develop into being an excellent teacher of your peers. You love travel and absorbing different cultures and could easily live abroad. You can be fanatical about your beliefs and tend to get on your soap box and alienate others – even without meaning to. That said, you are also very persuasive! Emotionally intense, your relationship is your bedrock, but you also need a lot of freedom. A night out at the theatre transports you into the fantasy world you yearn for.

TAROT CARD: The Hermit
PLANETS: Jupiter and Pluto
QUOTE: 'Comedy always works best when it is mean-spirited.' John Cleese

STRENGTHS: Insightful, positive.
WEAKNESSES: Dogmatic, forthright.

BORN ON THIS DAY:
John Cleese
(actor and writer)
Captain James Cook
(British admiral)
Erasmus
(humanist and theologian)
John Gotti
(American gangster)
Theodore Roosevelt
(US president)
Dylan Thomas
(poet)

MEDITATION:
Instinct is untaught ability.

October 28

You are a focussed and determined person who believes work is of utmost importance. You know about the importance of goals and are willing to undergo lengthy training to improve your skills. You are tough and have true grit – nothing fazes you. You have extraordinary self-discipline and understand and obey the rules of society. You can expect too much from others and judge them if they don't come up to your high standards. With your strong convictions, the realm of politics is well suited to you, as is the law. You have an earnest and sombre outlook yet have a gift for satire and a dry wit. In love you tend to play hard-to-get, which is very alluring to the opposite sex. You tend to overwork so being frivolous, singing and playing music brings the balance your require for contentment.

BORN ON THIS DAY:
Mahmoud Ahmadinejad
(Iranian president)
Bill Gates
(chairman of Microsoft)
Cleo Laine
(singer)
Joaquin Phoenix
(actor and musician)
Julia Roberts
(actor)
Evelyn Waugh
(writer)

MEDITATION:
If music be the food of love, play on.

TAROT CARD: The Wheel of Fortune
PLANETS: Saturn and Pluto
QUOTE: *'As we look ahead into the next century, leaders will be those who empower others.'* Bill Gates

STRENGTHS: Attentive, enticing.
WEAKNESSES: Critical, tough.

October 29

You are an innovator, a distinctive person with unusual tastes and a strong desire for experimentation. In your life you are always pushing boundaries and are attracted to explore metaphysics and occult sciences. You love to analyse and dissect information and are able to grasp deep abstract concepts. Your ability to observe from a detached viewpoint makes you an excellent trouble shooter or arbitrator. In your personal life you value truth and honesty in all your relationships. With your lover you demand a lot of personal space yet also desire passion and closeness. You tend to withdraw and remove yourself emotionally when things get too intense, and yet still want to remain friends. Exploring your deeper emotions with a therapist would be beneficial. Shiatsu is a good treatment to help shift your energy.

BORN ON THIS DAY:
Fanny Brice
(comedian and mimic)
Dan Castellaneta
(voice actor – voice of Homer Simpson)
Richard Dreyfuss
(actor)
Peter Green
(singer/songwriter, guitarist –
Fleetwood Mac)
Winona Ryder
(actor)
Rufus Sewell
(actor)

MEDITATION:
Remember that passion is universal humanity.

TAROT CARD: Justice
PLANETS: Uranus and Pluto
QUOTE: *'You go through spells where you feel that maybe you're too sensitive for this world.'* Winona Ryder

STRENGTHS: Inventive, a great problem solver.
WEAKNESSES: Emotionally guarded, slightly detached from reality.

October 30

You are a playful and yet serious person who is bright and good humoured one minute, then can be grave and sombre the next. Eternally youthful, you tend to look younger than you actually are. Your mind is intensely curious and you can dart from one topic to anther. You are a gifted writer as you can articulate the deep emotions people feel, and you have the added ability to laugh at the darker side of life. In relationships you love variety, but this leads you to flit from one person to another. It takes a long time for you to settle down and yet you yearn for emotional security. As you mature you appreciate that having lots of friends with varied interests will keep you stimulated and entertain you. In this way you can synthesize these two aspects of your personality.

TAROT CARD: The Empress
PLANETS: Mercury and Pluto
QUOTE: *'Assumptions are the termites of relationships.'* Henry Winkler

STRENGTHS: Fresh-faced and inquisitive.
WEAKNESSES: Solemn, short attention span.

BORN ON THIS DAY:
Charles Atlas
(bodybuilder)
Ezra Pound
(writer)
George Gilles de la Tourette
(neurologist)
Mario Testino
(photographer)
Henry Winkler
(actor)
Christopher Wren
(architect)

MEDITATION:
Laughter is a tranquillizer with no side effects.

October 31

You are a sensitive and impressionable person with a deep nostalgia for the past. Home and family are a central part of your life and you tend to be patriotic regarding your chosen country of residence. You seek success in life – you need to have a purpose and your choice of career is vitally important. Your concern for others propels you to help create change in people's lives, often through politics or working for a charity. In your personal life, once committed you give yourself totally. You are sensual and affectionate so your relationship needs to be deeply fulfilling. Your greatest desire is to be with someone who offers you the emotional security you crave and understands the depth of your feelings. You are an introspective person and can easily sink into a dark mood, but watching a romantic comedy will lighten you up.

TAROT CARD: The Emperor
PLANETS: Moon and Pluto
QUOTE: *'Scenery is fine – but human nature is finer.'* John Keats

STRENGTHS: Thoughtful and a born protector.
WEAKNESSES: Prone to pessimism, too self-analysing.

BORN ON THIS DAY:
John Candy
(comedian and actor)
John Evelyn
(diarist)
Peter Jackson
(filmmaker)
John Keats
(poet)
Juliette Low
(founder of the American Girl Scouts)
Jan Vermeer
(artist)

MEDITATION:
It doesn't hurt to be optimistic. You can always cry later.

141

November 1

BORN ON THIS DAY:

BORN ON THIS DAY:
Rick Allen
(drummer – Def Leppard)
Toni Collette
(actor)
Stephen T Crane
(writer)
Larry Flynt
(publisher)
Anthony Kiedis
(singer/songwriter –
Red Hot Chili Peppers)
Dizzee Rascal
(rapper and record producer)

MEDITATION:

If you surrender to the wind, you can ride it.

You are a champion and a passionate crusader with a strong will to succeed in life. You are a fighter and have enormous amounts of courage and emotional strength. You work with determination but can overdo it and exhaust yourself. You need a mission, a worthy cause to which you can dedicate yourself, heart and soul. You would do well in science or medicine as well as commerce, but whatever your work, you need to be constantly challenged and physically moving as you are impatient and restless if deskbound. In relationships you love the thrill of the chase, whatever your gender, and once you commit you are a fiercely loyal partner. You need to release your pent-up emotions and a combative game such as ice hockey or squash is well suited to your temperament.

TAROT CARD: The Magician
PLANETS: Mars and Pluto
QUOTE: *'Politics is my hobby. Smut is my vocation.'* Larry Flynt

STRENGTHS: Resolute, a campaigner.
WEAKNESSES: Prone to anxiety, emotionally withdrawn.

November 2

BORN ON THIS DAY:
Marie Antoinette
(French monarch)
Bunny Berigan
(musician and band leader)
Pat Buchanan
(US politician, writer and broadcaster)
K.D. Lang
(singer/songwriter)
Nelly
(rapper and entrepreneur)
James Knox Polk
(US president)

MEDITATION:

Self-confidence is the result of a successfully survived risk.

You are a sensual but self-controlled person with shrewd business acumen and the ability to handle large amounts of money. You are essentially quiet and gentle and prefer to live in the countryside and commune with nature. There is also another side to you which thrives in the powerful world of politics or exploring the mysteries of archaeology. You work hard and play hard and love good food and wine. When stressed you can easily over-indulge, then put yourself on a strict regime of self-denial. In relationships you are strongly emotional or else so self-contained that your partner spends a lot of time trying to fathom what you are feeling. This tendency to withdraw is an old pattern, and it is a good idea to make an effort and communicate your inner world with your beloved.

TAROT CARD: The High Priestess
PLANETS: Venus and Pluto
QUOTE: *'Let them eat cake.'* Marie Antoinette

STRENGTHS: Astute in business, good-natured.
WEAKNESSES: Prone to excess, at times emotionally inhibited.

November 3

You are a quick-witted and cheerful person who is a social butterfly. You can be devastatingly witty and your humour verges on the absurd. This ability is brilliant for a career as a stand-up comic or a comedy scriptwriter. You are always ready with a joke, but this can be your way of avoiding deeper emotions, batting questions away with a witty response rather than letting people see your weaknesses. At times you are overly flippant and the odd comment can catch people off guard. You are passionate with an urge to explore the secrets of how the universe works, and studying astronomy and astrology would fulfil you. In love you can blow hot or cold and you like to keep your options open. Fancy dress is a wonderful way for you to unwind and to explore your own varied personality.

TAROT CARD: The Empress
PLANETS: Mercury and Pluto
QUOTE: *'I think of [special effects] as magic tricks, as illusion.'* Tom Savini

STRENGTHS: Outgoing, a natural comedian.
WEAKNESSES: Facetious, non-committal.

BORN ON THIS DAY:
Adam Ant
(singer and guitarist)
Roseanne Barr
(actor and comedian)
Charles Bronson
(actor)
Leopold III
(Belgian royal)
Mutsuhito
(Japanese emperor)
Tom Savini
(film director)

MEDITATION:
Every survival kit should include a sense of humour.

November 4

You are a power-house of emotion, a person driven to explore the depths of the human condition and experience. You can swing from highs to extreme lows and sulk for weeks. You have an instinct for survival and can endure great emotional and physical pain. Your deep perceptiveness concerning other people, allied with your great intellect, would make you a superb psychologist or doctor. However if stressed your strong feelings can take over and compel you to make irrational and overly subjective decisions. Early in life you learn to be self-sufficient and keep many emotions hidden from public view. If extremely provoked, you can explode into volcanic rage. Passion is your middle name so a relationship is essential. Choose wisely, as they need to receive, and give you, strong emotional support.

TAROT CARD: The Emperor
PLANETS: Moon and Pluto
QUOTE: *'I think that's good that I have to watch how I act and what I say. I think that's a part of growing up.'* Sean Combs

STRENGTHS: Intuitive, determined.
WEAKNESSES: Unreasonable, short-tempered.

BORN ON THIS DAY:
Ariel Chiappone
(artist)
Sean 'Diddy' Combs
(rapper, record producer and fashion designer)
Don Eddy
(artist)
Robert Mapplethorpe
(photographer)
Matthew McConaughey
(actor)
Matthew Rhys
(actor)

MEDITATION:
People who fly into a rage always make a bad landing.

143

November 5

MEDITATION:
The desire for fame tempts even noble minds.

You are an outrageous person with an enormous amount of magnetism. You succeed where others may fail as you have a determination that never gives up. Your need is for recognition, to be someone, and you will do anything to achieve that. However, once you are well known you can complain about the lack of privacy. You can end up wearing dark glasses in the depths of winter in order to hide and your car could end up having tinted windows! You are a superb business person who is attracted to working in the glamorous world of the media. A born romantic you are an ardent lover and need a secure relationship to express your deepest emotions. As long as you are in charge all is well. You love to dress up for an occasion so a going to the theatre or opera – especially if you sit in a box – is perfect.

TAROT CARD: The Hierophant
PLANETS: Sun and Pluto
QUOTE: *'I'm not young. What's wrong with that?'* Vivien Leigh

STRENGTHS: Loving, purposeful.
WEAKNESSES: Obsessed with fame, domineering.

November 6

MEDITATION:
The truth told with bad intent beats all the lies you can invent.

You are a conscientious and passionate person with a real need to be of service to others. Truly sympathetic to the human condition, you are naturally drawn to the healing professions. You have clear insight and a gift for analysing people and situations. Highly critical, at times your scathing honesty is just too much for others to handle, but as you age, you learn to soften your approach. You have a tendency to support the underdog and a charitable nature. Health and your diet are of constant concern and you often experiment with the latest health-food trends. You are a very physical person so your partner needs to give you lots of affection and hugs for you to feel loved. Walking in nature restores your inner balance as your mental processes can get overactive.

TAROT CARD: The Lovers
PLANETS: Mercury and Pluto
QUOTE: *'We all know what happens to first ladies who shoot their mouths off.'* Maria Shriver

STRENGTHS: Benevolent, fervent.
WEAKNESSES: Unsparing, fault-finding.

November 7

You are an idealist, a graceful and intelligent person with both eloquence and charm. Well suited to the world of commerce, you have excellent negotiation skills and love creating peace and harmony. With an innate sense of fair play, injustice stirs you up to protest. You can be tough, and people can underestimate just how forceful you can be. You would do well in politics and management. If you feel insecure, you can be manipulative to get your own way. You need a close relationship to feel fulfilled and you are a passionate and romantic partner. You talk for hours on end with your beloved. However, if you compromise too much, you will end up fighting. Practising some form of martial arts or taking up fencing will benefit you immensely in releasing the aggression that you keep hidden.

TAROT CARD: The Chariot
PLANETS: Venus and Pluto
QUOTE: *'Be less curious about people and more curious about ideas.'* Marie Curie

STRENGTHS: Fluid, fair-minded.
WEAKNESSES: Domineering, at times scheming.

MEDITATION:
The softest things in the world overcome the hardest things in the world.

November 8

You are a quiet rebel, a person with strong desires and hidden depths. People find you mysterious and fascinating but they can feel that they never really know you completely. The mask you wear comes as a result of needing protection as you are very sensitive. You have a phenomenal memory and nothing is ever forgotten. This can be a real bonus if you are a writer, but it also means that you find it hard to let go of bad memories and heal old wounds. You can also be very controlling which makes for difficult business partnerships. In personal relationships you are devoted and steadfast, and expect your partner to be the same. Singing your heart out in private, or if your voice is good, at a karaoke night, is a wonderful way to release your pent-up energy.

TAROT CARD: Strength
PLANETS: Pluto and Pluto
QUOTE: *'No man knows till he has suffered from the night how sweet and dear to his heart and eye the morning can be.'* Bram Stoker

STRENGTHS: Non-conformist, philosophical.
WEAKNESSES: Dominant, emotionally delicate.

MEDITATION:
A bird doesn't sing because it has an answer, it sings because it has a song.

145

November 9

MEDITATION:

Quit whilst you are ahead.

You are a self-dramatizing and forceful person with a lot to say – there is never a dull moment when you're around. You take risks, love to gamble for high stakes and have a lust for extreme adventure. You have wide-ranging interests and cannot bear to be pinned down by one thing or one person. Your life is lived on a broad canvas that inspires less confident people. Your problem is when you adopt a 'holier-than-thou' attitude which comes from your fervent belief to improve yourself and others. You are loyal and generous to those you love and your word is your bond. In love you need someone who is willing to explore life with you, and is content to let you go off on your own travels. Gliding is a perfect sport for you, as you love flying and seeing the big picture.

TAROT CARD: The Hermit
PLANETS: Jupiter and Pluto
QUOTE: *'Never argue; repeat your assertion.'*
Robert Dale Owen

STRENGTHS: Dynamic, a thrill-seeker.
WEAKNESSES: Self-righteous, easily bored.

November 10

MEDITATION:

A small mind is obstinate. A great mind can lead and be led.

You are a purposeful and ambitious person. From early on in life you know what you want to achieve and set your sights high. You have the ability to tackle difficult issues, and with your strong moral and physical courage, you usually succeed. If, however, you fail and get overlooked on your way to the top, your frustration can create health issues. You are adept at regeneration and can transform raw materials into 'gold', whether it's a building, a company, or yourself. You are a pragmatic person but will not compromise your principles. This can lead to others seeing you as being inflexible. Relationships are serious for you, and you marry for love and financial security. Relaxation is vital for your emotional well-being. Your lack of flexibility would be remedied by a freestyle jazz dance form.

TAROT CARD: The Wheel of Fortune
PLANETS: Saturn and Pluto
QUOTE: *'Sticking to your values, listening to your instincts, making your own choices is so important.'* Brittany Murphy

STRENGTHS: Aspiring and resolute.
WEAKNESSES: Obstinate, materialistic.

November 11

You are an eccentric and unconventional person who needs a great deal of personal freedom. You love to shock people with your controversial views on life and have a way of delivering your ideas with power and passion. You can be deeply interested in the environment and will campaign on issues such as global warming. You love innovation and will be the first to buy a hybrid car or install solar panels in your roof. You are not traditional, and your life has to contain an edgy drama of danger and constant change. You are not naturally monogamous and when young you can embrace the idea of 'free love', however, you end up discovering just how jealous you can be! As you get older this becomes more an idea than a reality as you learn to appreciate intellectual companionship.

TAROT CARD: Justice
PLANETS: Uranus and Pluto
QUOTE: *'I'm not the kind of person who tries to be cool or trendy, I'm definitely an individual.'* Leonardo DiCaprio

STRENGTHS: An environmentalist, unorthodox.
WEAKNESSES: Distrustful of partners, devil's advocate in order to shock.

BORN ON THIS DAY:
Leonardo DiCaprio
(actor and film producer)
Fyodor Dostoevsky
(writer)
Demi Moore
(actor)
George Patton
(American WWII General)
Kurt Vonnegut
(writer)
Jonathan Winters
(comedian)

MEDITATION:
Don't blow it – good planets are hard to find.

November 12

You are a person who is in touch with the deepest dreams of the collective. You can create a vision that has power and a mesmerizing intensity that has qualities of a fairy tale or myth. This you do by your art, or your life itself, you are truly memorable and never forgotten. You are sensitive and deeply emotional, and at times can get overwhelmed by a huge sense of sadness at the suffering you see in the world. You can be quite inconsolable and are prone to addictions, until you learn to channel these feelings into your creativity. Your relationships are the stuff of great dramas, with intense highs and lows. You need a partner who is willing to stand by you and share the emotions with you. You adore the movies and a good old-fashioned romantic epic such as *Gone with the Wind* is food for your soul.

TAROT CARD: The Empress
PLANETS: Neptune and Pluto
QUOTE: *'The '60s was one of the first times the power of music was used by a generation to bind them together.'* Neil Young

STRENGTHS: Irrepressible, insightful.
WEAKNESSES: Highly sensitive, dependent.

BORN ON THIS DAY:
Roland Barthes
(writer)
Errol Brown
(singer – Hot Chocolate)
Booker T. Jones
(sinher/songwriter and musician)
Grace Kelly
(actor)
Auguste Rodin
(artist)
Neil Young
(musician, singer/songwriter and film director)

MEDITATION:
In the middle of difficulty lies opportunity.

147

November 13

MEDITATION:

Make others feel good about themselves in order to feel good about yourself.

You are a charismatic and intense person with deep emotions. Due to your sensitive and perceptive nature, you have the ability to tap into the mood of the people and deliver what they want. This can be through your creative gifts as a writer, actor or healer. You are very ambitious and want to make your mark on the world – from a very young age. You have a shrewd and canny mind and do well in business, especially in the stock market, as you have finely honed intuition. Relationships can be an emotional roller coaster, so you need a grounded partner who isn't easily put off by your volatile moods. However, negative emotions can take over and you can sink into the depths of self-pity. Homeopathy would be worth exploring as a way of healing and restoring emotional balance.

TAROT CARD: The Emperor
PLANETS: Moon and Pluto
QUOTE: *'Keep your fears to yourself, but share your courage with others.'*
Robert Louis Stevenson

STRENGTHS: Intuitive, determined.
WEAKNESSES: Overwhelmed by negativity and at times self-absorbed.

November 14

MEDITATION:

Snobbery's side-effect is ignorance – everyone has something to teach you.

You are a golden person with innate glamour and bewitching charm. You also have a penchant for investigating the darker aspects of life. With a strong appetite for sex, money and power you find it difficult to compromise. When pushed you stand up for what you believe in, even if it is the unpopular choice. This propels you towards centre stage, a place of leadership where you belong, and yet there is reluctance, as you fear being so exposed. You are incredibly hard-working and give yourself whole heartedly to any project you believe in. You can be a snob and intolerant of those who disagree with your deeply-held principles. Your partner needs to look good by your side, yet not to steal the spotlight from you. Ease off work and leave time for play and having fun.

TAROT CARD: The Hierophant
PLANETS: Sun and Pluto
QUOTE: *'Do you seriously expect me to be the first Prince of Wales in history not to have a mistress?'* Charles, Prince of Wales

STRENGTHS: A campaigner, enchanting.
WEAKNESSES: Haughty, and slightly superficial.

November 15

You are an intelligent person with a sharp mind and quick wit. You are a superb organizer and planner with a clear methodical approach. You can be ruthless, which is great when clearing out clutter as you have an ability to discard what is no longer useful. However, because you can get caught in every detail, you are apt to see, and point out the faults of others. You have good technical skills and tremendous physical stamina so sport is a likely profession. You can win against all odds as you have great determination. In relationships you need passion and also security – not easy to find in one person. Plus you can over organize and control your partner which is not conducive to happiness. Perfecting your body gives you huge satisfaction so weight training or yoga has immense appeal.

TAROT CARD: The Devil
PLANETS: Mercury and Pluto
QUOTE: *'I had a dream and it was fulfilled by meeting with Benny, Bjorn and Agnetha.'* Anni-Frid Lyngstad

STRENGTHS: Bright and efficient.
WEAKNESSES: Controlling and a fault-finder.

BORN ON THIS DAY:
Gesualdo Bufalino
(writer)
Petula Clark
(singer)
Gerhart Hauptmann
(dramatist)
Georgia O'Keefe
(artist)
Anni-Frid Lyngstad
(one quarter of Abba)
Randy Savage
(wrestler)

MEDITATION:
Nobody who ever gave his best regretted it.

November 16

You are a charming and delightful person with a quiet ambition and ideals to make the world a better place. You have impeccable good manners and always say the right thing, complimenting and appreciating people. With expensive taste you buy the best and can easily overspend as you cannot bear to have anything ugly around you. However, you are not weak, there is a core of steel within you and you can apply pressure when needed. Your work takes second place to your personal life and you tend to view marriage as an alliance. You are sensitive and intuitively know what your partner is feeling and what they need. You can be possessive and tend to get jealous if your partner doesn't pay enough attention to you. Restore the romance with a candlelit dinner.

TAROT CARD: The Chariot
PLANETS: Venus and Pluto
QUOTE: *'You're not going to do good work if you're not choosing something because it inspires you.'* Maggie Gyllenhaal

STRENGTHS: Caring, with genteel manners.
WEAKNESSES: Superficial, a spendthrift.

BORN ON THIS DAY:
Henri Bosco
(writer)
Salvatore Giuliano
(Italian bandit chief)
Maggie Gyllenhaal
(actor)
Diana Krall
(singer/songwriter and pianist)
Martha Plimpton
(actor)
Tiberius
(Roman emperor)

MEDITATION:
To do more for the world than the world does for you – that is success.

November 17

You are an enigma, someone that only a few really know, but all respect. You can be very secretive and suspicious. However, you are to be saluted as you have endured many struggles in your life and come through shining. Your heart is strong and you have developed enormous faith and optimism. Exploring the dark side of life fascinates you, and you revel in horror or occult stories. You have a keen intelligence and make astute judgments on situations and people. Nothing gets past your eagle eyes. Medical research, detective work and forensics all suit you. Emotionally you have strong desires and need for intimacy, so thrive in a committed relationship. Your partner needs to be someone you respect and your true equal. You need an active game such as squash where you let your emotions out.

BORN ON THIS DAY:
Nicolas Appert
(inventor)
Jeff Buckley
(singer/songwriter and guitarist)
Peter Cook
(comedian)
Rock Hudson
(actor)
Martin Scorsese
(filmmaker, actor and film historian)
Danny DeVito
(actor, film director and producer)

MEDITATION:
Like the moon – we all need a dark side.

TAROT CARD: The Star
PLANETS: Pluto and Pluto
QUOTE: *'There's no such thing as simple. Simple is hard.'* Martin Scorsese

STRENGTHS: Loyal and highly regarded.
WEAKNESSES: Reticent, distrustful.

November 18

You are a crusader, a person with an investigative mind. You are a fervent supporter of any cause you believe in. You can be restless in your search for the ultimate truth. You study many subjects – astronomy, psychology, philosophy and theology but until you find a spiritual path you can feel unfulfilled. You tend to rush forward without proper planning and can get careless and metaphorically tread on peoples toes. You adore sports that challenge and stretch you physically and emotionally. You have a passion for the theatre and make a great impresario or backer for a musical. Your lover is also your companion with your partner following your lead. Later in your life romance matters less to you than a spiritual connection. Opera helps you transcend daily life and is the ideal way for you to elevate any bad mood.

BORN ON THIS DAY:
Margaret Atwood
(writer)
Wolfgang Joop
(fashion designer)
Wilma Mankiller
(First female chief of Cherokee Nation)
Alan Moore
(writer)
Alan Shephard
(astronaut)
Owen Wilson
(actor)

MEDITATION:
The privilege of a lifetime is being who you are.

TAROT CARD: The Moon
PLANETS: Jupiter and Pluto
QUOTE: *'A ratio of failures is built into the process of writing. The wastebasket has evolved for a reason.'* Margaret Atwood

STRENGTHS: Enthusiastic, instinctive.
WEAKNESSES: Restless, impulsive.

November 19

You are a tenacious and committed person. You have a dark brooding intensity which makes you stand out from the crowd. With your fine rational intellect and thoughtful attitude, you have been seen as an old soul since your youth. You are most happy when you are working hard and you constantly set yourself new challenges. You fit well into society's hierarchy and your aim is to win and get to the top. Your weakness is a tendency for cynicism and evaluating everything on the physical level. You treat your love life as a project and you take time before you give yourself wholeheartedly. You tend to worry and get weighed down with responsibilities. Humour is your biggest asset and this gives you a much needed release for your energy. Playing practical jokes on your unsuspecting friends brings childlike joy.

TAROT CARD: The Sun
PLANETS: Saturn and Pluto
QUOTE: *'Forgiveness is a virtue of the brave.'* Indira Gandhi

STRENGTHS: Determined, industrious.
WEAKNESSES: Disillusioned and fretful.

BORN ON THIS DAY:
Jodie Foster
(actor)
Indira Gandhi
(Indian prime minister)
Larry King
(talkshow host)
Calvin Klein
(fashion designer)
Ferdinand Lesseps
(developer of the Suez Canal)
Meg Ryan
(actor)

MEDITATION:
Worry never fixes anything.

November 20

You are a person with a quiet strength, determination and a deep concern for others. You have an overwhelming desire to live a useful life and to be of practical service to the world. You have a great deal of common sense and are totally dependable; a true friend that others rely upon. You are sensitive to people's emotional problems and are drawn to the caring and healing professions. You are also fascinated by renovation and are quite prepared to roll up your sleeves and get involved with a rebuilding project. Your relationships are either all or nothing and you can spend a long time alone until you meet the right person, however, you can be very possessive and controlling which drives people away. Gardening is very nurturing for you and gets you in touch with the cycles of life.

TAROT CARD: Judgement
PLANETS: Venus and Pluto
QUOTE: *'I was the seventh of nine children. When you come from that far down you have to struggle to survive.'* Robert Kennedy

STRENGTHS: Trustworthy, purposeful.
WEAKNESSES: Domineering, covetous.

BORN ON THIS DAY:
Robert Byrd
(American politician)
Thomas Chatterton
(poet)
Bo Derek
(actor)
Mike D
(rapper – Beastie Boys)
Karl von Frisch
(zoologist and Nobel laureate)
Robert F. Kennedy
(American politician)

MEDITATION:
Gardens are a form of autobiography.

151

November 21

MEDITATION:

Whatever is good to know is difficult to learn.

You are a mystery, a person who at first can appear light-hearted and flirtatious, yet are also as deep and unfathomable as the ocean. You have a powerful imagination and are highly creative. You have an active and busy mind, always learning something new and you excel at being an educator. You are always on the phone connecting with your wide network and love passing on information – the role of the gossip columnist fits you like a glove! In love, you tend to have several affairs going at once, yet somehow you can get away with it due to your inordinate charm. If married, you need an easy going and practical partner who can inspire you and not worry about never fully understanding you. You are the eternal student – so someone whom you respect and takes the role of teacher – is your best alliance.

TAROT CARD: The Empress
PLANETS: Mercury and Pluto
QUOTE: *'A witty saying proves nothing.'*
Voltaire

STRENGTHS: Innovative, well-read.
WEAKNESSES: Fickle, a tattler.

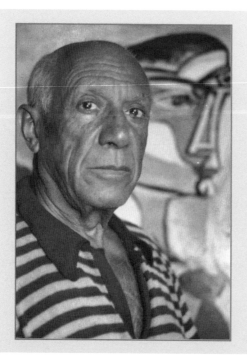

TYPICAL SCORPIO:
PABLO PICASSO

'If there were only one truth, you couldn't paint a hundred canvases on the same theme.'

SCORPIO TRAITS:
Scorpios are known for their steady, hypnotic gaze – their eyes stare right through to your soul and analyse you before letting you get close. Scorpios are ice cool and seldom give away their emotions with facial expressions such as blushing, frowning or grinning – smiles, even if somewhat rare, are always genuine.

November 22

You are an imaginative and sincere person with a strong sense of self. Emotionally resilient and compassionate, you can be very protective. You fiercely care for and mother people, especially children and the underprivileged. This draws you into the caring professions where you can rise to a top managerial position. You are not intimidated by people, whatever their status, and quite enjoy a fight as you revel in deep emotions. A position of power suits you as others feel they can lean and depend on you. Your relationships are complex – you are loyal and steadfast, but you can also be demanding and clingy. Family life can be richly rewarding as you long to recreate the perfect childhood. Bach flower remedies are ideally suited to you when you become stressed and over-emotional.

TAROT CARD: The Emperor
PLANETS: Moon and Pluto
QUOTE: *'Animals are such agreeable friends – they ask no questions; they pass no criticisms.'* George Eliot

STRENGTHS: Wholehearted, nurturing.
WEAKNESSES: Emotionally dependent, possessive.

BORN ON THIS DAY:
Wilhelm Friedemann Bach
(composer)
George Eliot
(writer)
Charles de Gaulle
(French president)
Terry Gilliam
(filmmaker and actor)
Scarlett Johannson
(actor)
Dora Maar
(artist and muse of Picasso)

MEDITATION:
In time of test, family is best.

TYPICAL SCORPIO:
JULIA ROBERTS

'I don't get angry very often. I lose my temper rarely. And when I do, there's always a legitimate cause. Normally I have a great lightness of being. I take things in a very happy, amused way.'

SCORPIO TRAITS:
Highly emotional with a passionate nature, in love Scorpios scrutinize before letting themselves go. They want to know exactly what they will be getting in return for their loyalty and devotion.

Sagittarius

November 23 – December 21

TAROT CARD: Temperance

ELEMENT: Fire

QUALITY: Mutable

NUMBER: 9

RULING PLANET: Jupiter

GEMSTONE: Topaz

COLOURS: Dark blue, purple

DAY OF THE WEEK: Thursday

COMPATIBLE SIGNS:
Leo, Pisces

KEY WORDS: Straightforward and bold, magnanimous and generous, expansive, inspirational, prone to exaggeration, loud mouthed, impractical and unstable

ANATOMY: Hips, thighs, liver, sciatic nerve

HERBS, PLANTS AND TREES: Pinks and carnations, peony, blackberry, ash, chestnut

KEY PHRASE:
I seek

Sagittarius is the optimist and teacher, the archer/centaur, half human half horse. As the sign that corresponds to the thighs in the body where the most powerful muscles are, Sagittarius has to be on the move and to travel long distances. Those born under this sign are keen on sport, and love horses. This is no surprise as their symbol is the centaur; half human, half horse. They seek the truth and are the like the archer who shoots his arrows – his piercing intellect – up into the sky, the higher realms.

This is the ninth sign of the zodiac when the nights are long. In Native American traditions it is the time of year to sit around the fire and tell stories. Sagittarians are the story tellers and adventurers of the zodiac. They are visionaries who live in the future.

PLANETARY RULER AND QUALITIES
Sagittarius is a mutable fire sign. As the last fire sign you take the creative flame and share it with others, so you naturally make an excellent teacher. Ruled by Jupiter, the giant of all the planets, Sagittarius is a big picture sign. Jupiter corresponds to Zeus, king of the gods who rules the skies. The stories of his sexual conquests are legendary, however his main concern is to father a race, which is why Jupiter is exalted in Cancer, the sign of family.

Jupiter is also a Santa Claus archetype – jovial, generous and on the large size. He was also known as the thunder god and is all-powerful, usually in a good way. Jupiter shows us what we have faith in, and our personal religion.

RELATIONSHIPS
Sagittarius is the life and soul of the party and a hearty companion. You love to socialize but also want freedom, and you don't like being pinned down. The other fire signs such as Leo are a good match as long as they are heading in the same direction. Air signs can be explosive, water signs give affection but are far too sensitive to Sagittarius' brashness. There is most affinity with the other sign ruled by Jupiter – Pisces – as you share the same philosophical outlook on life. The earth signs Taurus and Capricorn are best in a business relationship as long as your fire is allowed to burn brightly.

CONSTELLATION AND MYTH
The constellation Sagittarius represents the centaur Chiron who was a wise healer and tutor to many Greek heroes. According to legend, one day he was accidentally wounded in the thigh by one of Hercules' arrows which was dipped in the poisonous blood of the Hydra.

Because he was half immortal he couldn't die, but nor could he heal. After suffering a long time he eventually swapped places with Prometheus who had stolen fire to give to mankind and was being tortured by the gods as punishment. Chiron renounced his immortality and willingly went to his death. In acknowledgement of his sacrifice and past service the gods rewarded him by placing him in the heavens as a constellation.

STRENGTHS AND WEAKNESSES

Sagittarians are the missionaries, the explorers and lawyers of the world. Your enthusiasm and optimism is unchallenged. You have huge faith and confidence in your abilities, however, you can be unstable and over-enthusiastic, often dropping plans before completion. Sagittarians have no malice and you are direct and forthright in expressing your ideas. Your desire to influence others and tell them where they are going wrong can come across as opinionated and self-righteous. You are a natural storyteller and love to talk, but ignore subtle hints to stop! Sagittarians make excellent lawyers as you love the truth.

TYPICAL SAGITTARIUS:
TINA TURNER
'This is what I want in heaven… words to become notes and conversations to be symphonies.'

SAGITTARIAN POWERS: Keenly ambitious, truthful and sincere.

SAGITTARIAN NEGATIVES: Can be disorganized and a philanderer.

November 23

MEDITATION:

Meditation brings wisdom; lack of meditation leaves ignorance.

You are a positive thinker with a contagious enthusiasm for life. Extravagant with money, you enjoy gambling as you love to win and take risks. There is an innocence about you, and at times you can be quite childlike, even naïve. You live in the future and have an extraordinary intuitive ability to foresee trends. As an actor/producer/director in film or television you would be superb. Gregarious and full of bonhomie, you love parties and adore being the host as you love to show off, so the more grandiose and glamorous the event, the better. The lifestyle of a king or queen is what you aim for. You thrive on passion and all the drama and thrills of romance. Though frequently hurt in love, you bounce right back. Performing solo to an adoring crowd, is your idea of bliss.

TAROT CARD: The Hierophant
PLANETS: Sun and Jupiter
QUOTE: *'There's many a slip 'twix the cup and the lip.'* Billy the Kid

STRENGTHS: Positive thinker, intuitive.
WEAKNESSES: Show-off, at times naive.

November 24

MEDITATION:

Anyone can live sweetly, patiently, lovingly, purely, till the sun goes down.

You are a kind-hearted, warm and helpful person who has a gift of persuasion with clear, well-considered arguments. Your sense of humour borders on the outrageous, which delights and entertains others. You are a keen observer of the human condition, with the invaluable ability to laugh at yourself. When insecure your wit can have a sarcastic edge and you become highly critical and pedantic. With a sharp, enquiring mind, you have enormous talent as an educator and teacher. Talking and discussing ideas is vitally important for you, and your romantic liaisons need to meet your elevated criteria. You need space to roam as you are a lover of adventure and freedom. Escaping on your motorbike or getting on a plane to somewhere wild is exhilarating and keeps you young.

TAROT CARD: The Lovers
PLANETS: Mercury and Jupiter
QUOTE: *'Fame is being asked to sign your autograph on the back of a cigarette packet.'* Billy Connolly

STRENGTHS: Humorous, compelling.
WEAKNESSES: Critical, scathing.

November 25

You are a fun-loving and optimistic person who loves everything about life. You just adore people, and watching the world go by is your favourite occupation. You are a social animal, so need work that gives you a lot of room to move around during your day. You make a fantastic PR- or sales-person and as a born networker you have a wide circle of friends. As a result of this you hear of business opportunities and are prepared to take risks. You can be very lucky and this can result in some envy from others. Your romantic relationship is seen as a grand adventure and you need drama and passion. You have a knack in finding the right treat that uplifts your partner when they are down. Visiting the opera or an outdoor concert, preferably in a foreign city, suits your theatrical style.

TAROT CARD: The Chariot
PLANETS: Venus and Jupiter
QUOTE: *'A person always doing his or her best becomes a natural leader, just by example.'* Joe DiMaggio

STRENGTHS: Cheerful and positive.
WEAKNESSES: Restless, over dramatic.

BORN ON THIS DAY:
Christina Applegate
(actor)
Catherine of Braganza
(Consort of English King Charles II)
Alfred Camus
(writer)
Joe DiMaggio
(baseball player)
Amy Grant
(singer/songwriter)
Augusto Pinochet
(Chilean dictator)

MEDITATION:

Excess on occasion is exhilirating.

November 26

You are an irresistible and fascinating person with a thirst for all that life has to offer. You are on a constant search for knowledge, to look below the surface and explore the highs and depths of human emotions. You are always seeking challenges and love to be stretched to test your capabilities. This can make you an extremist and rather volatile and unpredictable. You pick up the atmosphere as soon as you walk in a room and no one can fool you; qualities of a brilliant detective. Although you live life on the edge, you yearn for the security a loving relationship can give you. Once committed you are a loyal and passionate partner. You can find it had to relax as you need a lot of mental and emotional stimulation. The funfair with all its thrilling and spectacular rides was designed just for you.

TAROT CARD: Strength
PLANETS: Pluto and Jupiter
QUOTE: *'I don't like to dwell on the past.'* Tina Turner

STRENGTHS: Captivating, enthusiastic.
WEAKNESSES: Volatile, a risk-taker.

BORN ON THIS DAY:
Carl Benz
(engineer and inventor)
Charles Brackett
(film writer and producer)
Charles Forte
(entrepreneur)
Rich Little
(comedian)
Charles Schulz
(cartoonist)
Tina Turner
(singer/songwriter, author and actor)

MEDITATION:

Your mind is your instrument. Learn to be its master and not its slave.

November 27

MEDITATION:

A calm mind is not disturbed by the waves of thoughts.

You are a flamboyant and joyful person with a huge love of people. Naturally gregarious, you are often to be found at the centre of the group entertaining everyone with your jokes and wise-cracks. You are talkative and can chat for hours, pontificating on your favourite subjects. Extremely honest and with a commitment to truth, you would make an excellent evangelical preacher. Constantly seeking knowledge, you never stop educating yourself and will travel to far-flung places for the sheer adventure of it. Your restless nature, however, can make you sloppy and careless. Your relationship needs to be fun and the person who makes you laugh is the one you will stay with. However, you will leave if you feel your partner is holding you back. Horse-riding is the ideal recreation for you and gives you the connection with nature you need.

TAROT CARD: The Hermit
PLANETS: Jupiter and Jupiter
QUOTE: *'If I'm free, it's because I'm always running.'* Jimi Hendrix

STRENGTHS: Cheeerful and sincere.
WEAKNESSES: Fidgety, slapdash.

November 28

MEDITATION:

One's first step in wisdom is to question everything.

As a person with expansive ideas yet with a cautious, conservative streak, you have a paradoxical nature. From youth you love life, and it gets better as you get older as people begin to take you more seriously. You have a deep desire to be respected and treated as an expert, and work extremely hard to achieve that position. You hugely enjoy sharing your knowledge and make a great mentor. You love to initiate new projects and have an urge to understand concepts that are new to you. In your life you explore new frontiers, stories of outer space inspire you and you could even end up working for NASA! A telescope or a sci-fi film is the ideal gift for you. Once committed, a romantic relationship is for keeps. You long for a family of your own and make a devoted and responsible parent.

TAROT CARD: The Wheel of Fortune
PLANETS: Saturn and Jupiter
QUOTE: *'A truth that's told with bad intent beats all the lies you can invent.'* William Blake

STRENGTHS: Explorer, wise mentor.
WEAKNESSES: Cautious, desires to be admired.

November 29

You are a person of high intelligence verging on genius. As a lover of freedom you cannot be pinned down and you are always seeking to explore new frontiers. You have original and innovative ideas and are often way ahead of your time. Science and religion are just two paths that you might follow. You desire to create grand epic visions, even when it isn't always practical. Whatever you do, you always stand out in the crowd as an oddball and eccentric. Group enterprises have enormous appeal for you. Relationships usually start as being good friends, and you need an intellectual and stimulating partner who shares your interests. Being an independent character, long distance affairs attract you and you can get embroiled in love triangles. Sky diving and adventure parks satisfy your need for thrills.

TAROT CARD: Justice
PLANETS: Uranus and Jupiter
QUOTE: *'Failures are finger posts on the road to achievement.'* C. S. Lewis

STRENGTHS: Bright, pioneering.
WEAKNESSES: Impractical, a dreamer.

BORN ON THIS DAY:
Louisa May Alcott
(writer)
Charles I
(English monarch)
Christian Doppler
(physicist)
C. S. Lewis
(writer)
Jacques Chirac
(French president)
Margaret Tudor
(Scottish monarch)

MEDITATION:
Be what nature intended you for and you will succeed.

November 30

You are an entertaining person with an irreverent and sometimes silly sense of humour. There is a Peter Pan character inside of you – ever youthful, never growing up. You live for adventure and love telling stories with a moral to them. Communication of ideas is your life's purpose, whether as a spokesperson, missionary or advertising copywriter. You can inspire others and lift their spirits. People come to you for information, advice and counsel and you love to guide and help them. You can spread yourself too thin and take on far too may projects, leaving them unfinished. Your tendency to flirt and wanderlust gets you into trouble in your relationships until you find the right person to travel through life with. If stressed you can be short tempered, so watching a Marx Brothers movie should cheer you up!

TAROT CARD: The Empress
PLANETS: Mercury and Jupiter
QUOTE: *'Attitude is a little thing that makes a big difference.'* Winston Churchill

STRENGTHS: Motivational, intrepid.
WEAKNESSES: Unfocussed, irritable.

BORN ON THIS DAY:
Shirley Chisholm
(first black American congresswoman)
Winston Churchill
(British prime minister)
Abbie Hoffman
(activist)
Ben Stiller
(actor and writer)
Jonathan Swift
(writer)
Mark Twain
(writer)

MEDITATION:
Only great passions, can elevate the soul to great things.

159

9

December 1

You are an enthusiastic and forthright person who lives life in the fast lane. Not noted for patience, you relish a challenge and move quickly from one project to the next. You are big-hearted and a lot of fun to be around. However, sensitivity isn't your strong suit and your comments, though often spot on, can be blunt and bruise people. You are fiery and have enormous drive and always look on the bright side of life. You love to gamble and are not averse to taking risks, so have all the qualities of an entrepreneur. Love affairs are dramatic, but your weakness is that you tend not to listen to what your partner is really saying as you are so busy rushing about. Physically, you can easily get burned out, so refuel your batteries with healthy 'super-foods' and the occasional day of complete rest.

BORN ON THIS DAY:
Woody Allen
(comedian, writer and film director)
Candace Bushnell
(writer)
Louis VI
(French monarch)
Bette Midler
(singer and actor)
Lee Travino
(professional golfer)
Madame Tussaud
(sculptor)

MEDITATION:
Always laugh when you can. It is cheap medicine.

TAROT CARD: The Magician
PLANETS: Mars and Jupiter
QUOTE: *'My one regret in life is that I am not someone else.'* Woody Allen

STRENGTHS: Tremendous drive and enthusiasm.
WEAKNESSES: Insensitive, blunt.

December 2

You are a gifted and confident person with a huge love of life. Highly sensual, warm and open, you are very attractive and people usually adore you. You are spontaneous, fun and intriguing, and yet you are prone to moodiness. Music and art play a big part of your life, whether as a hobby or as a career. You can create huge amounts of wealth through your talent and your ability to associate with influential people. You thrive on being at the cutting edge of the social and political scene. Your weakness is that you can live in a dream world, glossing over the gritty realities of life. A romantic partner who has your sense of fun and also enjoys living life on the edge will help you keep perspective and balance. You can overspend when upset, so having a massage would be a better way to cheer you up and help you unwind.

BORN ON THIS DAY:
Maria Callas
(opera singer)
Otto Dix
(artist)
Monica Seles
(champion tennis player)
Georges Seurat
(artist)
Britney Spears
(singer)
Gianni Versace
(fashion designer)

MEDITATION:
Cherish all your happy moments; they make a fine cushion for old age.

TAROT CARD: The High Priestess
PLANETS: Venus and Jupiter
QUOTE: *'I prepare myself for rehearsals like I would for marriage.'* Maria Callas

STRENGTHS: Genuine and passionate.
WEAKNESSES: Shopaholic, a dreamer.

December 3

You are an imaginative and highly creative person who loves to take big chances in life. You are fearless and have a tendency to take risks, whether in business, relationships or sport. You collect information and experiences, and throughout your life you will always experiment and never cease exploring. An expert communicator, you make a gifted writer and journalist – travel and philosophy being your specialities. There is a mischievous side to you, and you can completely win people over with a pithy one-liner. In love affairs you need a lot of freedom and pull away from strong shows of emotion. This infuriates your partners and you can leave many potentially good relationships as a result. You love socializing but can easily overdo it, so listening to music on headphones gives you the downtime you need.

TAROT CARD: The Empress
PLANETS: Mercury and Jupiter
QUOTE: *'A man's most open actions have a secret side to them.'* Joseph Conrad

STRENGTHS: Inspired, intrepid.
WEAKNESSES: Scared of commitment, emotionally inhibited.

BORN ON THIS DAY:
Charles VI
(French monarch)
Joseph Conrad
(adventurer and writer)
Anna Freud
(psychoanalyst and writer)
Jean Luc Goddard
(film director)
Daryl Hannah
(actor)
Ozzy Osbourne
(singer/songwriter – Black Sabbath)

MEDITATION:
Mistakes are the portals of discovery.

TYPICAL SAGITTARIUS:
BRAD PITT

'Success is a beast. And it actually puts the emphasis on the wrong thing. You get away with more instead of looking within.'

SAGITTARIUS TRAITS:
The Sagittarian male is more like a little boy than a man, especially when they are turning on the charm. They are very popular because of their ability to laugh, which means they usually have loyal followers. They tend to have an inability to stay in one place for long because the call of the good times is too strong.

When they turn on the tears, they tend to bring out a woman's mothering instinct and they may manipulate this to their advantage.

9 ♐

You are an emotional and dramatic person whose heart rules your head. You are a true optimist, with a sensitive and caring nature. Whatever happens you are convinced that things will turn out alright. People can mislead you, as you are easily deceived by those less scrupulous than you. Your boundless faith always inspires others, and you have a tireless enthusiasm which makes you very popular. Whatever your field of work, it is the people you interact with that matter most to you. You have a yen for travelling and tend to become restless when in a relationship. Much as you like cosy domesticity, the urge to adventure is strong and you can suddenly pack your bags and move on – having children helps you settle down. Vigorous swimming followed by a relaxing sauna is ideally suited to your temperament.

BORN ON THIS DAY:
Gae Aulenti
(architect and artist)
Tyra Banks
(model and TV personality)
Jeff Bridges
(actor)
Edith Cavell
(nurse and WWI hero)
Dennis Wilson
(drummer and founding member of
The Beach Boys)
Jay-Z
(rapper/record label owner)

MEDITATION:
The wisest men follow their own direction.

TAROT CARD: The Emperor
PLANETS: Moon and Jupiter
QUOTE: *'I realize that patriotism is not enough. I must have no hatred or bitterness towards anyone.'* Edith Cavell

STRENGTHS: Optimistic, kind-hearted.
WEAKNESSES: Gullible, restless.

December 5

You are a larger-than-life person with a huge creative imagination. With a big heart and powerful vision, you can inspire many people. There is tremendous warmth radiating from you, which draws a crowd to follow you. Everything you touch has originality and flair and the stage or a big corporation is your natural habitat. You need to lead the show and be in the spotlight – if not you can get quite petulant and throw a temper tantrum. Pride will be your biggest downfall. You are a romantic through and through and adore being in love. As long as you shower as much attention on your partner as you want them to give you, everything will go smoothly. A workout down the gym, where you can show off your prowess, is wonderful for your self-confidence.

BORN ON THIS DAY:
Bhumibol Adulyadej
(King of Thailand)
José Carreras
(opera singer)
Walt Disney
(animator, filmmaker
and entrepreneur)
Werner Heisenberg
(scientist and Nobel laureate)
Little Richard
(singer/songwriter and pianist)
Christina Rossetti
(poet)

MEDITATION:
Courage is doing what you're afraid to do.

TAROT CARD: The Hierophant
PLANETS: Sun and Jupiter
QUOTE: *'It's kind of fun to do the impossible.'* Walt Disney

STRENGTHS: Natural leader, inventive.
WEAKNESSES: Prone to temper tantrums, proud.

December 6

You are a quietly charming person who is innately modest, yet can also take centre stage and the leadership position when prompted. You are dedicated to high ideals and also work hard to achieve your goals. Words and sounds fascinate you, and you convey your love of life with great enthusiasm as a writer or musician. You are very thorough and do your homework in preparation for any major task you embark on. You can get obsessive about collating information or never throwing anything away as it 'might come in useful one day'. You are a devoted and affectionate partner when committed, and can be shocked if your beloved strays. At these times you can come across as moralistic and judgmental. Being outdoors in the wilderness or moorland excites and expands your vision.

TAROT CARD: The Lovers
PLANETS: Mercury and Jupiter
QUOTE: *'A song without music is a lot like H_2 without the O.'* Ira Gershwin

STRENGTHS: Steadfast, meticulous.
WEAKNESSES: Obsessive and at times deprecating.

BORN ON THIS DAY:
Judd Apatow
(film and TV director and producer)
Ira Gershwin
(lyricist)
Lester M. Gillis aka Baby Face Nelson
(American gangster)
Richard Krajicek
(champion tennis player)
Agnes Moorhead
(actor)
Silvia Townsend Warner
(writer)

MEDITATION:
Man's greatness lies in his power of thought.

December 7

You are a warm and sincere person with a genuine love of people. You have a fine intellect and a passion for communicating your inspirational ideas and concepts. You thrive on hanging out with friends as you like to know what's going on. Very popular, you have a wicked sense of humour. You are generous with your time and money, but you can be gullible and extravagant. As such a positive person, you have a tendency to rely a bit too much on luck to extricate yourself from difficult situations. Injustice makes you angry and you can be a vehement supporter of the underdog. In love you are passionate, but not sentimental, and view marriage as a shared journey of like minds. When unhappy, beauty inspires you, so treat yourself and your partner to a night out at the ballet.

TAROT CARD: The Chariot
PLANETS: Venus and Jupiter
QUOTE: *'Even if I don't want to slow down, I'm slowing down.'* Eli Wallach

STRENGTHS: A philanthropist, understanding.
WEAKNESSES: Over-trusting, rely too much on luck.

BORN ON THIS DAY:
Lord Darnley
(husband of Mary Queen of Scots)
Nicholas Hoult
(actor)
James Keach
(actor)
Hermann Maier
(champion Olympic skier)
Damian Rice
(singer/songwriter and musician)
Eli Wallach
(actor)

MEDITATION:
A day without sunshine is like night.

December 8

MEDITATION:
Nothing great was ever achieved without enthusiasm.

You are an intense and intoxicating person, with mesmerizing charisma. Hugely courageous, you dive into life experiences with a passion. You are an entrepreneur and enjoy taking on enormous challenges. An explorer of the unknown, you have enormous mental and physical courage and can withstand large amounts of pain. You can argue fiercely for your beliefs and are known for your stubbornness. With your investigative mind you would perform well in the courtroom as a lawyer or working in the field of psychiatry. When you enter a relationship you commit yourself one hundred percent and you demand that your partner is both loyal and faithful, but this can lead to many suspicious jealous out-bursts. Lighten up and let loose your emotions at a wild rock concert.

TAROT CARD: Strength
PLANETS: Pluto and Jupiter
QUOTE: *'I have to be a star like another man has to breathe.'* Sammy Davis, Jr.

STRENGTHS: Entrancing, fearless.
WEAKNESSES: Obstinate, insecure.

December 9

MEDITATION:
Learning never exhausts the mind.

You are an ebullient and intuitive person with big dreams. Life is all or nothing for you and you have a utopian vision. Always seeing the best in people, your enthusiasm is contagious, so you can easily rally support for your ventures. You are a wanderer, constantly moving, always restless, and a weakness is that you tend not to finish what you have started. You are naturally joyful and always look on the bright side of life. Generous and kind, you throw yourself wholeheartedly into your work. You have a tendency to exaggerate and be over-dramatic in your emotions, so a theatrical career is suited to you. You are constantly seeking variety in your relationships, so you need a partner who can entertain you. Jogging or running are ideal for you to work off your excess nervous energy.

TAROT CARD: The Hermit
PLANETS: Jupiter and Jupiter
QUOTE: *'I don't think anybody can be told how to act... you have to find your own way through it.'* Dame Judi Dench

STRENGTHS: Cheerful, passionate.
WEAKNESSES: Tendency to overreact, restless.

December 10

You are a positive and trustworthy person with a strong belief in the abundance of the Universe, but still able to make wise investments. Although you love adventure and will gamble on enterprises that take your fancy, you have a tough business mind that directs you to make canny decisions. You would make a gifted producer or director, or both. Your dry sense of humour and broad intellect endear you to many influential people. Your weakness is that you want to run the show, and can get quite pompous and self-righteous. Along with your work, your relationship is the source of your greatest joy. A traditionalist, you are loyal and work hard to maintain the security of your family. Overwork is a tendency and a day-trip to a museum or art gallery reconnects you to your creativity.

TAROT CARD: The Wheel of Fortune
PLANETS: Saturn and Jupiter
QUOTE: *'Behaviour is what a man does, not what he thinks, feels or believes.'* Emily Dickinson

STRENGTHS: Wry, dependable.
WEAKNESSES: Sententious, a moralizer.

BORN ON THIS DAY:
Kenneth Branagh
(actor)
Emily Dickinson
(poet)
Michael Clark Duncan
(actor)
William Lloyd Garrison
(activist)
Dorothy Lamour
(actor)
Olivier Messiaen
(composer and musician)

MEDITATION:
Instruction does much, but encouragement does everything.

December 11

You are a friendly, easy-going person with a strong idealistic streak. Concerned by social issues, you are a natural campaigner, humanitarian and reformer. You love technology and connecting with people across the globe via the internet. You seek truth and will suddenly change your whole life to go off on a completely different tangent. You take risks with no thought of personal danger, and usually things work out well. The world of academia is suited to you as you are very cerebral. With your love of anything new, you frequently take on too many projects and spread yourself too thin; you can be frustratingly absent-minded. In personal relationships you are looking for a companion, someone who is your equal and doesn't mind sharing you with your friends. Let your mind have a break and enjoy a light-hearted comedy.

TAROT CARD: Justice
PLANETS: Uranus and Jupiter
QUOTE: *'If one is forever cautious, can one remain a human being?'* Aleksandr Solzhenitsyn

STRENGTHS: Compassionate, an activist.
WEAKNESSES: Easily distracted, risk taker.

BORN ON THIS DAY:
Hector Berlioz
(composer)
Ursula Bloom
(writer)
David Brewster
(scientist – inventor of the kaleidoscope)
Charles IV
(French monarch)
Carlo Ponti
(film producer)
Aleksandr Solzhenitsyn
(writer and Nobel laureate)

MEDITATION:
You can never learn less; you can only learn more.

165

December 12

You are an affectionate person who is a deeply romantic soul. You have great insight and are extremely sensitive to how others feel. Always willing to help people less fortunate, you are naturally charitable. Less scrupulous people can take advantage of your good nature but you are immensely forgiving. Your weakness is that you can be over-sentimental, verging on being gushy. With your magnificent creative talents you can capture the minds and hearts of your generation. Careers as a poet, artist or singer all appeal; your problem is choosing just one path. Relationships can be idealized as you tend to fall hopelessly in love and are often attracted to people you feel you can save. Recognizing this pattern will help you to find a more stable partner who will support you. Sailing is the perfect recreation for you.

TAROT CARD: The Empress
PLANETS: Neptune and Jupiter
QUOTE: 'I'm not looking for the secret to life… I just go on from day to day.' Frank Sinatra

STRENGTHS: Altruistic, empathetic.
WEAKNESSES: Effusive, idealistic.

MEDITATION:
Think of all the beauty still left around you and be happy.

December 13

You are a romantic and creative person with a love of action and a zest for life. Striking and dramatic, you make a vivid impression on people. You have a gift for prophecy and your vision leads you and others forward. You are an innovator and can persuade and convince people as you speak from your heart. Whatever your experiences, you have faith and believe the best in people. You can throw caution to the wind and be over-trusting and naïve, especially in financial matters and you may lose money by making a bad investment. A partner who has a good dose of common sense would be a good bet for you. You can be overcome by emotional unrest and suddenly leave in search of new horizons. To satisfy your need for variety, consider getting involved with charity work overseas.

TAROT CARD: The Emperor
PLANETS: Moon and Jupiter
QUOTE: 'I've retired so many times now it's getting to be a habit.' Dick Van Dyke

STRENGTHS: Enthusiastic, pioneering.
WEAKNESSES: Gullible and, at times, reckless.

MEDITATION:
Nothing is so exhausting as indecision.

December 14

You are a person who is pure of heart with a noble spirit. A naturally positive thinker, your optimism and immense courage can propel you into a leadership position in your career. You have the ability to see the potential in people and others value you as their mentor. You love to uphold justice, and with your theatrical flair, you would make an excellent courtroom lawyer or judge. You have an autocratic style so this will upset those who prefer equality, and they will resist taking orders from you. As a fiery person you can be highly volatile if triggered and throw a dramatic scene. However, you don't hold grudges and all is forgotten very quickly. Love is an intense experience for you, but your passions can change overnight. The sport of kings – horse racing – gives you immense pleasure.

TAROT CARD: The Hierophant
PLANETS: Sun and Jupiter
QUOTE: *'I delight in what I fear.'* Shirley Jackson

STRENGTHS: Virtuous, valiant.
WEAKNESSES: Domineering, prone to exaggeration.

BORN ON THIS DAY:
Jane Birkin
(actor)
George VI
(English monarch)
Shirley Jackson
(writer)
Raj Kapoor
(actor)
Nostradamus
(prophet)
Margaret Chase Smith
(American politician)

MEDITATION:
A leader leads by example, whether he intends to or not.

December 15

You are a visionary, a person who thinks big, yet also has an eye for every detail. When inspired, yours is a grand vision and you are not afraid to tackle projects on a large scale. Always socially concerned, you are thoughtful and want what you produce to be of use to others. You are discriminating and know what's really important in life – your outlook is based on reason. You need a good education and will continue to study all your life, seeking out the right courses to improve your skills. You can be both prudish and an outrageous flirt, so therefore give out mixed messages to potential lovers. You seek someone who shares your vision and who is equally dedicated to a cause. Time off is rare as you work so hard – gardening helps to ground you and allows for mediation.

TAROT CARD: The Devil
PLANETS: Mercury and Jupiter
QUOTE: *'Formula for success: Rise early, work hard, strike oil.'* John Paul Getty

STRENGTHS: Insightful, learned.
WEAKNESSES: Prim, overloaded.

BORN ON THIS DAY:
Gustave Eiffel
(architect)
John Paul Getty, Sr
(entrepreneur)
Henry VI
(English monarch)
Don Johnson
(actor)
Nero
(Roman Emperor)
Edna O'Brien
(writer)

MEDITATION:
The moon is a friend for the lonesome to talk to.

167

December 16

You are an honest and optimistic person with a positive approach to life's problems. Whatever challenges you come up against, you get through with a philosophical attitude and bounce back. You have strong opinions and you speak your mind with candour and passion; plus you have a wonderfully mischievous side to your personality. At ease with people from all spheres of society, you are gifted at coordinating people to collaborate on important humanitarian causes. With your social graces you make a superb fund-raiser. Romantic and charming, you view marriage as an epic love story or a strategic alliance. On the negative side, you contain your deep emotions and everyday domestic chores bore you. However, you know how to cheer your partner up with a well-timed, extravagant treat that bowls them over.

MEDITATION:

If you do not hope, you will not find what is beyond your hopes.

TAROT CARD: The Chariot
PLANETS: Venus and Jupiter
QUOTE: *'Music is a higher revelation than all wisdom and philosophy.'*
Ludwig van Beethoven

STRENGTHS: Thoughtful, socially adept.
WEAKNESSES: Emotionally contained, crave excitement.

December 17

You are a sensual person with a thirst for self-knowledge. Life has to be stimulating for you to feel alive and you throw yourself into the primal emotions of lust, love, hate and jealousy in your quest to understand human nature. You have a vein of optimism that carries you through the darkest despair, and your faith, though often tested, is strong. You want to make a difference in life and work obsessively hard to achieve wealth as you appreciate the power it brings. The role of publisher suits you, as does that of a doctor. You are not afraid of stirring things up just to be controversial and people either love or hate you. All your relationships are deep and passionate, as nothing superficial will satisfy you. Your weakness is your possessiveness. Rock climbing is your kind of sport.

MEDITATION:

Time is a great healer.

TAROT CARD: The Star
PLANETS: Pluto and Jupiter
QUOTE: *'I really believe my greatest service is in the many unwise steps I prevent.'* William Mackenzie King

STRENGTHS: Soulful, hopeful.
WEAKNESSES: Controlling, a devil's advocate.

December 18

You are an energetic and expansive person with a passion for exploration. This is both mental and physical and you often end up living far from your birthplace. You have an overdose of optimism and love to gamble with high stakes. As such you are the epitome of the entrepreneur and speculator. As you get older, your social conscience develops and you become an ardent campaigner for humanitarian causes. 'Carpe Diem' is your motto and despite your concern for others, you tend not to recognize the harsher realities in your own life. You can easily put on weight as you don't know the meaning of the word limitation. As a lover of freedom, marriage isn't natural for you. However, you are incurably romantic, and as long as your partner allows you to roam, you can be content.

TAROT CARD: The Moon
PLANETS: Jupiter and Jupiter
QUOTE: *'I dream for a living.'* Steven Spielberg

STRENGTHS: Communicative, a crusader.
WEAKNESSES: Blindly optimistic, prone to excess.

BORN ON THIS DAY:
Franz Ferdinand
(Austrian archduke)
Betty Grable
(singer, dancer and actor)
Mary Queen of Scots
(Scottish monarch)
Brad Pitt
(actor and film producer)
Keith Richards
(musician, singer/songwriter –
The Rolling Stones)
Steven Spielberg
(film producer and director)

MEDITATION:
Learn from yesterday, live for today.

December 19

You are a person with a deep love of the past and excitement about the future. You respect tradition and learning and are willing to work and study hard to become an writerity on your chosen subject. You love old buildings and value education, so are attracted to work in a university or museum. In your social life, there is a contrast in your personality; either you let your hair down and are the life and soul of the party, or you act like a controlling parent. You appreciate your creature comforts and can be too materialistic; you are not happy unless your bank account is healthy. You take relationships seriously and with your innate sense of morality are faithful and loyal. There is a wanderlust in you that the occasional camping trip with close friends or family would satisfy.

TAROT CARD: The
PLANETS: Saturn and Jupiter
QUOTE: *'A good book is the precious lifeblood of a master spirit.'* John Milton

STRENGTHS: Exuberant, loyal.
WEAKNESSES: Over-serious, materialistic.

BORN ON THIS DAY:
Jake Gyllenhaal
(actor)
Richard Hammond
(TV personality)
John Milton
(writer)
Philip V
(Spanish monarch)
Edith Piaf
(singer/songwriter and actor)
Alberto Tomba
(champion Olympic skier)

MEDITATION:
Wealth is the ability to fully experience life.

December 20

MEDITATION:

*Leave no stone
unturned.*

You are a generous and friendly person with a calm, serene countenance. You have a vivid imagination and the ability to communicate your ideas, and would thrive in a creative profession. You are expansive and love discussing philosophical concepts with your many friends. You are at ease with yourself and others feel at ease in your company. As a *bon viveur* you enjoy the good things in life and will share your great fortune with others who are less blessed. You have integrity and moral strength, and throughout your life you search for both beauty and truth. Your relationship needs to be with someone who can teach you about emotions. At times you can be lazy and over-indulge in food and wine, thus putting on weight. Horse-riding is the kind of exercise that both thrills and motivates you.

TAROT CARD: Judgement
PLANETS: Venus and Jupiter
QUOTE: *'I live in the present, taking one day at a time.'* Uri Geller

STRENGTHS: Magnanimous, genuine.
WEAKNESSES: Prone to lethargy, greedy.

TYPICAL SAGITTARIUS:
JENNY AGUTTER

'When you look at a photo album it's lovely to remember being so young but it's also good to know you grew up! '

SAGITTARIUS TRAITS:
Sagittarian women are prone to be independent and love their freedom. They do not take kindly to receiving orders, so if you want them to do something it is best to ask nicely. She needs a real man and doesn't deal well with weakness, so her partner needs to remember to be polite and firm. They can be charming and can easily captivate their audience. Talkative, outspoken and forthright, they are natural communicators.

December 21

You are a free spirit, a vociferous and articulate person. You are both the eternal student and also a wise teacher. You thrive on expanding your mind and increasing your knowledge. A gifted orator, you love debating and can take the opposition view just for the fun of it. However, you have a tendency for you to be intoxicated by the sound of your own voice. No one can doubt your sincerity and conviction when you espouse a cause and you can persuade people to rally around you. You have the ability to be very successful in your chosen field once you learn to have confidence in your abilities. In your relationship you need an intellectual rapport as ideas are so vitally important to you. Give vent to your feelings by singing your heart out, either in a choir or on your own in the bath.

BORN ON THIS DAY:
Benjamin Disraeli
(British prime minister)
Jane Fonda
(actor)
Samuel L. Jackson
(actor)
Keifer Sutherland
(actor, director and producer)
Rebecca West
(writer)
Frank Zappa
(guitarist and composer)

TAROT CARD: The Empress
PLANETS: Mercury and Jupiter
QUOTE: *'A consistent soul believes in destiny, a capricious one in chance.'*
Benjamin Disraeli

STRENGTHS: Gifted speaker, strong-minded.
WEAKNESSES: Vocally unrestrained and at times self-absorbed.

MEDITATION:
Think big, and discover how to make your dreams real.

TYPICAL SAGITTARIUS:
BENJAMIN DISRAELI

'Life is too short to be little. Man is never so manly as when he feels deeply, acts boldly and expresses himself with frankness and with fervour.'

SAGITTARIUS TRAITS:
Sagittarian men are rarely on their own; it is far more likely that you will find them surrounded by a crowd. Their optimism about life can sometimes border on blind faith. They are always chasing high dreams, but they can also fall heavily if these dreams do not come true. However, a Sagittarius man usually has exceptionally good luck which seldom runs out. In matters of the heart, they tend to look beyond external appearances, as looks mean little to them.

Capricorn

December 22–January 20

TAROT CARD: The Devil

ELEMENT: Earth

QUALITY: Cardinal

NUMBER: 10

RULING PLANET: Saturn

GEMSTONES: Blue sapphire, lapis lazuli

COLOURS: Navy, blue, black

DAY OF THE WEEK: Saturday

COMPATIBLE SIGNS:
Taurus, Virgo, Scorpio, Pisces

KEY WORDS: Earthy good humour,
prudent and self-sacrificing,
trustworthy and loyal, serious and
business like, industrious, ambitious,
miserly, stiff and rigid, status seeking

ANATOMY: Knees, joints,
skeletal system, bones

HERBS, PLANTS AND TREES: Ivy, magnolia,
pine, elm, pansy

KEY PHRASE:
I achieve

Capricorn is the architect of the zodiac. It corresponds to the knees and those born under the sign find that arthritis can be a problem in later years. The knees represent humility and Capricorns can suffer from too much self-effacement and not enough self-confidence.

Capricorn is the sign that marks the Winter Solstice and the longest night of the year in the northern hemisphere. This ancient festival has been celebrated for over 5,000 years and represents the turning point, when the Sun changes direction and the days start to get longer. The New Year also falls in the sign of Capricorn and Old Father Time is an apt symbol. Capricorns improve with age as they gain experience of life.

Capricorns are the backbone of society and value anything that is old and traditional. Like the mountain goat they slowly build upwards in their lives and their goal is to reach the top. Capricorn represents the height of achievement and the recognition that comes from years of work.

PLANETARY RULER AND QUALITIES

Capricorn is a cardinal earth sign. As the last earth sign it is the master builder and governs mountains and buildings. It is governed by Saturn, the furthest planet that can be seen with the naked eye. Saturn is the ringed planet and is concerned with limitations and boundaries. Planets represent energy and Saturn conserves, restricts and governs time.

RELATIONSHIPS

Capricorn is polite and well-mannered, and will always do the 'right thing'. All earth signs are sensual as they enjoy their bodies. The male is likely to be dressed in a suit and quite formal and knows how to make a relationship work. The female is always more sensual than she appears and she likes to be the boss. Marriage is a contract that is taken seriously by you. When you commit, it's for the long haul. When young, a Capricorn will be attracted to someone older. You relate well to Cancerians as this is a traditional father/mother partnership. The most attractive signs for marriage are Taureans and Scorpios, and Aries make better partners than you might think. Virgos are great friends and excellent business partners and, for Capricorns in the media, Pisces is an imaginative ally.

CONSTELLATION AND MYTH

Capricornus is the constellation of The Sea Goat, a goat with the tail of a fish. This might relate to the story of Pan who, when fleeing from the sea monster Typhon, jumped into

the Nile. The part that was underwater turned into a fish, while his top half remained that of a goat.

In the Greek myths, Saturn corresponds to Cronus who was one of the children of the original creator god Ouranus. Cronus killed his father with his mother's help and the Golden Age of Time began. Capricorn is the Father Archetype, yet often the actual father is a remote figure for those born under this sign.

STRENGTHS AND WEAKNESSES

Capricorn is concerned with self-mastery. You are devoted to duty and fulfil your responsibilities. You provide security, a well-organized home, or business with firm foundations. You work extremely hard and can be workaholic. This makes for a serious and often materialistic life with not much time for fun, which you can see as a waste of time. You preserve the status quo and can be very resistant to change or innovation as you are loathe to take risks. Capricorns are careful, especially with money, so you can be stingy. You can be pompous and judgemental – the typical grumpy old man or woman.

TYPICAL CAPRICORN: ELVIS PRESLEY
'Adversity is sometimes hard upon a man; but for one man who can stand prosperity, there are a hundred that will stand adversity.'

CAPRICORN POWERS: Practical, good organizational skills, strong work ethic.

CAPRICORN NEGATIVES: Materialistic, excessive perfectionism.

173

December 22

You are a sensitive and strong person with a tough exterior but a marshmallow-soft inner centre. You are capable of immense self-control and are the ultimate professional, totally dedicated to your career and able to work long hours to achieve that coveted promotion. Your heart is tender, and you can be quite soppy, easily bursting into tears when stories of orphaned children appear on the news. You are not one to blow your own trumpet and your charitable work is done quietly with no fuss. You are a superb manager and people feel that you listen to their concerns, so you would excel in Human Resources. Marriage is almost essential as you need a partner to feel complete. A family get-together is your idea of happiness, and you're the perfect person to make it happen.

BORN ON THIS DAY:
Peggy Ashcroft
(actor)
Jean-Michel Basquiat
(artist)
Ralph Fiennes
(actor)
Maurice and Robin Gibb
(musicians – the Bee Gees)
Giacomo Puccini
(composer)
Diane Sawyer
(journalist)

MEDITATION:
When one door closes another door opens.

TAROT CARD: The Emperor
PLANETS: Moon and Saturn
QUOTE: *'I veer away from trying to understand why I act. I just know I need to do it.'* Ralph Fiennes

STRENGTHS: Modest, committed.
WEAKNESSES: Tendency to overwork, sentimental.

December 23

You are an assertive and purposeful person with high ambitions and deep desire for recognition. With a strong belief in yourself and a willingness to work very hard, you have the abilities of a natural leader. You can't bear to be in a subordinate position, but luckily for you, people generally agree that you are right person to be in charge. Once in the right position, you lead with your heart and radiate warmth. You achieve superb results because of the care and preparation that you put into your projects. Be aware of a tendency to let power to go to your head; you can turn into a dictator and lord it over people! In relationships, your partner has to be your equal and yet mustn't outshine you or you will not flourish. Your creativity needs an outlet, and singing for the fun of it is a natural talent.

BORN ON THIS DAY:
Akihito
(emperor of Japan)
Bob Kurland
(basketball player)
Aleksander Mikhailovich
(artist)
Harriet Monroe
(poet)
Nick Moran
(actor, writer and producer)
Helmut Schmidt
(German chancellor)

MEDITATION:
Happiness is a state of mind.

TAROT CARD: The Hierophant
PLANETS: Sun and Saturn
QUOTE: *'Whoever wants to reach a distant goal must take small steps.'* Helmut Schmidt

STRENGTHS: Warmhearted, creative.
WEAKNESSES: Power-hungry, dictatorial.

December 24

You are a modest yet highly successful person who enjoys helping others. Highly skilled, you pride yourself on the professionalism of your work. You are not known for being showy, and prefer to keep behind the scenes as you are quite shy. You are interested in diet and nutrition so you can do well in the health industry. You excel at streamlining systems and finding the most efficient methods. However, you tend to find fault in everything as you have very high standards. With friends you can relax and have a wicked sense of humour. In relationships you are content to settle down early as you love caring for people, and a family brings you great joy. Decluttering and reorganizing your home is one of the most enjoyable things you can do in your spare time.

TAROT CARD: The Lovers
PLANETS: Mercury and Saturn
QUOTE: *'I'm not a paranoid deranged millionaire. Goddamit, I'm a billionaire.'*
Howard Hughes

STRENGTHS: Efficient, comical.
WEAKNESSES: Critical, self-effacing.

BORN ON THIS DAY:
Michael Curtiz
(film director)
Ava Gardner
(actor)
George I
(Greek monarch)
Howard Hughes
(aviator and film producer)
Stephenie Meyer
(writer)
Benjamin Rush
(a Founding Father of the United States)

MEDITATION:
It's the possibility of having a dream come true that makes life interesting.

December 25

You are a charming and well-mannered person who knows the rules of etiquette and abides by them. Although you have a love of tradition you can be progressive in your views. You have an innate sense of justice and your words – though always polite – are powerful when directed to upholding the truth. Entering the legal profession as an advocate, or following a career as a foreign diplomat, are both attractive paths for you. A weakness is your indecision and you can sit on the fence for a long time. Your relationship is a true partnership, and you seek an ally; a partner who shares your ambitions. You are loyal and tender, and thrive on entertaining your mutual business contacts. Obsessed with looking good, you need to be stylish even when you exercise, so tennis or cricket has great appeal.

TAROT CARD: The Chariot
PLANETS: Venus and Saturn
QUOTE: *'I drink beacuse I'm thirsty.'*
Shane MacGowan

STRENGTHS: Refined, logical.
WEAKNESSES: Tentative, poorly motivated.

BORN ON THIS DAY:
Cab Calloway
(singer/songwriter and bandleader)
Catherine of Aragon
(English monarch)
Quentin Crisp
(writer)
Helena Christensen
(supermodel)
Shane MacGowan
(singer/songwriter – The Pogues)
Annie Lennox
(singer/songwriter – Eurythmics)

MEDITATION:
Life is like a giant canvas.

December 26

You are a charismatic and dedicated person with huge powers of endurance. Whatever you start you finish and you are able to confront tremendous obstacles and challenges. Physically and emotionally strong, you take pride in keeping yourself in good shape and keep improving your qualifications. As a leader you are strong and decisive so you are suited to a position of responsibility. However, you can be too tough and unable to see that others can't keep up with you. When you apply your powerful will toward helping the underdog you come into your own. You have traditional values so marriage is for keeps and you will make every effort to ensure it works. You can be too serious and austere so your down time needs to be fun. You enjoy thrills so an exciting ride at a theme park could do the trick.

BORN ON THIS DAY:
Charles Babbage
(mathematician)
Thomas Gray
(poet)
Phil Spector
(music producer)
Mao Tse-Tung
(Chinese political leader)
Lars Ulrich
(drummer – Metallica)
Richard Widmark
(actor)

MEDITATION:
*Without hard work,
nothing grows but weeds.*

TAROT CARD: Strength
PLANETS: Pluto and Saturn
QUOTE: *'In time of difficulties, we must not lose sight of our achievements.'* Mao Tse-Tung

STRENGTHS: Emotionally strong, a good leader.
WEAKNESSES: Severe in manner, exacting.

December 27

You are an enthusiastic and dedicated person with a great sense of adventure. You are fearless and have few concerns about the future as you have faith in your abilities and are willing to put in a lot of effort to achieve your dreams. You speculate to accumulate and your confidence and dignity ensures that people value and look up to you. You adore travel and have a broad outlook on life. Once wealthy you donate to worthy causes. Although you are a consummate professional, you love playing practical jokes on people – much to their annoyance. When young, your relationships are free and easy and you can be quite cavalier with your affections. As you mature you begin to appreciate your need for a partner who is also your best friend. Your favourite way to relax is walking or hill climbing.

BORN ON THIS DAY:
Gerard Depardieu
(actor)
Marlene Dietrich
(actor and singer)
Oscar Levant
(composer, writer and actor)
Louis Pasteur
(chemist)
Michael Pinder
(singer/songwriter and pianist –
The Moody Blues)
Emilie de Ravin
(actor)

MEDITATION:
*The steeper the mountain,
the harder the climb.*

TAROT CARD: The Hermit
PLANETS: Jupiter and Saturn
QUOTE: *'Superstitions are habits rather than beliefs.'* Marlene Dietrich

STRENGTHS: Fearless, humanitarian.
WEAKNESSES: Arrogant, a prankster.

December 28

You are a sophisticated and practical person who aims high in life and usually succeeds. You have a huge amount of common sense and a quiet charm that grows on people. Steadfast and dependable, you can be too serious and so focused on self-advancement that you don't stop to smell the roses. You are the backbone of any organization you care to work for, but you have your eyes set on the top job. You love old things and appreciate craftsmanship and will pay top dollar for quality. Cheap stuff just doesn't do it for you. You approach relationships cautiously and take time to evaluate the merits of potential partners. Once committed you are a sensual lover with a witty sense of humour. Purposeless fun is much needed in your life – playing kids games would do it.

TAROT CARD: The Wheel of Fortune
PLANETS: Saturn and Saturn
QUOTE: *'I don't tolerate fools but then they don't tolerate me…'* Maggie Smith

STRENGTHS: Refined, witty.
WEAKNESSES: Serious, self-absorbed.

BORN ON THIS DAY:
Nigel Kennedy
(violinist)
Stan Lee
(comic book writer)
Sienna Miller
(actor)
Dame Maggie Smith
(actor and filmmaker)
Denzel Washington
(actor)
Woodrow Wilson
(US president)

MEDITATION:
Stay young – carry your childhood with you.

December 29

You are an eccentric person with a highly original way of doing things. Highly intelligent, your mental powers can verge on genius. You are quick to take on new concepts. Concerned with promoting a cause, you are attracted to local politics and actively serving your community. Having space and freedom is crucial for your well-being and being tied to a routine job is an anathema. Being self-employed and running your own enterprise is far more in keeping with your style. At times you are rather cool and distant and people can think you're ignoring them. In relationships you tend to take your time and seek a partner who'll be a friend, be materially successful, and keep you on your toes. Social activities that involve some fun, such as line dancing, are entertaining and good relaxation for you.

TAROT CARD: Justice
PLANETS: Uranus and Saturn
QUOTE: *'Selfishness is the greatest curse of the human race.'* William E. Gladstone

STRENGTHS: Innovative, clever.
WEAKNESSES: Standoffish, withdrawn.

BORN ON THIS DAY:
Bernard Cribbins
(actor)
Marianne Faithfull
(singer)
William E. Gladstone
(British prime minister)
Jude Law
(actor)
Mary Tyler Moore
(actor)
Jon Voight
(actor)

MEDITATION:
Our perception is shaped by our previous experiences.

177

December 30

MEDITATION:

Common sense is not so common.

You are a disciplined and sombre person, yet have a youthful air about you. You impress people with your mental agility and logical, well-considered arguments. Light-hearted but never superficial, what you say is taken seriously. You have an extensive vocabulary yet choose your words carefully. With acute powers of observation, writing is an attractive career for you, and you have the skill and dedication to be very successful. You also have an innate sense of rhythm and dexterity so could well be a gifted musician. In your intimate relationship you settle down, but need intellectual stimulation and variety to keep your love alive. At times you read too much into things and can be wary of showing your deeper emotions, much to the frustration of your partner. Twitter was invented just for you!

TAROT CARD: The Empress
PLANETS: Mercury and Saturn
QUOTE: *'A woman's guess is much more accurate than a man's certainty.'* Rudyard Kipling

STRENGTHS: Intelligent, a wordsmith.
WEAKNESSES: Wary of showing feelings, overly analytical.

December 31

MEDITATION:

It is easier to be wise for others than for ourselves.

You are a determined and ambitious person, in tune with your emotions, with the added ability to touch the public's mood. You are both shrewd at business and thoughtful, and have a practical, hands-on approach to helping people with their problems. Your organizational skills are impressive and as you get older you spend time using your talents in charitable work. Emotionally you are vulnerable, and are nostalgic for your childhood. Your weakness is over-sensitivity and you take any criticism personally. You have a keen intellect and an excellent memory, perfect for a career in acting or writing. Relationships are crucial for you and you long to create a traditional family life. With your connection to your internal rhythm, drumming would be a brilliantly therapeutic and enjoyable activity.

TAROT CARD: The Emperor
PLANETS: Moon and Saturn
QUOTE: *'I love life because what more is there?'* Sir Anthony Hopkins

STRENGTHS: Considerate, artistic.
WEAKNESSES: Emotionally naive, sensitive to criticism.

January 1

You are a person with initiative and a tremendous drive to succeed. Intensely ambitious, you never stop creating and overcoming challenges. Highly competitive and focussed, you have the attributes of an athlete or business tycoon, and you are quite willing to undertake the rigorous training needed to get to the top. You surround yourself with the trappings of success; the right car and home are important to you as you feel they prove your worth. You can be blind to others' feelings, and at times you ride roughshod over weaker opponents; you are also a poor loser. Your lover needs to be someone you are proud of, and once you are sure that they admire you too, will be a devoted partner. Your energy needs to be released through a tough physical workout at the gym.

TAROT CARD: The Magician
PLANETS: Mars and Saturn
QUOTE: *'Either life entails courage, or it ceases to be life.'* E. M. Forster

STRENGTHS: Motivated, energetic.
WEAKNESSES: Intimidating, a bad loser.

BORN ON THIS DAY:
E. M. Forster
(writer)
Guccio Gucci
(fashion entrepreneur)
Grandmaster Flash
(musician and DJ)
J. Edgar Hoover
(FBI director)
J.D. Salinger
(writer)
Verne Troyer
(actor)

MEDITATION:
Years teach us more than books.

January 2

You are a friendly and reliable person with a great deal of common sense. Ever the realist, you know and appreciate the material world and have excellent organizational skills. Budgeting is your forte; you can be frugal when needed, and have a good eye for a bargain. With a deep love of all things that combine beauty and usefulness, you would make a superb architect or furniture designer. The role of financial manager would also suit you. You can be controlling and rigid in your outlook and are thrown off track when people don't follow the rules. You are a sensual lover, and once committed, are loyal and faithful. Learning to be flexible is your biggest challenge. With your love of nature and artistic colour sense, gardening is the ideal hobby.

TAROT CARD: The High Priestess
PLANETS: Venus and Saturn
QUOTE: *'It's one thing to have talent. It's another to figure out how to use it.'* Roger Miller

STRENGTHS: Amiable, pragmatic.
WEAKNESSES: Domineering, obstinate.

BORN ON THIS DAY:
Kate Bosworth
(actor)
Louis Breguet
(industrialist and pioneer pilot)
Didier Daurat
(aviator)
Lucy Davis
(actor)
Cuba Gooding Jr
(actor and film producer)
Roger Miller
(singer/songwriter and musician)

MEDITATION:
The secret of success is to know something nobody else knows.

179

January 3

MEDITATION:

Every survival kit should include a sense of humour.

You are a highly intelligent person who loves to talk and is always learning new things. You appear conventional and serious until you relax, when you display a silly and surreal sense of humour. As a gifted communicator whose opinions carry weight, careers as varied as a minister or a political satirist are suitable. With your ready wit you attract friends of all ages and people just adore being in your company. You love playing practical jokes on friends, but can't bear to be laughed at yourself. You are very adaptable and keep up with the latest trends, especially gadgets that aid communication. Your relationships are diverse but the person who sees through your many masks and captures your heart is for keeps. Fancy dress parties allow you to indulge your fun side and entertain others.

TAROT CARD: The Empress
PLANETS: Mercury and Saturn
QUOTE: *'Acting is like lying. The art of lying well. I'm paid to tell elaborate lies.'* Mel Gibson

STRENGTHS: Great sense of humour, talented conversationalist.
WEAKNESSES: Insecure, furtive.

January 4

MEDITATION:

Beauty is truth, and truth is beauty.

You are a caring and kind person who is polite, courteous and well-mannered. You are protective and considerate of people's feelings both at home and at work. As such you are suited to being in a leadership position where taking care of others is the priority and you make an excellent parent. You are a great organizer and capable of paying thorough attention to detail. Your family is important to you and you can be faced with making a choice between home life and your career. Having a home-based business would be an ideal solution. Your relationship keeps you stable and you do need to be needed. You can suffer extreme mood swings and get caught in depression. Activities such as sailing or swimming give you the peace and connection with your inner self that are good for your mind and soul.

TAROT CARD: The Emperor
PLANETS: Moon and Saturn
QUOTE: *'Errors are not in the art but in the artificers.'* Isaac Newton

STRENGTHS: Thoughtful, solicitous.
WEAKNESSES: Temperamental, reliant on others.

January 5

You are a supremely self-confident and creative person. Your aspiration is to be at the top, and you will dedicate your life to achieving just that. There is something of the star about you and you revel in being in the spotlight. Although you work hard you also have time to laugh and play too, which endears you to others. Your enthusiasm and warm-heartedness, added to your desire to make the world a better place, make you a wonderful fundraiser for charity. You are cautious when making decisions, especially those that involve money. A weakness is that you can be too controlling and not allow others to show initiative. When you fall in love it tends to be forever and you are a loyal and passionate partner. Playing children's games is a wonderful way for you to show your silly side.

TAROT CARD: The Hierophant
PLANETS: Sun and Saturn
QUOTE: 'A dream is a scripture, and many scriptures are nothing but dreams.' Umberto Eco

STRENGTHS: Creative, warm-hearted.
WEAKNESSES: Controlling, over-cautious.

BORN ON THIS DAY:
Robert Duvall
(actor and director)
Umberto Eco
(writer)
Vinnie Jones
(soccer player and actor)
Diane Keaton
(actor, director and producer)
Marilyn Manson
(singer and musician)
Charlie Richmond
(entrepreneur)

MEDITATION:
Go confidently in the direction of your dreams.

January 6

You are a reserved and gentle person with a talent for finding the right turn of phrase. With a deep love of the spoken word you are articulate and your humour can be hilarious. You are logical and methodical, and get immense satisfaction from following routines. You make a superb editor and are constantly correcting yourself, but also correcting others. Learning to overlook people's mistakes is a life-long lesson. People respect you for your achievements and your success is built on a solid foundation of hard work. You tend to avoid risks and can't bear to make mistakes. Your relationships are enduring, but you need your partner to be youthful in outlook, or you will stray. Worrying is your weakness and aromatherapy massage is virtually essential to help you unwind.

TAROT CARD: The Lovers
PLANETS: Mercury and Saturn
QUOTE: 'I want to express myself in a different way. I have a performing inclination.' Rowan Atkinson

STRENGTHS: Very funny, expressive.
WEAKNESSES: Cautious, critical.

BORN ON THIS DAY:
Rowan Atkinson
(actor and writer)
Khalil Gibran
(poet)
Joan of Arc
(French heroine)
Nigella Lawson
(food writer and broadcaster)
Loretta Young
(actor)
Malcolm Young
(guitarist and songwriter – AC/DC)

MEDITATION:
It is hard to fail, but it is worse never to have tried to succeed.

181

January 7

You are a refined and graceful person with immense style and elegance. You are socially adept and know how to play your cards right so you succeed in business. There is a strong sense of purpose in your life – you know where you are going and work steadily to get there. You are able to surround yourself with the most influential people who can advance your career. The worlds of fashion, architecture and finance all have appeal for you. At times you plan too strategically and lack spontaneity. You want people to like you, so you find it hard to say no, which can get you into trouble. You are an appreciative lover and a delightful companion. You can be combative under your peaceful exterior, so sports such as rally driving or fencing are immensely satisfying.

BORN ON THIS DAY:
Nicolas Cage
(actor)
Gerald Durrell
(naturalist)
Johann Christian Fabricius
(zoologist)
Lewis Hamilton
(champion F1 racing driver)
Butterfly McQueen
(actor)
John E. Walker
(chemist, Nobel Prize laureate)

MEDITATION:
Well done is better than well said.

TAROT CARD: The Chariot
PLANETS: Venus and Saturn
QUOTE: *'Shock is still fun. I won't ever shut the door on it.'* Nicolas Cage

STRENGTHS: Graceful, driven.
WEAKNESSES: Calculating, inability to say no.

January 8

You are a sensual and magnetic person with a powerful presence. With your penetrating mind and high intelligence you work effectively and laboriously to succeed in the commercial world. Money and the ease of mind it gives you, is all-important. As a result of your success you can become suspicious of others' motives. You have a strength of character that helps you get through the tough times in your life. Although you are emotionally reserved you have enormous compassion for your fellow man, and you are well qualified to work on regeneration projects. When stressed you can become bogged down in pessimism. A solid relationship gives you much-needed emotional security and you are fiercely protective of your family. A frivolous night out with your friends is a great way to let your hair down.

BORN ON THIS DAY:
Dame Shirley Bassey
(singer)
David Bowie
(musician)
Graham Chapman
(comedian)
William Hartnell
(actor)
Steven Hawking
(theoretical physicist and writer)
Elvis Presley
(singer and actor)

MEDITATION:
If the world seems cold to you, kindle fires to warm it.

TAROT CARD: Strength
PLANETS: Pluto and Saturn
QUOTE: *'Ambition is a dream with a V8 engine.'* Elvis Presley

STRENGTHS: Passionate, bright.
WEAKNESSES: Distrustful, cynical.

January 9

You are a buoyant and optimistic person who can also be deadly serious; a combination that is disarming and enigmatic. You love being in a position of writerity, are extremely ambitious and enjoy getting older as people treat you with more respect. You are open-minded, love exploring fresh fields and expanding your circle of influence, often travelling overseas with your work. Since knowledge is so important to you, your ideal role is that of mentor or educator. The legal profession, or even the constantly evolving world of the internet, may also beckon. Ever restless and needing constant change and stimulus, it's not easy for you to settle down with just one person or career. You are a charming lover, easy-going and fun to be with. As you love one-to-one combat, a game of snooker or squash is your ideal workout.

TAROT CARD: The Hermit
PLANETS: Jupiter and Saturn
QUOTE: *'If a thing is worth doing, it is worth doing slowly… very slowly.'* Gypsy Rose Lee

STRENGTHS: Liberal, optimistic.
WEAKNESSES: Determined, unsettled.

BORN ON THIS DAY:
Simone de Beauvoir
(writer and philosopher)
Gypsy Rose Lee
(entertainer)
Richard Nixon
(president of the United States)
Paolo Nutini
(singer/songwriter and guitarist)
Jimmy Page
(musician and producer)
Imelda Staunton
(actor)

MEDITATION:
You gain strength, courage and confidence with every experience.

January 10

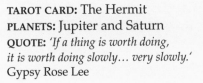

You are a conscientious and caring person who is a true professional. A superb planner and indefatigable worker, you usually achieve success early in life. One problem is that you tend to take on too much and suffer from the weight of competing demands on your time. Learning to trust and delegate is a big lesson for you. You love anything classic, well-made and stylish and architecture, furniture design and antiques are all areas of interest to you. In relationships you tend to hold back until you're 100 per cent sure, then you commit wholeheartedly. You're the one in charge and will do everything in your power to protect your loved ones. Behind the scenes you reveal your sensuality and often bawdy sense of humour. A good belly laugh does you the world of good.

TAROT CARD: The Wheel of Fortune
PLANETS: Saturn and Saturn
QUOTE: *'I wish I knew what I know now before.'* Rod Stewart

STRENGTHS: Diligent, protective.
WEAKNESSES: Prone to stress, unable to delegate.

BORN ON THIS DAY:
Annete von Droste
(poet)
George Foreman
(champion boxer)
Barbara Hepworth
(sculptor)
Frank Sinatra Jr
(singer/songwriter)
Rod Stewart
(singer/songwriter and musician)
Robert Woodrow Wilson
(astronomer)

MEDITATION:
In love beggar and king are equal.

January 11

MEDITATION:

*Wisdom is the sharing of
wise experiences and
knowledge.*

You are a friendly and sociable person who is also self-contained and independent. You have a logical mind and a clear perception of events; you can be very objective about things. You are a gifted organizer and forward planner and you have a love of order, but also of change. Ideally you can bridge the old with the new but at times you struggle when you have to choose between tradition and innovation. You need to be in control, to be the authority and can dig your heels in if someone challenges you. This attitude comes from deeper feelings of insecurity which you tend to cover up. You are attracted to unusual types, and your relationships tend to be unconventional, though a part of you yearns for security. Being out in the fresh air suits you, so take time off walking in wide open spaces.

TAROT CARD: Justice
PLANETS: Uranus and Saturn
QUOTE: *'There are many paths, but only one journey.'* Naomi Judd

STRENGTHS: Cordial, independent.
WEAKNESSES: Controlling, self-conscious.

January 12

MEDITATION:

*The only way to retain love
is to give it away.*

You are a dreamy and sensitive person who also desires material success. Outwardly you come across as business-like and professional, in control of your emotions, but scratch the surface and you are a real softy. Artistic and prepared to work long and hard, you can establish an excellent career for yourself in theatre, art or creative writing. Your sensitivity also makes you a compassionate counsellor as you are willing to help people on a practical level. Your weakness is that you can take on others' emotional burdens and then lose confidence in yourself. In love you are tender-hearted and devoted to your beloved. However, you can become very needy and dependent. Singing opens your heart, and an evening at a karaoke bar is terrific fun for you and allows you to gain confidence in yourself.

TAROT CARD: The Hanged Man
PLANETS: Neptune and Saturn
QUOTE: *'Education is dangerous – every educated person is a future enemy.'* Hermann Goering

STRENGTHS: Creative, considerate.
WEAKNESSES: Lacking in confidence, insecure.

January 13

You are a tough yet tender person with a practical, no-nonsense approach to life. You are in touch with your emotions and self-aware, and enjoy spending a great deal of time alone. Some might say you are too self-absorbed. Looking good and feeling good are important to you as you are not overly robust. You have a close relationship with your family and often keep in contact with childhood friends. Work is important and you take pride in maintaining a high standard in all that you do. You are happiest working in established companies. You get the best from people as you truly listen to them and empathize. In relationships you are often attracted to an older partner. You will commit early as you need to find your 'other half'. Time spent in nature, especially in forests, really boosts your energy.

TAROT CARD: Death
PLANETS: Moon and Saturn
QUOTE: *'Failure is simply the non-presence of success.'* Orlando Bloom

STRENGTHS: Confident, compassionate.
WEAKNESSES: An introvert, slightly egocentric.

BORN ON THIS DAY:
Orlando Bloom
(actor)
Patrick Dempsey
(actor)
Jan van Goyen
(artist)
Ian Hendry
(actor)
John McNaughton
(film director)
Sophie Tucker
(singer)

MEDITATION:
Life is an adventure – dare it.

January 14

You are a vibrant and forceful person whose warmth and radiance is felt by all who meet you. A natural leader, you are cut out for high-flying business roles. You are a polished professional and had big plans for success from an early age. As you are ambitious, you are happiest when juggling a variety of responsibilities. Your reputation matters to you and you take care to keep your personal life private. Although you appear supremely confident there is a always a voice of self-doubt inside. At times you can come across as vain and self-centred, but people forgive you since you really do know how to show the way and have fun. A naturally amorous and expressive lover, you devote yourself to your partner and family. Charades is a great game for you and your friends.

TAROT CARD: Temperance
PLANETS: Sun and Saturn
QUOTE: *'You are an athlete when you're onstage. You can't get tired.'* Faye Dunaway

STRENGTHS: Animated, competent.
WEAKNESSES: Arrogant, sanctimonious.

BORN ON THIS DAY:
Sir Cecil Beaton
(photographer)
Richard Briers
(actor)
Faye Dunaway
(actor)
Dave Grohl
(musician, singer/songwriter – Foo Fighters)
Jack Jones
(singer and actor)
Berthe Morisot
(artist)

MEDITATION:
The wisest mind has something yet to learn.

January 15

You are a deeply caring person with a strong work ethic. You work tirelessly on behalf of others, wanting to serve and help them in a practical way. With a clear, logical mind, your communication skills are superb, and you consider precisely what you want to say. It is rare that you get caught off guard. You make a brilliant orator and writer especially on subjects involving a lot of research. When upset you can be cranky and over-fastidious. A serious student, you love learning and do so all your life. You choose friends carefully and they get to know the softer, more sentimental side of you. In relationships you are at first cool and emotionally reserved; once you feel safe you become a thoughtful and romantic lover. Pruning the garden is an ideal way to unwind.

TAROT CARD: The Devil
PLANETS: Mercury and Saturn
QUOTE: *'A man who won't die for something is not fit to live.'* Martin Luther King, Jr

STRENGTHS: Logical mind, brilliant orator.
WEAKNESSES: Over-serious, fussy.

BORN ON THIS DAY:
Lloyd Bridges
(actor)
Martin Luther King, Jr
(civil rights leader)
Molière
(playwright)
James Nesbitt
(actor)
Ivor Novello
(entertainer)
Aristotle Onassis
(shipping magnate)

MEDITATION:
Motivation determines what you do.

January 16

You are a popular and socially aware person with an alluring aura. You mix in influential circles and have many friends in high places. A canny business mind, combined with a dry wit, gives you an advantage in the world of commerce. Immensely stylish, you dress well with a chic, understated look, and you apply your good taste to everything you own. Interior design and fashion are just two possible careers. You are intensely pragmatic, but can sometimes get trapped in negative thinking and become cynical. Partnership is essential for you, whether personal or business, as you need someone to bounce ideas off. A born romantic, you court your lover and take great pleasure in buying them gifts. An art exhibition is the perfect romantic and cultural experience for you.

TAROT CARD: The Tower
PLANETS: Venus and Saturn
QUOTE: *'Ambition, if it feeds at all, does so on the ambition of others.'* Susan Sontag

STRENGTHS: Elegant, beguiling.
WEAKNESSES: Contrary, sceptical.

BORN ON THIS DAY:
John Carpenter
(film director)
James May
(TV personality)
Andre Michelin
(co-founder of Michelin Tyre Company)
Kate Moss
(supermodel)
Susan Sontag
(writer)

MEDITATION:
Problems are only opportunities with thorns on them.

186

January 17

You are an enigmatic and passionately dedicated person with a tough inner core. Tenacious and ambitious, you apply yourself to your career and will sacrifice personal pleasures to attain your goals. Keen to understand yourself and human emotions, you are attracted to the fields of psychology and psychiatry. In your youth you can be self-conscious and shy, but as you get older you become more self-assured and confident. You are a trustworthy and loyal friend and have a wicked sense of humour. You live by a high moral code and can impose your standards on others, demanding that they behave in a certain way. In relationship you need a faithful partner as you can be jealous and possessive. To keep your marriage alive, an expensive dinner and a night out at a hotel with your beloved has the thrill you seek.

TAROT CARD: The Star
PLANETS: Pluto and Saturn
QUOTE: *'A man wrapped up in himself makes a very small bundle.'*
Benjamin Franklin

STRENGTHS: Mysterious, comical.
WEAKNESSES: Moralistic, with a jealous streak.

BORN ON THIS DAY:
Anne Brontë
(writer)
Al Capone
(American gangster)
Jim Carrey
(actor and comedian)
Benjamin Franklin
(founding Father of the United States)
Muhammad Ali
(champion boxer)
Michelle Obama
(First Lady of the United States)

MEDITATION:
Great effort springs naturally from a great attitude.

January 18

You are a big-hearted, extravagant and hard-working person. A builder and adventurer, you are on a quest to discover yourself and the world. You never cease from garnering knowledge and distilling it into your own unique brand of wisdom. Not suited to be an underling, you thrive when self-employed. A shrewd gambler, your intuition is strong, so you make calculated risks and solid investments. Your business interests are varied and could encompass a travel company, horse riding school, or running a casino. A problem you have is wasting nervous energy, always seeking new ventures. Love affairs are many; it's later in life that you settle down with your intellectual equal. You are a generous partner and shower your lover with gifts. A sporty type, you love being outdoors, so soccer or rowing is excellent.

TAROT CARD: The Moon
PLANETS: Jupiter and Saturn
QUOTE: *'Beware of snobbery; it is the unwelcome recognition of one's own past failings.'* Cary Grant

STRENGTHS: Intuitive, benevolent.
WEAKNESSES: Tendency to overwork, restless.

BORN ON THIS DAY:
Raymond Briggs
(writer and illustrator)
Kevin Costner
(actor)
Manuel Garcia
(matador)
Cary Grant
(actor)
Oliver Hardy
(actor)
A.A Milne
(writer)

MEDITATION:
You can do it if you believe you can.

187

January 19

MEDITATION:

The more alternatives, the more difficult the choice.

You are a helpful and trustworthy person that others depend upon. Intensely ambitious, you make a sure and steady climb to the top. Always working, you need material security and recognition for your accomplishments. Status really matters to you. There are times when you can get overwhelmed with the monumental tasks you have set yourself, so it is vital to make time to be with friends into your busy schedule. Remember, it can be lonely at the top. A lover of tradition, you have a strong set of values and marriage suits you. Your partner gives you much-needed balance and you are attracted to an emotional person who just adores you. You maintain a well-organized household and strive to ensure that everyone feels secure. Letting your hair down with some light-hearted fun will lighten your load.

TAROT CARD: The Sun
PLANETS: Saturn and Saturn
QUOTE: *'All that we see or seem is but a dream within a dream.'* Edgar Allan Poe

STRENGTHS: Reliable, determined.
WEAKNESSES: Tendency to overwork, uptight.

TYPICAL CAPRICORN:
JENSON BUTTON

'When it comes to my racing career I'm very driven and very selfish. People who are around me at races will know that I'm a different person here (at the circuit) than in my personal life. I completely blank people at races. I need to be focussed. I'm rude.'

CAPRICORN TRAITS:
It is not easy to get close to a Capricorn man, as he builds up an exterior barrier which is difficult to breach. He has fierce ambitions and determination, which he will pursue with a strong resolve. He prefers intimate dinners to large parties, as underneath the exterior he is shy and unable to express his feelings openly.

January 20

You are a practical and peaceful person with good old-fashioned traditional values. You are patient and well-disciplined and always stay the course. Physically and emotionally you improve with age and assume the role of the elder with immense style and grace. You work hard to achieve material success as it buys you the home and the security you need. It often takes early success, however, to give you the self-confidence to meet challenges. Your weakness is that you can be too possessive of things and people and become reliant on the same familiar routines. You are a trustworthy and generous friend and love to invite people over for dinner parties. Your relationship means a great deal to you and you tend to meet your life partner at an early age. A treat that helps loosen you up is an aromatherapy massage, worth every penny.

TAROT CARD: Judgement
PLANETS: Venus and Saturn
QUOTE: *'Mars is there, waiting to be reached.'* Buzz Aldrin

STRENGTHS: Dependable, calm.
WEAKNESSES: Controlling, afraid of change.

BORN ON THIS DAY:
Buzz Aldrin
(astronaut)
George Burns
(entertainer)
Federico Fellini
(filmmaker)
Stonewall Jackson
(US military)
David Lynch
(director and screenwriter)
Aristotle Onassis
(shipping tycoon)

MEDITATION:
You are the master of your fate; you are the captain of your soul.

TYPICAL CAPRICORN:
FAYE DUNAWAY

'Softness and femininity like yours, people don't expect of me; so when they find me emotional and capable of real vulnerability, they're surprised.'

CAPRICORN TRAITS:
A Capricorn woman can enjoy the role of wife or mother as much as that of company director, but they will demand the same respect and security. Whatever her appearance on the outside, whether she is a supermodel or a scientist trying to save mankind, inside is a woman looking for security, writerity and respect. The Capricorn woman seeks recognition above all else, and it doesn't seem to matter how she gets it.

Aquarius

January 21–February 19

THE STAR.

TAROT CARD: The Star

ELEMENT: Air

QUALITY: Fixed

NUMBER: 11

RULING PLANET: Uranus

GEMSTONES: Traditional blue sapphire and lapis lazuli

COLOURS: Turquoise

DAY OF THE WEEK: Saturday

COMPATIBLE SIGNS: Aries, Gemini, Libra, Sagittarius

KEY WORDS: Gregarious and social, humanitarian, idealistic, inventive, innovative, genius, cool, aloof, zany impractical schemes, fixed ideas

ANATOMY: Calves, ankles and the circulatory system

HERBS, PLANTS AND TREES: Solomon's seal, orchid, fruit trees, elderberry, olive

KEY PHRASE:
I invent

Aquarius is the idealist and humanitarian of the zodiac. It governs the calves and ankles and the circulatory system, which can leave those born under this sign prone to problems such as cramps. The symbol of Aquarius is the water-bearer and the glyph looks like radio or air waves. It marks the time of year when the days are getting longer and, in many parts of the world, the rains begin. It is the 11th sign of the zodiac, when the energy is outgoing and universal. Aquarius is the inventor and rebel of the zodiac.

PLANETARY RULER AND QUALITIES
Aquarius is a fixed air sign. As the last air sign it wants to communicate to the world and Aquarians love the internet. Aquarius is governed by both Saturn and, more recently, Uranus and as a consequence there are two types of Aquarians. Those who are more Saturnian are traditionalists and love law and order. The Uranian types are eccentric and unconventional.

Uranus was discovered in 1777, at the time of the French Revolution, The American War of Independence and the Industrial Revolution in Great Britain. The phrase of the revolution – 'liberty, equality, fraternity' – is highly relevant to this sign.

Uranus is an extremely bizarre planet. It takes 84 years to orbit and is tilted at a very odd angle. It is said that at the ages of 21, 42, 63 and 84 we have the urges to start anew, to break free of restriction and shock convention.

RELATIONSHIPS
Aquarians have lots of friends and like to hang out with groups of people. You are naturally friendly but can appear cool in your more intimate relationships.

The male can be quite whacky and non-conformist. The female can appear beautiful yet distant – a typical ice queen. An Aquarian never follows the crowd, and your relationships are often unconventional. You need freedom and space. Long-distance relationships can work for you. You need to be mentally stimulated by your partners so Gemini and Libra suit you well. You are intrigued by Scorpio's depth but can be put off by its emotional intensity. Best friends are Sagittarians and fellow Aquarians.

CONSTELLATION AND MYTH
Aquarius is the constellation of the water bearer and Aquarian myths are concerned with great floods. The Greeks associated Aquarius with Ganymede, the beautiful Trojan

boy who was the cup-bearer of the Gods. In this cup was ambrosia, the nectar of immortality, so Aquarius is connected with the concept of a divine substance which nourishes all life – a life-giving drink.

Aquarius also connects to the myth of Prometheus who stole fire to give to mankind and was punished by the gods. Prometheus displays the rebel aspect of Aquarius.

STRENGTHS AND WEAKNESSES

Aquarians are idealists, seeking the best for humanity, and you have an ability to remain detached and see life from a higher perspective. You search for universal truths, and you are highly original, progressive and willing to experiment. You also have a keen intellect, are faithful and loyal to friends and marvellous at doing a good turn. You have a reforming spirit.

Your weaknesses are that you can be contrary and unpredictable. You often fail to understand why others are so emotional. You can sometimes get stuck in the past and are also prone to have fixed opinions.

TYPICAL AQUARIUS:
PAUL NEWMAN
'You only grow when you are alone.'

AQUARIUS POWERS: An eclectic way of seeing things.

AQUARIUS NEGATIVES: A know-it-all attitude tends to put others off.

January 21

You are a bright and breezy person with a cheerful manner. A brilliant communicator, you are the archetypal traveller on the super-highway that is the internet. Science and computers play an important role in your life and you could be a journalist or work in advertising, as the media invigorates you. A natural mimic, you are witty and great fun to be around so you have a large, ever-changing group of friends. Incredibly restless, your weakness is spreading yourself too thin, always jumping from one new idea to the next and never focussing. In relationships you are easy-going and view your partner as your best friend. They need to be a down-to-earth type who helps keep your feet on the ground. Talking a lot tires you, so chill out with some soothing meditation music.

BORN ON THIS DAY:
Emma Bunton
(singer/songwriter – Spice Girls)
Christian Dior
(fashion designer)
Geena Davis
(actor)
Placido Domingo
(singer)
Jill Eikenberry
(actor)
Jack Nicklaus
(professional golfer)

MEDITATION:
*Teach love to those
who hate.*

TAROT CARD: The World
PLANETS: Mercury and Uranus
QUOTE: *'A woman's perfume tells more about her than her handwriting.'* Christian Dior

STRENGTHS: Scintillating, conversationalist.
WEAKNESSES: Agitated and, at times, tense.

January 22

You are a sensitive and helpful person with a keen intelligence. You are totally devoted to the truth and to helping people have a better life. Eccentric and unorthodox in your approach, you are essentially well meaning. Being self-employed suits you best, although you are attracted to being part of a small team and social work has enormous appeal. Working for a charity is ideal as long as you are allowed a lot of freedom to implement your original ideas. In personal relationships you can be cool and detached on the outside, but underneath your heart is soft and tender. Emotionally you can suddenly cut off and your partner needs to shower you with affection without being clingy, which takes some skill! Flower remedies are very helpful for you to relax and get in touch with hidden feelings.

BORN ON THIS DAY:
Linda Blair
(actor)
George Gordon, Lord Byron
(poet)
John Hurt
(actor)
Michael Hutchence
(singer/songwriter – INXS)
Piper Laurie
(actor)
Rasputin
(monk and mystic)

MEDITATION:
*Keep your heart open
to dreams.*

TAROT CARD: The Emperor
PLANETS: Moon and Uranus
QUOTE: *'Always laugh when you can. It is cheap medicine.'* Lord Byron

STRENGTHS: Accommodating, soft-hearted.
WEAKNESSES: Aloof, restless.

January 23

You are a flamboyant and creative person who is sincere and honest. You are naturally generous and extremely chivalrous. A born idealist, you are attracted to campaign for social reform. With a regal and dignified manner, you appear to have innate confidence. However, that is not always true as there are times when you lack assertiveness and if you are not in the leadership position you can get very downhearted. Although you can be arrogant at times your need for affection and admiration makes you vulnerable and very lovable. When you're in love – which is frequently – you shine as romance is second nature to you. However, you can get over-dramatic and sabotage a good relationship because it isn't exciting enough. A thrilling sport such as skiing or snowboarding will lift you out of negative moods.

TAROT CARD: The Hierophant
PLANETS: Sun and Uranus
QUOTE: *'Things are never so bad they can't be made worse.'* Humphrey Bogart

STRENGTHS: Artistic, valiant.
WEAKNESSES: Self-doubting, self-important.

BORN ON THIS DAY:
Humphrey Bogart
(actor)
John Browning
(inventor)
Edouard Manet
(artist)
Princess Caroline of Monaco
(daughter of Prince Rainier)
Tiffani Thiessen
(actor)
Louis Zukofsky
(poet)

MEDITATION:
Begin with the end in mind.

January 24

You are a methodical and industrious person with great capacity for research. With an excellent systematic mind, analysing and synthesizing is what you do best. You have the abilities necessary to be a graphic designer or an astrologer. The mind/body connection fascinates you, and health and healing play an important role in your life, either through personal ill health or the desire to help others. Working in alternative medicine also attracts you. You can be rather clinical at times and people can feel as though you are scrutinizing them too closely. In relationships you are friendly and affectionate, but need a passionate partner to set you on fire and bring you out of yourself. You can get lethargic, so a trip to a theme park, with all the thrills of the roller coaster, will infuse you with physical energy.

TAROT CARD: The Lovers
PLANETS: Mercury and Uranus
QUOTE: *'A little disdain is not amiss; a little scorn is alluring.'* William Congreve

STRENGTHS: Curative abilities, investigative mind.
WEAKNESSES: Lethargic, dispassionate.

BORN ON THIS DAY:
John Belushi
(actor and comedian)
Ernest Borgnine
(actor)
William Congreve
(playwright and poet)
Neil Diamond
(singer/songwriter)
Adrian Edmonson
(comedian)
Jools Holland
(musician, band leader and TV presenter)

MEDITATION:
Know yourself and you will win all battles.

193

January 25

MEDITATION:

*He who angers you
conquers you.*

You are an intellectual and affable person who is artistic and a natural peacemaker. A great observer of people, you are a talented writer and love mixing in literary circles. Dreamy and introspective, you have a magnetism and charm about you. You have a sympathetic nature, are well liked and have a wide circle of friends. At times people aren't sure of your intentions, as you don't like offending anyone, so you will sit on the fence rather than taking sides. Indecision is your bugbear. Your gracious manners make you superb at public relations and you are a naturally good host. In relationships you tend not to communicate your feelings and the best partner for you is a fiery or water type who helps you explore deep emotions. Pilates is a form of exercise which focusses you on your body and would help ground you.

TAROT CARD: The Chariot
PLANETS: Venus and Uranus
QUOTE: *'People ask for criticism, but they only want praise.'* W. Somerset Maugham

STRENGTHS: Compassionate, charming.
WEAKNESSES: Indecisive, muddle-headed.

January 26

MEDITATION:

*Happiness is the sense that
one matters.*

You are a powerful and magnetic person with an almost hypnotic quality about you. Extraordinarily charismatic, you are someone that people do not forget easily. You are dedicated to excelling at whatever you do and have amazing stamina. Once committed, you never give up on a project. You pride yourself on doing a thorough job and set high standards. You excel at business, are a brilliant entrepreneur and are not fazed at handling large amounts of money. Your weakness is jealousy, which comes from a sense of insecurity when young. A committed relationship is the making of you, as you allow yourself to be vulnerable you become more open and loveable. You love the dark and the eclectic, so a rock concert or a jazz club are natural places for you to hang out and enjoy yourself.

TAROT CARD: Strength
PLANETS: Pluto and Uranus
QUOTE: *'I never take anything for granted. I may slip any minute.'* Eartha Kitt

STRENGTHS: Alluring, staying power.
WEAKNESSES: Jealous, perfectionist.

January 27

You are an adventurous and daring person with a pioneering spirit. Highly independent, you do your own thing with considerable originality and self-confidence. Your bold, adventurous spirit is much admired by more timid souls. However, you can charge ahead in your enthusiasm and lack sensitivity to see that you may be treading on others' toes. Your life can evolve in a way that inspires others. A superb teacher, explorer, film or theatre director, your career choices are many and varied. A rolling stone, you have a problem settling down and in your intimate relationships you need a great deal of freedom. Daring sports where you feel challenged are vital if you are at all restricted in your daily life. Hang gliding, skiing or jumping from a plane are just a few you might try.

TAROT CARD: The Hermit
PLANETS: Jupiter and Uranus
QUOTE: *Everything's got a moral, if only you can find it.'* Lewis Carroll

STRENGTHS: Adventurous, original.
WEAKNESSES: Unsettled, insensitive.

BORN ON THIS DAY:
Mohammed Al-Fayed
(entrepreneur)
Mikhail Baryshnikov
(dancer and actor)
Lewis Carroll
(writer)
Bridget Fonda
(actor)
Wolfgang Amadeus Mozart
(composer)
Kaiser Wilhelm
(German emperor)

MEDITATION:
He who fears being conquered is sure of defeat.

January 28

You are an ambitious, hard-working person who has lofty ideals and a desire to make the world a better place. You're a rugged individualist who also has a deep sense of honour and is highly principled. People respect your authority as you communicate well and treat them as your equal. You are broad-minded and although you are generally law-abiding, there is a part of you that rebels and may suddenly act irrationally. Breaking the rules in this way can get you into a lot of trouble. Your creativity is extraordinary and you will spend long hours perfecting your skills. A committed relationship with someone you adore will bring you deep joy. You need to take time out to exercise as you can have problems with stiffness in the joints. Yoga, which increases your flexibility, is ideal.

TAROT CARD: The Wheel of Fortune
PLANETS: Saturn and Uranus
QUOTE: *'Be as smart as you can, but remember that it is always better to be wise than to be smart.'* Alan Alda

STRENGTHS: Highly principled, creative.
WEAKNESSES: Workaholic, rebellious.

BORN ON THIS DAY:
Alan Alda
(actor, director and screenwriter)
Colette
(writer)
Jackson Pollock
(artist)
Nicolas Sarkozy
(French president)
Dick Taylor
(bassist)
Elijah Wood
(actor)

MEDITATION:
Laugh at yourself first, before anyone else can.

195

January 29

MEDITATION:

We must never cease from exploration.

You are a clear-headed, logical person with a passion for changing the world. You value the truth above all things and are not afraid of talking about subjects that others find shocking. You are the revolutionary or campaigner whose objective is not to fight, but to persuade others to come round to your point of view. You can be a law unto yourself and incredibly stubborn if people try to force you to do anything against your will. Friends really matter and you love being in groups. You are of a scientific and intellectual bent so you tend to gravitate toward careers where your mind is fully engaged. Intimate relationships are your weakness as it isn't easy for you to connect with deep emotions. A fiery partner can get through your defences and humour always works. A rhythmic exercise like jogging is great for you.

TAROT CARD: Justice
PLANETS: Uranus and Uranus
QUOTE: *'Freud is the father of psychoanalysis. It has no mother.'* Germaine Greer

STRENGTHS: Judicious, peaceful revolutionary.
WEAKNESSES: Fear of intimacy, bull-headed.

January 30

MEDITATION:

Reason and judgement are the qualities of a leader.

You are a gifted communicator and ever-changing person whose intelligence borders on genius. Extremely agile in your thought processes, you pick up new ideas and make connections immediately. You love words and have an extensive vocabulary, so work as a copywriter, playwright or songwriter suits you well. You are an idealist and have a social conscience, so as you mature you feel the need to be useful rather than squander your energy on trivial things. Relationships are your lifeblood as you are essentially a people person. However, intimacy can be uncomfortable as you feel out of your depth when it comes to emotions. Communicating from your heart rather than your head is a life-long lesson. Yoga is a great way to help you tune into, and become aware of, your body.

TAROT CARD: The Empress
PLANETS: Mercury and Uranus
QUOTE: *'Ask the right questions if you're to find the right answers.'* Vanessa Redgrave

STRENGTHS: Clever, a quick thinker.
WEAKNESSES: Scared of deep emotions, a fantasist.

January 31

You are a popular and intelligent person who is both kind and supportive. Very much your own person, you won't follow the rules. You do things differently and can come up with amazingly creative solutions. With a cool exterior, underneath you are warm and caring, and need to feel that what you accomplish has true value. Owning or managing a restaurant or hotel appeals to you as you enjoy nurturing people and giving them an experience they will remember. Your originality needs channelling into something productive or else you switch off and let your moods get the better of you. A childhood sweetheart can be your soulmate as you need a true friend and someone who connects you to your roots. Taking care of yourself by balancing your erratic emotions with acupuncture or homeopathy is a priority.

TAROT CARD: The Emperor
PLANETS: Moon and Uranus
QUOTE: *'I was equally in love with singing and acting from an early age.'* Minnie Driver

STRENGTHS: Individual, popular.
WEAKNESSES: Moody, emotionally erratic.

BORN ON THIS DAY:
Minnie Driver
(actor)
Zane Grey
(writer)
Derek Jarman
(film director)
Norman Mailer
(writer)
Franz Schubert
(composer)
Justin Timberlake
(singer/songwriter, dancer and record producer)

MEDITATION:
Dream the impossible dream.

February 1

You are a frank and outspoken person with radical views of how the world can be put to rights. Your intellect is sharp and you are quick to react to hypocrisy, often through the use of humour. You adore poking fun at the establishment and bureaucracy. You can motivate people into action, so politics, with the cut and thrust of debate, is the perfect arena for your talents. A good friend and neighbour, you are the ideal spokesperson for a group. You make friends easily, but because you have so many it is difficult to have a close relationship with anyone in particular. Intimate relationships are not easy as you love freedom and need to be able to do your own thing. You can be highly strung and get burnt out so an exercise like t'ai chi, which uses your body but stills the mind, is beneficial for you.

TAROT CARD: The Magician
PLANETS: Mars and Uranus
QUOTE: *'A wise man will make more opportunities than he finds.'* Francis Bacon

STRENGTHS: Witty, excellent orator.
WEAKNESSES: Insensitive, edgy.

BORN ON THIS DAY:
Sir Francis Bacon
(statesman and writer)
Clark Gable
(actor)
Terry Jones
(actor and writer)
Brandon Lee
(actor)
Lisa Marie Presley
(singer and actor)
Boris Yeltsin
(first Russian president)

MEDITATION:
Challenges are what make life interesting.

197

February 2

MEDITATION:

Courage faces fear and thereby masters it.

You are a sensual and kind-hearted person with a large dose of originality. You need the comforts of a solid home base and financial security, and work hard to acquire them. You are confident in your abilities and have a high opinion of yourself. This propels you into a position of leadership as you have progressive ideas combined with a practical realism. Some people envy this and find you smug and self-satisfied. However, you enjoy being yourself and tend to ignore what others think of you. Your love life is based on friendship and you need a partner who you respect intellectually. Once you settle down, you are devoted and extremely affectionate and tactile. Bodywork is good for you as you can get sluggish and lethargic; shiatsu or deep tissue massage are ideal.

TAROT CARD: The High Priestess
PLANETS: Venus and Uranus
QUOTE: *'A man's errors are his portals of discovery.'* James Joyce

STRENGTHS: Confident, kind-hearted.
WEAKNESSES: Smug, self-centred.

February 3

MEDITATION:

Learn to smile at every situation.

You are a friendly and light-hearted person with a quick and agile mind. Intensely curious, you love the hustle and bustle of city life. You thrive on the stimulus of meeting new people and exchanging ideas. With a clear, logical mind and honest and reasonable approach, you inspire confidence in others. You are a great negotiator, as you are able to see things from a higher perspective. Public relations, journalism and advertising are all suitable careers. However, you are an ideas person and need others to handle the practical details. Easily bored, you are always moving on to the next challenge. Your relationships can be very cerebral, so learning about emotional intelligence would be highly beneficial for you. Turning off the computer in the evening is crucial if you want your mind to relax.

TAROT CARD: The Empress
PLANETS: Mercury and Uranus
QUOTE: *'It is not easy to be a pioneer – but oh, it is fascinating!'* Elizabeth Blackwell

STRENGTHS: Light-hearted, logical.
WEAKNESSES: Easily bored, uncomfortable with emotions.

February 4

You are an altruistic and thoughtful person with a strong urge to change things for the better. You're the campaigner who firmly, and with clear expression, voices what others can't or won't say. Working for an aid organization or a charity is ideal for you. Deeply connected to your early home life, your own personal story is the basis for your idealism and shows your ability to share yourself with others. Your weakness is a tendency to sulk or use tears to get your own way. A relationship which provides warmth and a sense of security – yet also allows you room to express your individuality – is the solution. You love kitchen gadgets and experimenting with exotic styles of cooking, which is a delightful way for you to find contentment and peace within.

TAROT CARD: The Emperor
PLANETS: Moon and Uranus
QUOTE: *'I realized that if I had to choose, I would rather have birds than airplanes.'* Charles Lindbergh

STRENGTHS: Charitable, supportive.
WEAKNESSES: Sulky, insincere sorrow.

MEDITATION:
In the middle of difficulty lies opportunity.

February 5

You are an inspired person with the potential to be a creative genius. You are a visionary who takes on new ideas enthusiastically and can be an accomplished inventor. With a strong sense of individuality, you need to express your uniqueness through creative work. Never the shrinking violet, you naturally take the lead. An important aspect of your drive to succeed is to see your name 'up in lights'. Acting, whether professionally, or as an amateur, is very fulfilling for you as you need to feel feted by others. However, you can be vain and take great offence if people ignore you. Love plays a large part in your life and you always believe the best of your partners. This can lead to you being deeply disappointed, so you rely heavily on your friends to console you. Channel your heartbreak into creativity; it will reward you.

TAROT CARD: The Hierophant
PLANETS: Sun and Uranus
QUOTE: *'Be just and if you can't be just, be arbitrary.'* William S. Burroughs

STRENGTHS: Natural leader, originality.
WEAKNESSES: Vanity, hatred of being ignored.

MEDITATION:
Vanity is the quicksand of reason.

February 6

MEDITATION:
Live – because life is everything.

You are a kind and thoughtful person with a love of organizing. You aim to be useful and are a humanitarian at heart, so healthcare is a good industry for you. Always finding new methods and systems to make life easier, you are excellent at office or hospital administration. You love the efficiency of computers and will be up to date with the latest technology. Perfectionism is your weakness as your standards are so high. A bit of a paradox, you can be very gregarious and also at times a loner. In relationships you are an affectionate and gentle lover, and you need someone who tenderly encourages you to explore your sensual nature. Getting messy is so contrary to your nature that it is actually a great way for you to release your inhibitions. Mud wrestling may be a stretch too far, but you get the idea!

TAROT CARD: The Lovers
PLANETS: Mercury and Uranus
QUOTE: *'Every man gotta right to decide his own destiny.'* Bob Marley

STRENGTHS: Thoughtful lover, efficient.
WEAKNESSES: Introverted, an idealist.

February 7

MEDITATION:
Remember to take one day at a time.

You are a stylish and eccentric person who enjoys a rich social life. People-watching and chatting with friends are your favourite pastimes. A lover of beauty, you are superbly suited to working in the arts or the fashion industry. With a gift for mimicry and a cosmopolitan sense of humour, you can shock others, but in the best possible way, with no intention of hurting them. You are an innovator and part of the avant garde set. If people take advantage of your good nature and kindness you can be quite forthright in stepping away from your involvement. A born lover, relationships are the breath of life for you. However, you can over-intellectualize your partner and neglect to connect with them emotionally. You often stay up late socializing with friends, so need some quiet time at home relaxing, listening to music or reading.

TAROT CARD: The Chariot
PLANETS: Venus and Uranus
QUOTE: *'A day wasted on others is not wasted on one's self.'* Charles Dickens

STRENGTHS: Stylish, sociable.
WEAKNESSES: Intellectually superior, emotionally inept.

February 8

You are an intense and brooding person with a sense of mystery about you. Your enigmatic personality is compelling and draws people to you. As a tremendous actor, or working in business, your strong will and confidence in your abilities commands respect and admiration. People can even be overwhelmed, and view you with a sense of awe. On the downside, you are capable of using your powers to gain advantage over others and may be ruthless in your desire for success. You also have a tendency to seek more freedom than is realistic. In a committed relationship your sensuality and passion can be expressed as long as you choose a partner who understands your complexity. Exploring caves or going on a murder mystery weekend are the kinds of activities that turn you on.

TAROT CARD: Strength
PLANETS: Pluto and Uranus
QUOTE: *'Art is not a study of positive reality, it is the seeking for ideal truth.'* John Ruskin

STRENGTHS: Passionate, mysterious.
WEAKNESSES: Manipulative, ruthless.

BORN ON THIS DAY:
Neal Cassady
(poet)
John Grisham
(writer)
Jack Lemmon
(actor and director)
Nick Nolte
(actor)
John Ruskin
(writer and art critic)
John Williams
(composer and conductor)

MEDITATION:
With hope, you can get through the toughest times.

February 9

You are an avant-garde and worldly person with a huge zest for life. Incredibly enthusiastic and open to experiment, you are a risk-taker and a bit of a daredevil. Well-suited to being an entrepreneur, you are unlikely to be able to stick to a regular office job. Your vast imagination and future-orientated way of thinking lends itself to work on innovative projects. What you lack is patience and attention to detail, so you need someone else to check for mistakes. You mix in a wide circle of bohemian types and have many friends from different cultures. Your intimate relationship has to be based on intellectual rapport and your partner needs to have the same adventurous spirit as you. Trekking or camping in the wilderness is your idea of a fun weekend.

TAROT CARD: The Hermit
PLANETS: Jupiter and Uranus
QUOTE: *'Life is about losing and about doing it as gracefully as possible… and enjoying everything in between.'* Mia Farrow

STRENGTHS: Adventurous, energetic.
WEAKNESSES: Impatient, picky.

BORN ON THIS DAY:
Mia Farrow
(actor)
Carole King
(singer/songwrtier and musician)
Gypsy Rose Lee
(exotic dancer)
Carmen Miranda
(singer and actor)
Joe Pesci
(actor and comedian)
Alice Walker
(writer)

MEDITATION:
Love grows by giving.

February 10

You are a self-sufficient, independent person with a great deal of common sense. You have a realistic approach to life and are immensely disciplined. With crystal-clear thinking, you set goals and will work your utmost to attain them. Supremely ambitious, you have a stoical acceptance of what it takes to get to the top and your personal life can suffer as a result. You are attracted to working in policy or for a think-tank as you are always looking to the future. You are friendly and charitable and will offer practical assistance to those in need. In relationships you need an equal and someone who can shake up your somewhat Spartan attitude. Humour is your soft spot and a stand-up comedy night or trip to the theatre to see a farce can help to revitalize and balance you.

BORN ON THIS DAY:
Bertolt Brecht
(writer)
Roberta Flack
(singer/songwriter and pianist)
Boris Pasternak
(writer)
Mark Spitz
(champion Olympic swimmer)
Sir John Suckling
(poet)
Robert Wagner
(actor)

MEDITATION:
The most beautiful things in the world are neither seen nor touched.

TAROT CARD: The Wheel of Fortune
PLANETS: Saturn and Uranus
QUOTE: *'I was spawned by some pretty good people in this business – Mr. Astaire, Mr. Tracy.'* Robert Wagner

STRENGTHS: Clear thinker, ambitious.
WEAKNESSES: Aloof, neglectful.

February 11

You are a quirky and offbeat person who is eminently sociable. You have the ability to be a friend to all types of people from all walks of life. People warm to your eccentric ways and the sense of camaraderie that you create. You are an innovator – whether in the world of engineering, computing or fashion – and your creativity makes its mark. Always controversial, your life is never dull. You are restless and crave novelty; you are prone to get up and leave abruptly if bored. In relationships you can try to fit your partner into a mould and need to learn to listen rather than fix them. With a tendency to be highly strung, you seek a distinctive form of exercise that releases nervous tension. Experiment with martial arts such as qi gong, kendo and karate until you find the ideal one for you.

BORN ON THIS DAY:
Jennifer Aniston
(actor)
Yukio Hatoyama
(Japanese prime minister)
Leslie Nielsen
(actor and comedian)
Mary Quant
(fashion designer)
Burt Reynolds
(actor)
William Fox Talbot
(photographer and inventor)

MEDITATION:
You were born to be an original.

TAROT CARD: Justice
PLANETS: Uranus and Uranus
QUOTE: *'Fashion is not frivolous. It is a part of being alive today.'* Mary Quant

STRENGTHS: Sociable, inventive.
WEAKNESSES: Anxious, controlling.

February 12

You are an imaginative and realistic person who can get along with all sorts of people. Your natural sympathy and compassion touches people's hearts and they feel you are their friend. Your understanding nature, combined with your intelligence, takes you into the caring and medical professions. There is a strongly spiritual side to you and you may experiment with psychic studies, tarot or astrology. You would also make a brilliant interfaith minister. A weakness is your tendency to daydream and suddenly drift off into another realm, and you definitely hold a utopian vision of how the world could be. An intimate relationship needs to combine friendship with unconditional love, which is a tall order for anyone to fulfil. Music is the ideal way to lose yourself in reverie, undisturbed by mundane reality.

TAROT CARD: The Hanged Man
PLANETS: Neptune and Uranus
QUOTE: *'A man's friendships are one of the best measures of his worth.'* Charles Darwin

STRENGTHS: Benevolence, sagacity.
WEAKNESSES: Dreamer, high expectations.

BORN ON THIS DAY:
Judy Blume
(writer)
Charles Darwin
(naturalist)
Abraham Lincoln
(US president)
Anna Pavlova
(ballerina)
Christina Ricci
(actor)
Franco Zeffirelli
(film director)

MEDITATION:
The journey is the reward.

February 13

You are a controversial and fascinating person with an engaging and provocative manner. You love to rebel against the status quo and shock people, yet paradoxically you have a soft, romantic side. If you fulfil your potential you can become incredibly successful and really make a difference to the world. Expressing the caring and kind-hearted side of your nature is vital and social work suits you, as does writing poetry. If you get pulled down by your negative emotions you can be maudlin and fall victim to addictions. A gift of whacky humour can lift you and others up. In relationships you can be vulnerable and when you mature you realize just how rewarding being supported emotionally is for you. A sport like golf, that acts like a walking meditation, is a godsend.

TAROT CARD: Death
PLANETS: Moon and Uranus
QUOTE: *'I don't like doing most things unless I can do them quite well.'* Oliver Reed

STRENGTHS: Enchanting, good sense of humour.
WEAKNESSES: Over-emotional, negative.

BORN ON THIS DAY:
Stockard Channing
(actor)
Peter Gabriel
(musician – lead singer Genesis)
Kim Novak
(actor)
Oliver Reed
(actor)
Jerry Springer
(TV personality)
Robbie Williams
(singer/songwriter)

MEDITATION:
Act as if what you do makes a difference.

203

February 14

MEDITATION:

To think is easy.
To act is hard.

You are a passionate and idealistic person who lives life to the full. You have a grand, romantic vision of life and are able to express yourself with creative flair and originality. Always experimenting, you can live on the edge, and are not averse to taking risks. You can blow hot and cold and need to find a way to express your strong emotions. This energy is best channelled into a cause that you believe in and you make an excellent defender of the underdog. You gravitate towards groups as you love to take centre stage, so you are the ideal political leader. In an intimate relationship you need to be adored and in return you are tremendously loyal. Your energy can dip suddenly and you need to protect your nervous system with herbal remedies rather than chemical stimulants.

TAROT CARD: The Hierophant
PLANETS: Sun and Uranus
QUOTE: *'It's not so much knowing when to speak, but when to pause.'* Jack Benny

STRENGTHS: Enthusiastic, imaginative.
WEAKNESSES: Erratic, volatile.

February 15

MEDITATION:

Don't count the days,
make the days count.

You are a kind and devoted person who has a love of routine. Your ability to dissect problems, clearly organize your thoughts, and then come up with constructive solutions, make you a great architect or designer. You also possess technical skills and you can take up dressmaking and carpentry. If a friend wants to declutter, then you are the right one to help. You are a purist and like nothing better than cleaning and throwing stuff away. However, you can take over and become overly critical about the way people live. To have a successful relationship you need to learn that you cannot control everything. You make a loving and nurturing parent, who knows how to fuel the imagination of children. Learning massage is a wonderful way for you to give and receive the physical affection you need.

TAROT CARD: The Devil
PLANETS: Mercury and Uranus
QUOTE: *'I've loved the stars too fondly to be fearful of the night.'* Galileo Galilei

STRENGTHS: Organized, caring.
WEAKNESSES: Perfectionist, dominating.

February 16

You are a charming and well-mannered person who is a true humanitarian. You have a high IQ and are very knowledgeable. Cultured and civilized, you are naturally drawn to the art world and museums where your intellect is stimulated. You are immensely talkative and need the stimulus of city life and a variety of sophisticated people around you, although the countryside gives you inner peace. Your true purpose is fulfilled when you find a cause you can support that improves the quality of people's lives. In love you can be over-idealistic and subject your partner to unrealistic expectations. For a long-term relationship, you need someone who can be firm with you, while allowing you to express yourself. Singing in a choir would be a wonderful way for you to connect you with your emotions.

TAROT CARD: The Tower
PLANETS: Venus and Uranus
QUOTE: *'I feel kind of like the black sheep in Congress, but here I am.'* Sonny Bono

STRENGTHS: Knowledgeable, humanitarian.
WEAKNESSES: Chatterbox, unrealistic.

BORN ON THIS DAY:
Iain Banks
(writer)
Sonny Bono
(entertainer and Congressman)
Sarah Clark
(actor)
John McEnroe
(champion tennis player)
Christopher Marlowe
(writer)
Andy Taylor
(musician – Duran Duran guitarist)

MEDITATION:
Always forgive your enemies.

February 17

You are a deep and fascinating person who lives life to the full. You love to probe and discover the hidden aspects of people, starting with knowing all about yourself. Being psychoanalysed at an early age is likely, and it could become your career. Your mind is razor-sharp and you love investigating with scientific precision, yet there is also a dark and sensual side to your nature. You are self-reliant and a born survivor with immense resilience. However, you can detach yourself from people and shut down as an emotional defence mechanism. In relationships it's all or nothing and you need a partner who matches your intensity, or you can get obsessed with your own self-importance. Gardening or renovating your home can be the best physical exercise because you achieve something satisfying while doing it.

TAROT CARD: The Star
PLANETS: Pluto and Uranus
QUOTE: *'The way I see it, you should live everyday like its your birthday.'* Paris Hilton

STRENGTHS: Resilience, intensity.
WEAKNESSES: Detached, arrogant.

BORN ON THIS DAY:
Billie Joe Armstrong
(singer/songwriter and guitarist – Green Day)
Paris Hilton
(socialite and media personality)
Michael Jordan
(basketball player)
Ruth Rendell
(writer)
Denise Richards
(actor)
Sidney Sheldon
(writer)

MEDITATION:
He who hesitates is lost.

February 18

11

BORN ON THIS DAY:
Helen Gurley Brown
(publisher)
John Hughes
(film director)
Toni Morrison
(writer, editor and professor)
Yoko Ono
(artist and musician)
Molly Ringwald
(actor)
John Travolta
(actor, singer, dancer, writer
and film producer)

MEDITATION:

*We are masters of
our own fate.*

You are an electrifying, optimistic person with a daring vision. You have an outrageous sense of humour and a passion for travel and new experiences. A larger-than-life character, people take notice of you. You can't bear to be hemmed in and are constantly breaking new ground in your desire to know everything. Philosophy and anthropology are just two subjects that might be the foundation of your career. You make a superb teacher as you have a fine grasp of complex concepts. Always promoting your pet cause, you can be over-moralistic, often ending up preaching to anyone who'll listen. Domestic life is not for you, so your personal relationships tend to be free and open as you value your independence so highly. The best present anyone could ever give you is flying lessons.

TAROT CARD: Jupiter and Uranus
PLANETS: The Moon
QUOTE: *'Art is my life and my life is art.'*
Yoko Ono

STRENGTHS: Optimistic, enquiring, humourous.
WEAKNESSES: Moralizing, restless.

TYPICAL AQUARIUS:
MICHAEL JORDAN

'To be successful you have to be selfish, or else you never achieve. And once you get to your highest level, then you have to be unselfish. Stay reachable. Stay in touch. Don't isolate.'

AQUARIUS TRAITS:
The Aquarian male hates violence and seeks to maintain a harmonious and peaceful lifestyle. Friends come easily to him, although he will carefully avoid getting too involved in other people's problems. His strengths lie in his determination and unshakeable stability and his ability to take advantage of any opportunity that comes his way. He is both shrewd and inventive, but has a tendency towards privacy.

February 19

You are an honest and dependable person with shrewd business acumen. A deep thinker with a future-orientated outlook, you are guaranteed to come up with inspired solutions to the most difficult problems. You are well suited to a management position or teaching, where you can use your talents as a wise mentor. A team player, you see the best in people and can help them find their true vocation. You're a true egalitarian and a natural at working with all sorts of people. In relationships, you can remain cool and detached and you certainly don't go in for dramatic displays of emotion. Your partner needs to be able to lure you away from the workplace. You love being surprised, so letting your lover treat you to a fine meal at a restaurant with an unusual cuisine has great appeal.

TAROT CARD: The Sun
PLANETS: Saturn and Uranus
QUOTE: *'I only make movies to finance my fishing.'* Lee Marvin

STRENGTHS: Wise mentor, democratic.
WEAKNESSES: Cool, unemotional.

BORN ON THIS DAY:
Prince Andrew
(British royal)
Nicolaus Copernicus
(astronomer)
Lee Marvin
(actor)
Merle Oberon
(actor)
Smokey Robinson
(singer/songwriter and
record producer)
Ray Winstone
(actor)

MEDITATION:
*Fortune favours
the brave.*

TYPICAL AQUARIUS:
TONI MORRISON

'At some point in life the world's beauty becomes enough. You don't need to photograph, paint or even remember it. It is enough.'

AQUARIUS TRAITS:
An Aquarian female needs freedom and plenty of it. She is a loyal partner, but hates to feel trapped, so allow her to enjoy her freedom and in return she will reward you with affection. Position and power are more important to her than material possessions. She is true and honest not only to herself, but to anyone who is lucky enough to be her friend. She finds it hard to show her emotions, but once her guard is down it is possible to discover her passionate side.

Pisces

February 20 – March 20

THE MOON.

TAROT CARD: The Moon

ELEMENT: Water

QUALITY: Mutable

NUMBER: 12

RULING PLANET: Neptune

GEMSTONE: Moonstone

COLOURS: Soft, sea greens and blues

DAY OF THE WEEK: Thursday

COMPATIBLE SIGNS: Taurus, Cancer, Scorpio, Capricorn

KEY WORDS: Selfless and compassionate, sensitive and kind, receptive and intuitive, creative and spiritual, vague and forgetful, indecisive and weak-willed

ANATOMY: Feet, lymphatic system

HERBS, PLANTS AND TREES: Lime, mosses, cucumber, melon, waterlily

KEY PHRASE:
I dream

Pisces is the last sign of the zodiac and the most selfless of all the signs. Pisces governs the feet and, represented by the symbol of the fishes, it is most at home living near and relaxing in water. Those born under the sign are daydreamers and mystics and spend most of their time in the world of the imagination. Pisces governs the restless time of year when spring is anticipated but has not yet arrived. The contrast with the following sign, Aries, is dramatic.

PLANETARY RULER AND QUALITIES

Pisces is a mutable water sign. As the last water sign, it is connected with the 12th house of the birth chart. This is akin to the womb and the collective unconscious. It's governed by Jupiter which rules religion and Neptune which rules mysticism.

Neptune is a mysterious planet over a million miles from earth. It takes 165 years to travel through the zodiac. The planet was discovered in 1846 when Romanticism was sweeping Europe, and it represents music, paintings and poetry that uplift the soul. In ancient mythology Neptune is God of the Sea, governing the deep and unfathomable underwater world. Neptune rules over fashion, the media and the mood of the people. Pisces can get overwhelmed by emotions and plunge to the depths of despair and addiction.

Neptune in our astrological birth charts shows us the highest vibration of universal love. It can be illusion and disillusion, imagination or deception, the psychic or the addict.

RELATIONSHIPS

Pisces are very adaptable so can appear to be all things to all people. You live through others, but can lose your identity and feel overwhelmed, especially in a group. Pisces women are soft and feminine, with an ethereal quality. The male is passionate, poetic and extremely sensitive. Pisces can be easily hurt and often fall in love with unsuitable people. You are best suited to the other water signs, Cancer and Scorpio because you have a mutual empathy and share your sensitive feelings. Sagittarians are exciting partners whose sense of humour can lift the Piscean moodiness – co-ruled by Jupiter, you share the same ideals. Fellow Pisces are also a good match. Best friends are Leos and Capricorns and you get on well with Taureans and Librans.

CONSTELLATION AND MYTH

Pisces is the faint constellation of The Fishes. According to ancient myth, Aphrodite and her son Eros were pursued by the monster Typhon, and to escape him they turned

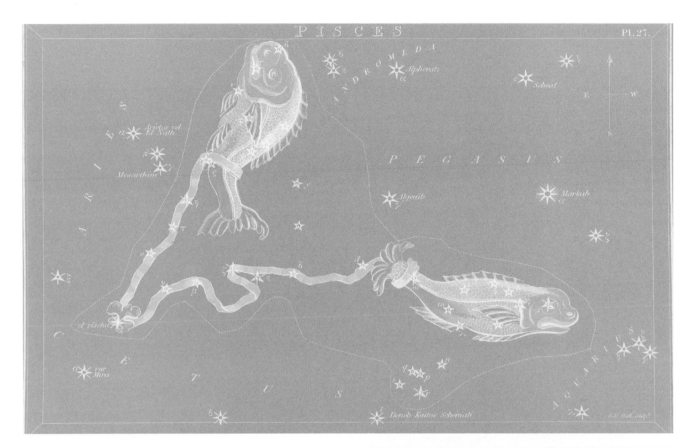

themselves into fish and swam away, tying their tails together so they would not be parted. The story reveals how the Goddess of love can transform herself to escape the monstrous. In 7BC there was a triple conjunction of Saturn and Jupiter in Pisces, which is said to be the Star of Bethlehem heralding the birth of Jesus Christ.

STRENGTHS AND WEAKNESSES

Pisces are the most creative of all the signs, but there is often a price to be paid. You can suffer for your art, or sacrifice yourself to help others. This is the sign of the carer, the truly charitable, the archetype of the saviour and priest.

When having fun Pisces are to be found at the seaside, in art galleries, theatres, concert halls or at the movies. You need to give yourself extra time to arrive for appointments as you can easily get lost or distracted. Your forgetfulness is endearing or frustrating. Pisces forgive others their faults with grace. You live in a realm of enchantment where anything is possible. You are motivated in your search for wholeness and transcendence.

TYPICAL PISCES: ELIZABETH TAYLOR
'Big girls need big diamonds.'
PISCES POWERS: Creative imagination, artistic talent.
PISCES NEGATIVES: Impressionable, indecisive.

February 20

MEDITATION:

The time is always right to do what is right.

You are a caring and capable person with both an awareness and a deep sensitivity to others' feelings. You desire to be of service and inspire people to enjoy life. With your vivid imagination and the practical ability to translate your ideas into material results, you do well in any artistic ventures. You are warm and tactile and people feel at ease in your company. Partnerships are essential to you, and yet can let you down. Romantically you are looking for an ideal which doesn't exist. You need a partner who showers you with affection, and yet you are never satisfied. What you are seeking is spiritual solace, and that connection comes when you give to others. Charity work can appeal to you and volunteering in a soup kitchen would be richly rewarding.

TAROT CARD: The High Priestess **PLANETS:** Venus and Neptune **QUOTE:** *'Let the work of change begin.'* Gordon Brown	**STRENGTHS:** Tactile, charitable. **WEAKNESSES:** Unrealistic, dissatisfied.

February 21

MEDITATION:

If you believe you can, you probably can.

You are a humorous and highly intelligent person with a great sense of fun. A brilliant mimic with a love of words and images, you are a natural actor or screen-writer. Whatever you do, it absorbs you totally and your mind works overtime. You have a fertile imagination and are extremely talkative, loving to discuss your work with anyone who cares to listen. Although you are very sociable, you can also be shy and nervous. Your biggest gift is the ability to inspire magic in people, but you also have a tendency to daydream and be caught up in fanciful, impractical projects. You enjoy the good things in life but are not fervent about getting ahead financially. In love, you are tender and playful and need to be on the same wavelength as your partner. Going to a movie allows you escape your mental chatter.

TAROT CARD: The Empress **PLANETS:** Mercury and Neptune **QUOTE:** *'A poet is a professional maker of verbal objects.'* W. H. Auden	**STRENGTHS:** Humorous, imaginative, affectionate. **WEAKNESSES:** Shy and impractical.

February 22

You are a compassionate and thoughtful person who is very warm and generous. Extremely emotional, you are always in touch with your feelings. You know instinctively what people are feeling and they can count on you for comfort and a sympathetic ear. Helping others is your *raison d'être* and you would make a superb counsellor, minister of religion or healer. Your biggest weakness is your extreme sensitivity, and you can be offended by the slightest thing. In relationships you come alive, and an appreciative partner can help you flourish. Domestic life suits you and you are content to play the parental role. Living and being by water is a priority, so installing a water feature – such as a miniature waterfall or pond in your garden – relaxes you and restores your wellbeing.

TAROT CARD: The Emperor
PLANETS: Moon and Neptune
QUOTE: *'Happiness and moral duty are inseparably connected.'* George Washington

STRENGTHS: Compassionate, generous.
WEAKNESSES: Over-emotional, thin-skinned.

BORN ON THIS DAY:
Sir Robert Baden-Powell
(founder of the Boy Scouts)
Drew Barrymore
(actor, film director and producer)
Steve Irwin
(herpetologist)
Sir John Mills
(actor)
Rembrandt Peale
(artist)
George Washington
(first US president)

MEDITATION:
Nourish the mind like you would your body.

February 23

You are a gloriously confident and loving person. Totally immersed in discovering yourself, you are a dreamer and creator of a magical life; you seem to have the Midas touch. You have the gift of playfulness and people feel young and alive in your company. Always drawn to centre-stage, the worlds of theatre, television or the movies beckon. You need others' admiration and applause to feel validated. However, you are easily upset and need to retreat to lick your wounds if someone criticizes you. Reaching out to help others by entertaining them is the perfect solution. You cherish your illusions and seek to make them come true. In love you shine, every cell of your being vibrates with joy. You need a partner who is faithful as you can't bear competition.

TAROT CARD: The Hierophant
PLANETS: Sun and Neptune
QUOTE: *'As happy a man as any in the world, for the whole world seems to smile upon me!'* Samuel Pepys

STRENGTHS: Confident, high-spirited.
WEAKNESSES: Vulnerable, attention-craving.

BORN ON THIS DAY:
Kristin Davis
(actor)
Michael Dell
(founder of Dell computer)
Peter Fonda
(actor)
George Friederich Handel
(composer)
Samuel Pepys
(naval administrator and diarist)
Baron Rothschild
(entrepreneur/financier)

MEDITATION:
Convince yourself that you have no limits.

February 24

MEDITATION:

*Winning isn't everything,
but wanting to win is.*

You are a devoted and thoughtful person. You have a rich imagination combined with a practical and methodical mind. Your abilities are profound as you are able to access the wider picture through your intuition and psychic powers and bring your vision into manifestation. Attracted to healing as a profession, you are caring and sensitive in your approach so would make an ideal counsellor or health practitioner. Concerned about nutrition, a vegetarian or macrobiotic diet has great appeal. Your health is vulnerable as you have a tendency to get anxious over the tiniest of things. In relationships, you can fall in love with a fantasy, so you need to make sure you truly know someone before committing. When you find the right person your nurturing side blossoms and you are a gentle and affectionate partner.

TAROT CARD: The Lovers
PLANETS: Mercury and Neptune
QUOTE: *'For me it's always about first impressions. I trust my instincts.'* Billy Zane

STRENGTHS: Caring, imaginative.
WEAKNESSES: Worrier, fanciful.

February 25

MEDITATION:

*Dreams seldom
materialize on their own.*

You are a cultured and charming person with a love of beauty and harmony. With a clear, balanced mind and a gift of eloquence, you are a natural diplomat and peacemaker. Love is all-important for you and your relationships are an integral part of your life. People can let you down as you have unrealistic ideals and in business and personal life you need to manage your expectations. Your creativity is an expression of your love and you make a mesmerizing dancer or actor. People can feel transported to another realm through your art. Once you recognize that your need for love can only be filled by a connection with the divine, your relationships dramatically improve. A tear-jerker movie is your idea of a great night out, as it gives you the opportunity to feel your emotions.

TAROT CARD: The Chariot
PLANETS: Venus and Neptune
QUOTE: *'The Beatles saved the world from boredom.'* George Harrison

STRENGTHS: Eloquent, a pacifist.
WEAKNESSES: Unrealistic ideals, vulnerable.

February 26

You are an emotionally complex person with tremendous courage and determination. Your life has an epic quality to it; a story of agony and ecstasy. Highly emotional and willing to face the depths of your being, you prefer time alone when you can analyse and sort yourself out. This 'cave' is vital for you, but you can get trapped in self-absorption. Your fascination with emotions, together with a brilliant intellect, can lead you into a career as a psychoanalyst or medical researcher. All of your relationships are eventful, and your passion and intensity can flare up or down – your partner is in for a turbulent time. However, you are the most exciting lover and no one can ever accuse you of being boring! A night out at a rock concert allows you to release all that excess energy.

TAROT CARD: Strength
PLANETS: Pluto and Neptune
QUOTE: *'Adversity makes men, and prosperity makes monsters.'* Victor Hugo

STRENGTHS: Fortitude, perseverance.
WEAKNESSES: Egotistical, emotionally erratic.

BORN ON THIS DAY:
Michael Bolton
(singer/songwriter and guitarist)
Johnny Cash
(singer /songwriter, musician and actor)
Fats Domino
(singer/songwriter and pianist)
Victor Hugo
(writer)
John Harvey Kellogg
(doctor and inventor)
Levi Strauss
(fashion designer)

MEDITATION:
The best way to prepare for life is to begin to live.

February 27

You are an intensely passionate and fiery person with a generous heart. A seeker of truth, you are attracted to higher education and philosophy. Deeply spiritual, you tend to avoid the conventional religions of your native country, experimenting with those of a foreign culture. You are able to find meaning in the tragic and negative situations in life. As a creative person with 'big picture' mentality, you need a lot of freedom to explore and move around. Movies are an ideal career path for you, especially directing. The roles of therapist or teacher are also suitable. In relationships, you are very open and giving, but you have high expectations. You can be deeply disappointed in love, and easily get caught sacrificing things you love which leads to resentment. Being actively involved with an overseas charity helps you to rise above everyday problems.

TAROT CARD: The Hermit
PLANETS: Jupiter and Neptune
QUOTE: *'Into each life some rain must fall.'* Henry Wadsworth Longfellow

STRENGTHS: Sensual, generous.
WEAKNESSES: High expectations, restless.

BORN ON THIS DAY:
Lawrence Durrell
(writer)
Henry Wadsworth Longfellow
(poet)
Adrian Smith
(guitarist and songwriter – Iron Maiden)
Timothy Spall
(actor)
John Steinbeck
(writer)
Elizabeth Taylor
(actor)

MEDITATION:
Never say more than is necessary.

February 28

MEDITATION:
There is more to life than increasing its speed.

You are an empathic and resourceful person with a combination of common sense and imagination. Not overtly ambitious, you are content to work behind the scenes. Your intuitive gifts make you very popular as you know what people need and can give it to them. This talent makes you an ideal composer, architect or set designer. You love a challenge and are an excellent organizer. As you are deeply caring and can inspire people, you also make a great fund-raiser. When you fall in love you can be secretive and shy and keep your feelings hidden. Once you decide on your perfect mate – which can take some time as you have very high standards and expectations – you are faithful and loyal. You love a spectacle so a night at a *Son et Lumière* would be heaven for you.

TAROT CARD: The Wheel of Fortune **PLANETS:** Saturn and Neptune **QUOTE:** *'I'm the one by the backdoor – I am not the one in the middle of the party.'* Stephanie Beacham	**STRENGTHS:** Compassionate, loyal. **WEAKNESSES:** Unforthcoming, coy.

February 29

MEDITATION:
Happiness depends upon ourselves.

You are a trustworthy and progressive person who is very much the humanitarian. There is an edgy quality to you and a hint of danger, which is very exciting. An idealist, you dream of a better world where equality and freedom exists for everyone. You have respect for the rules of society, yet also push the boundaries. A born campaigner for social reform, politics is a natural career path. However, you can get on your soapbox and come across as hectoring others. Your saving grace is your quirky sense of humour. In relationships, you need a lot of time on your own and can be emotionally reserved. Yet under your cool exterior you are tender and devoted. Playing a team game such as cricket or baseball is wonderful for you, as you delight in the camaraderie.

TAROT CARD: Justice **PLANETS:** Uranus and Neptune **QUOTE:** *'For changes to be of any true value, they've got to be lasting and consistent.'* Tony Robbins	**STRENGTHS:** Dependable, visionary. **WEAKNESSES:** Intimidating, emotionally reserved.

March 1

You are a warm and optimistic person with a soft and sentimental heart. Extremely gifted, especially at music, you have the imagination and the initiative to be a pioneer. You think on your feet, but can be impetuous and rush ahead without considering all the angles, much to the chagrin of others. With your courage and compassion you do well when actively helping others, especially if travel is an essential part of the job. You are not afraid to speak your mind, but can have a reputation for being temperamental. This comes from an inner fear of not being recognized for your abilities. A loving relationship will go a long to way helping you find balance in your life. You fall in love easily, and are very romantic. An active sport that lets you express all your frustrations such as rally driving is perfect.

TAROT CARD: The Magician
PLANETS: Mars and Neptune
QUOTE: *'I see my purpose in life as making the world a happier place to be in.'*
David Niven

STRENGTHS: Talented, kindhearted.
WEAKNESSES: Unpredictable, outspoken.

BORN ON THIS DAY:
Harry Belafonte
(musician and activist)
Frédéric Chopin
(composer)
Roger Daltrey
(musician, singer/songwriter –
The Who)
Ron Howard
(actor and director)
Glenn Miller
(bandleader and musician)
David Niven
(actor)

MEDITATION:
Go confidently in the direction of your dreams.

March 2

You are a sweet-tempered and affectionate person with a love of the simple pleasures in life. Extremely sensuous, you adore the sights, smells and sounds of nature and are happiest in the countryside. You need to put down roots so your creativity can blossom. Cooking is a fabulous experience for you and you present food as an art form. Entertaining groups of people is your forte and you are sensitive to their needs, so a career in public relations is excellent. You have an ability to be content, but need to be careful not to become lazy or over-indulge your sweet tooth. Romance is never far from your mind and you are a delightful and thoughtful lover. Your weakness is being overly possessive. Trust is a important lesson for you. Relax and tend to your garden.

TAROT CARD: The High Priestess
PLANETS: Venus and Neptune
QUOTE: *'There are few things as seemingly untouched by the real world as a child asleep.'*
John Irving

STRENGTHS: Affable, loving, contented.
WEAKNESSES: Over-indulgence, possessiveness.

BORN ON THIS DAY:
John Irving
(writer)
Tom Wolfe
(writer)
Jon Bon Jovi
(singer/songwriter – Bon Jovi)
Daniel Craig
(actor)
Chris Martin
(singer/songwriter – Cold Play)
Lou Reed
(singer / songwriter and musician –
The Velvet Underground)

MEDITATION:
If at first you don't succeed, try, try again.

March 3

You are a curious and highly articulate person with a youthful air about you. Connected totally to your inner dream world, ideas come to you in a flash and you can't help but share them with everyone. A born communicator and natural filmmaker, you are attracted to television and the internet in particular for its immediacy. With a delightful, lighthearted sense of humour, you are quixotic and almost fairylike in your energy. Children just adore you they sense that you are still a child at heart. In relationships, you need a lot of space and variety and can't bear to feel hemmed in. Your restlessness can result in you being fickle. However, you can also become dependent on your partner to give you the stability you need. Dancing freestyle is wonderful for you to express your individuality.

BORN ON THIS DAY:
Alexander Graham Bell
(inventor and scientist)
Alfred Bruneau
(musician and composer)
Alexandre Decamps
(artist)
Perry Ellis
(fashion designer)
Jean Harlow
(actor)
Ronan Keating
(singer – Boyzone)

MEDITATION:
The power of imagination makes us infinite.

TAROT CARD: The Empress
PLANETS: Mercury and Neptune
QUOTE: *'Before anything else, preparation is the key to success.'* Alexander Graham Bell

STRENGTHS: Idealistic, expressive.
WEAKNESSES: Capricious, reliant.

March 4

You are a versatile and sensitive person with a colourful imagination. Artistically gifted, your ability to touch people's deepest feelings with your creativity can make you a well-known and loved artist. Candidly photo-graphing or painting people is your strength as you can capture emotion brilliantly. Plus you are quiet and unobtrusive so they never know you're there and you seldom offend. You wear your heart on your sleeve and can be moody and ultra-emotional, veering on high drama. To overcome this is a challenge, and channelling your feelings into an artistic project is the perfect solution. When you fall in love you commit wholeheartedly as you long for a family and tend to marry young. Being with loved ones changes you for the better and this is when your zany sense of humour comes out to play.

BORN ON THIS DAY:
Joan Greenwood
(actor)
Patrick Moore
(astronomer)
Paula Prentiss
(actor)
Theodor Seuss
(artist, cartoonist and writer)
Antonio Vivaldi
(composer)
Bobby Womack
(singer/songwriter and musician)

MEDITATION:
Discontent is the source of all trouble.

TAROT CARD: The Emperor
PLANETS: Moon and Neptune
QUOTE: *'Don't cry because it's over. Smile because it happened.'* Theodor Seuss

STRENGTHS: Creative, tactful.
WEAKNESSES: Over-dramatic, temperamental.

March 5

You are an articulate and fiery person with a flair for the dramatic. Warm and friendly, you offer encouragement and inspiration to all. You need to be respected and admired, so seek a leadership position in whatever field you enter. Your talents are spectacular either as a musician, actor, or in business. Taking the lead is natural, however, you are sensitive to what people think of you and need constant reassurance. From time to time your moodiness and self-pity get the better of you and you become withdrawn. Then you are liable to create a dramatic scene just so people pay attention! With a vivid imagination and love of fantasy, you love being in love and express your whole heart as the most romantic and tender of lovers. Watching the sunset touches the essence of you and reconnects you to your source.

TAROT CARD: The Hierophant
PLANETS: Sun and Neptune
QUOTE: *'When I left school I was full of angst… I channelled it all into comedy.'*
Matt Lucas

STRENGTHS: Encouraging, expressive.
WEAKNESSES: Volatile and, at times, reticent.

BORN ON THIS DAY:
Sir Rex Harrison
(actor)
Matt Lucas
(actor, writer and comedian)
Eva Mendes
(actor)
William Oughtred
(mathematician and inventor of the slide rule)
Elaine Paige
(singer and actor)
Howard Pyle
(artist)

MEDITATION:
What you dislike in another take care to correct in yourself.

March 6

You are an adaptable and discerning person with a soft and shy nature. Artistically talented, your vivid imagination plays an important role in your career choice. Your music and poetry can inspire others to a state of transcendence. You have a 'feel' for things and act on your hunches and are also able to pay great attention to detail. These abilities make you a success in business as you have an uncanny knack of knowing when to take risks. However, you are a daydreamer and sometimes want to escape, so you can be prone to addictions. As you become materially successful, you become philanthropic and give generously of your time and money to help others. In relationships, you need a partner who keeps up with your ever-changing interests. You are a bit of a softy and need to feel cared for.

TAROT CARD: The Lovers
PLANETS: Mercury and Neptune
QUOTE: *'If you desire faith, then you have faith enough.'* Elizabeth Barrett Browning

STRENGTHS: Intuitive, philanthropic.
WEAKNESSES: Romanticist, obsessive.

BORN ON THIS DAY:
Tom Arnold
(actor and comedian)
Cyrano de Bergerac
(playwright)
Elizabeth Barrett Browning
(poet)
Lou Costello
(actor and comedian)
Alan Davies
(actor and comedian)
Frankie Howerd
(actor and comedian)

MEDITATION:
Imagination is the eye of the soul.

217

March 7

MEDITATION:
Smile, it makes a world of difference.

You are a gracious and gentle person with an ethereal and entrancing quality. You love glamour and beauty and are attracted to the art world, photography and the theatre. With your delicacy of touch and elegant good taste you are also at home in the fashion business. Wherever you work it has to be aesthetically pleasing as ugliness is abhorrent to you. With a dignified manner and charm you are the perfect host as you can make everyone feel at ease. A weakness is your indecisiveness as you want to please people and keep everyone happy. In your personal relationship you can be 'in love with love' and can't bear to be alone so can cling on to a bad relationship. Romance is your lifeblood so an intimate candlelight dinner followed by dancing feeds your soul.

TAROT CARD: The Chariot
PLANETS: Venus and Neptune
QUOTE: *'There is no such thing as bad weather, only inappropriate clothing.'* Ranulph Fiennes

STRENGTHS: Accommodating, honourable.
WEAKNESSES: Indecisive, a people pleaser.

March 8

MEDITATION:
Each day is an entirely new creation.

You are an extraordinary person with a quiet yet powerful strength and captivating manner. Never superficial, highly intuitive and emotionally courageous, you are a person who doesn't flinch from facing the darker sides of life. With an intellectual and analytical mind, you are fascinated by exploring reincarnation, the ancient wisdom traditions and metaphysics. Maths, computing, politics or biology are more traditional career options. Your weakness is that you can be overly-suspicious of people's motives. In relationships, you need a lot of love and are very vulnerable. This can result in you being very jealous and possessive. With maturity, and over time, you can relax and trust your partner. You need excitement and passion and the opera or a murder mystery is the perfect escape from reality.

TAROT CARD: Strength
PLANETS: Pluto and Neptune
QUOTE: *'I'm looking at life, and I'm putting nothing off.'* Lynn Redgrave

STRENGTHS: Spiritually engaged, courageous.
WEAKNESSES: Suspicious, possessive.

March 9

You are an exuberant and generous person who is always looking for a new adventure. You adore travel and seek to constantly expand your mind with books, films and the internet. The life of an explorer or philosopher is definitely one for you. However, you are never satisfied with sticking to one thing, lack focus and can get overwhelmed by all your projects and end up achieving very little. You have an endearing naivety and can make people laugh, so everyone wants to be your friend. They are astounded by your optimism and positive outlook. In love you are affectionate and enjoy companionship, but get itchy feet and can only be happy with someone who understands your need for freedom. Hiking is one sport you enjoy, especially along the coastline or by lakes.

TAROT CARD: The Hermit
PLANETS: Jupiter and Neptune
QUOTE: *'I could have gone on flying through space forever.'* Yuri Gagarin

STRENGTHS: Inquiring, adventurous.
WEAKNESSES: Unfocussed, restless.

BORN ON THIS DAY:
Howard Aiken
(computing pioneer)
Juliette Binoche
(actor)
John Cale
(singer/songwriter and musician – Velvet Underground)
Bobby Fischer
(chess player)
Yuri Gagarin
(astronaut)
Keely Smith
(singer)

MEDITATION:
To become a champion, fight one more round.

March 10

You are a cautious yet charitable person with genuine kindness. You have a deep sense of duty and are traditional in your outlook, with good old-fashioned values. With shrewd perception and compassion, plus an awareness of people's emotions, you are a talented psychologist or counsellor. However, you have a tendency to take on others' burdens in your desire to be helpful, which can lead to burnout. You are prone to worry and pessimism, so finding a spiritual or religious path is vital for your long-term wellbeing. In your relationships, you thrive on intimacy but also desire security and will take your time seeking a partner who can give you that. You love your family yet are also self-sufficient. A sport that is really you is ice-skating; romance and discipline combined. Perfect!

TAROT CARD: The Wheel of Fortune
PLANETS: Saturn and Neptune
QUOTE: *'I knew what I wanted to do even when I was a little girl.'* Sharon Stone

STRENGTHS: Considerate, perceptive.
WEAKNESSES: Defeatist, fretful.

BORN ON THIS DAY:
Jeff Ament
(bassist – Pearl Jam)
Bix Beiderbecke
(jazz pianist and composer)
Prince Edward
(British royal)
Rick Rubin
(co-founder of Def Jam records)
Sharon Stone
(actor and film producer)
Timbaland
(rapper and music producer)

MEDITATION:
Regret for wasted time is a waste of time.

March 11

You are a brilliantly inventive person who is usually way ahead of their time. You are not afraid to experiment and come up with whacky and original ideas. As a storyteller you are second to none, and can take people on a magical mystery adventure. The wondrous world of science fiction is your speciality. You are both a scientist and an artist; someone who can use both their left and right brain, which is a rare combination. You are incredibly social and have a wide-ranging circle of friends, some of whom are eccentrics and oddballs. In your romantic relationships, you are loyal and devoted and require a strong intellectual connection. However, you need to spend time alone, so can appear emotionally distant and cool. For total relaxation and entertainment, you appreciate a witty, satirical comedy show.

BORN ON THIS DAY:
Douglas Adams
(writer)
Thora Birch
(actor)
Alex Kingston
(actor)
Johnny Knoxville
(TV personality)
Rupert Murdoch
(entrepreneur)
Harold Wilson
(British prime minister)

MEDITATION:
Anger is never without a reason, but seldom a good one.

TAROT CARD: Justice
PLANETS: Uranus and Neptune
QUOTE: *'I'm an optimist, but an optimist who carries a raincoat.'* Harold Wilson

STRENGTHS: Avant-garde, imaginative.
WEAKNESSES: Unforthcoming, aloof.

March 12

You are an unworldly, impressionable person who is extremely altruistic. You are so sensitive that it's as if you have no skin, so you have to develop a protective layer around you. You have an elusive and mystical quality about you and can be hard to pin down. As you get older its easier for you to get in touch with, and draw on, the extraordinary psychic and artistic gifts that you have. Helping others comes easily to you, and you're the one who volunteers to run the homeless shelter or local stray cat's home. In relationships, you can get caught in fantasy and suffer from unrequited love; you have difficulty maintaining permanence in your romantic life. A down-to-earth type is what you need. The opera was invented just for you – it's a memorable night out that will have a long-lasting effect.

BORN ON THIS DAY:
Pete Doherty
(singer/songwriter and guitarist –
Babyshambles)
Sammy 'The Bull' Gravano
(American gangster)
Steve Harris
(bassist – Iron Maiden)
Jack Kerouac
(writer)
Liza Minnelli
(actor and singer)
Googie Withers
(actor)

MEDITATION:
Everything has beauty, but not everyone sees it.

TAROT CARD: The Hanged Man
PLANETS: Neptune and Neptune
QUOTE: *'If moderation is a fault, then indifference is a crime.'* Jack Kerouac

STRENGTHS: Big-hearted, gifted.
WEAKNESSES: Over-sensitive, irresolute.

March 13

You are a caring and kind person who is a born romantic. You have a quiet enigmatic quality that is very alluring. Totally aware of your feelings, you can ride an emotional roller coaster at times and soon learn to protect yourself from harsh environments. You have an excellent memory and a gift for listening; talents which make you an imaginative writer, poet or lyricist. You are trustworthy and able to keep secrets; the ideal best friend. With a decidedly theatrical leaning, you would also make a brilliant set designer. In relationships, you need to be careful not to become the doormat as you are incredibly giving to others and tend to neglect your own needs. You tend to pick up any infection going, so you need to support your immune system and detox on a regular basis.

TAROT CARD: The Emperor
PLANETS: Moon and Neptune
QUOTE: *'Never regret yesterday. Life is in you today, and you make your tomorrow.'* L. Ron Hubbard

STRENGTHS: Good listener, trustworthy.
WEAKNESSES: Emotionally unstable, neglectful of personal needs.

BORN ON THIS DAY:
Adam Clayton
(bassist – U2)
L. Ron Hubbard
(science fiction writer and founder of Scientology)
William H. Macy
(actor)
Marthe Robin
(mystic)
George Seferis
(writer and Nobel prize winner)
Hugo Wolf
(composer)

MEDITATION:
Hope is grief's best music.

March 14

You are a person with natural charisma. A great actor, you can exude confidence and charm, enlivening all you meet. No one can question the enormous creative and leadership gifts you possess. However, underneath there is a shy and brooding persona, and you can be racked with self-doubt. These moods can suddenly descend, much to the chagrin of colleagues and loved ones. You have a soft and generous heart and working in the public sector in a leadership position is suited. The stage also whispers seductively, as being in the spotlight is your natural habitat. Relationships are your life and you relish all types of emotion, so heartbreak, dramatic break-ups and passion make you feel alive. Hot saunas match your temperament, as do beach holidays in tropical parts of the world.

TAROT CARD: The Hierophant
PLANETS: Sun and Neptune
QUOTE: *'Be like a duck. Calm on the surface, but always paddling like the dickens underneath.'* Michael Caine

STRENGTHS: Magnetism, assertive.
WEAKNESSES: Downcast, romantically vulnerable.

BORN ON THIS DAY:
Jamie Bell
(actor)
Sir Michael Caine
(actor)
Billy Crystal
(actor)
Albert Einstein
(physicist)
Quincy Jones
(composer)
Hank Ketcham
(cartoonist)

MEDITATION:
A smile is a curve that sets everything straight.

March 15

BORN ON THIS DAY:
Andrew Jackson
(US president)
Fabio Lanzoni
(model)
Mike Love
(musician – The Beach Boys)
Eva Longoria Parker
(actor)
Lynda La Plante
(writer)
Lawrence Tierney
(actor)

MEDITATION:
Great minds rise above misfortune.

You are a sentimental and affectionate person with a healing touch. Reiki, massage and shiatsu are all modalities you might explore as a career. You have the rare knack of combining perceptive insights with practical and efficient solutions. There is a strong desire in you to serve others and you're the ideal person to do voluntary work overseas. At times you can become fretful and uptight about getting everything perfect. This can affect your digestive system so the occasional detox would do you the world of good. Letting go of minor details and working as part of a team would be highly beneficial. In relationships, your partner can get confused as you can drift off one minute and be efficient and attentive the next. Your sense of humour and ability to laugh at yourself saves the day.

TAROT CARD: The Devil
PLANETS: Mercury and Neptune
QUOTE: *'Any man worth his salt will stick up for what he believes…'* Andrew Jackson

STRENGTHS: Restorative powers, warm-hearted.
WEAKNESSES: Fretful, perfectionist.

March 16

BORN ON THIS DAY:
Bernardo Bertolucci
(film director)
Rosa Bonheur
(artist)
Michael Bruce
(musician)
Robert Scott Irvine
(artist)
Jerry Lewis
(comedian)
James Madison
(US president)

MEDITATION:
It is idle to dread what you cannot avoid.

You are an artistic and easy-going person who is inspired by a love of truth. Your soul is that of a poet or mystic and you have a deeply sympathetic and agreeable nature. People adore being around you as you create an enchanted fairyland world usually only seen in movies. You could be the director or writer of an epic love story and your life is a grand romance. You love giving cocktail parties with a witty and fascinating group, especially arty or literary types. Being in love is so important, you can become dependent on your partner and avoid any form of confrontation as you fear being rejected. Your emotions can overwhelm you which makes you vulnerable to colds and flu. Building up your immune system with vitamins and using flower remedies is very helpful to stop you getting run down.

TAROT CARD: The Chariot
PLANETS: Venus and Neptune
QUOTE: *'I get paid for what most kids get punished for.'* Jerry Lewis

STRENGTHS: Supportive, mystical.
WEAKNESSES: Needy, scared of rejection.

March 17

You are a compassionate and responsive person with a radar for those in trouble that you can help. As a natural healer, your mind focusses on deep subjects, and you are attracted to study psychology, medicine and techniques such as hypnosis. Your motivation is to understand the great mysteries of life and death. Perceptive and dedicated, you can be very successful once you find your niche. When tired you can be cantankerous and scathing, especially of people who underestimate your intelligence – you don't suffer fools gladly. Relationships are the centre of your life and you are fiercely loyal to those you love. You can overflow with feelings and need a partner who can support your emotional nature and ground you. A daily swim or rigorous yoga session is a way to balance you and restore your equilibrium.

TAROT CARD: The Star
PLANETS: Pluto and Neptune
QUOTE: *'I may be helping to bring harmony between people through my music.'*
Nat King Cole

STRENGTHS: Receptive and insightful.
WEAKNESSES: Bad-tempered, cutting.

BORN ON THIS DAY:
Nat King Cole
(singer/songwriter and pianist)
Lesley-Anne Down
(actor)
Kate Greenaway
(writer and illustrator)
James Irwin
(astronaut)
Rob Lowe
(actor)
Rudolf Nureyev
(ballet dancer)

MEDITATION:
*If you want time,
you must make it.*

March 18

You are a benevolent and kind person with a far-ranging imagination. You have a strong sense of moral integrity and are very spiritual, always believing the best in people. With your tender heart you can be gullible and taken in by any sob story, so people can easily deceive you. Career-wise you are creative and extremely versatile so have many options open to you. Choosing just one profession can be difficult, but you need to feel it has meaning and contributes to improving people's lives. In your love affairs you need an intellectual equal and someone who stimulates your fertile imagination. You also need lot of time alone to do your own thing. You favour adventure rather than the conventional holidays – travelling across the desert on a camel has more appeal for you than a beach resort.

TAROT CARD: The Moon
PLANETS: Jupiter and Neptune
QUOTE: *'In war . . . there are no winners, but all are losers.'* Neville Chamberlain

STRENGTHS: Imaginative, kind, bounteous.
WEAKNESSES: Overtrusting, easily deceived.

BORN ON THIS DAY:
Luc Besson
(writer and director)
Neville Chamberlain
(British prime minister)
Rudolf Diesel
(inventor of the diesel engine)
Robert Donat
(actor)
Queen Latifah
(singer and actor)
Vanessa Williams
(actor, model, singer)

MEDITATION:
*Difficulties strengthen
the mind.*

March 19

You are a sympathetic and helpful person who has a strong moral integrity and genuine concern for others. Serious-minded and self-reflective, you have a quiet demeanour that belies an inner core of strength. You are a skilled business person capable of managing large groups as you have acute sensitivity for how people feel. This ability keeps you in tune with the public mood and you would do well in the fashion or movie industry. However, if you do not receive constant appreciation of your efforts, you can become defensive and critical, in order to hide your lack of confidence. In relationships you are romantic and loving and once you commit your word is your bond. You need to lighten up and the ballet is the kind of fantasy world you find delightful.

BORN ON THIS DAY:
Ursula Andress
(actor)
Sir Richard Burton
(explorer)
Glenn Close
(actor)
Wyatt Earp
(US lawman)
David Livingstone
(explorer)
Bruce Willis
(actor)

MEDITATION:

Nothing is impossible to a willing heart.

TAROT CARD: The Sun
PLANETS: Saturn and Neptune
QUOTE: *'I am prepared to go anywhere, provided it be forward.'* David Livingstone

STRENGTHS: Sensitive, benevolent.
WEAKNESSES: Overly wary, timid.

March 20

You are a demonstrative and loving person with a huge desire to express yourself creatively. You have a soft and gentle touch and everything you do is imbued with beauty and grace. Whether as a massage therapist, a garden designer or a carpenter, you relish being hands-on in your work and connecting with people. You enjoy life and believe it has to be lived in each moment – you really know how to relax. Totally subjective and with a tendency to be over-emotional, you respond intuitively to any situation. Being logical just isn't your thing. At times you are so changeable that you can drive others to distraction. Being in love is bliss; you blossom as your best qualities emerge. You are quite happy pottering around on your own, and it's important that you let others know this.

BORN ON THIS DAY:
Holly Hunter
(actor and producer)
William Hurt
(actor)
Henrik Ibsen
(playwright)
Spike Lee
(director)
Vera Lynn
(actor and singer)
Michael Redgrave
(actor, director and writer)

MEDITATION:

Never lose a chance of saying a kind word.

TAROT CARD: Judgement
PLANETS: Venus and Neptune
QUOTE: *'A thousand words will not leave so deep an impression as one deed.'* Henrik Ibsen

STRENGTHS: Communicative, deeply perceptive.
WEAKNESSES: Hot-blooded, erratic.